Mezzofanti's Gift

ALSO BY MICHAEL ERARD

Um . . . :
Slips, Stumbles, and Verbal Blunders,
and What They Mean

Mezzofanti's Gift

The Search for the World's Most
Extraordinary Language Learners

MICHAEL ERARD

DUCKWORTH OVERLOOK

London and New York

First published in the UK in 2013 by
Duckworth Overlook

LONDON
30 Calvin Street, London E1 6NW
T: 020 7490 7300
E: info@duckworth-publishers.co.uk
www.ducknet.co.uk
For bulk and special sales, please contact
sales@duckworth-publishers.co.uk
or write to us at the address above

First published in the US in 2012 by
Free Press, a division of Simon and Schuster, Inc.

A catalogue record for this book is available
from the British Library

ISBNs
Paperback: 978-0-7156-4568-0
Kindle: 978-0-7156-4701-1
ePub: 978-0-7156-4702-8
Library PDF: 978-0-7156-4703-5

Printed and bound in the UK by
CPI Group (UK) Ltd, Croydon, CR0 4YY

For Misty

Contents

Part 1
QUESTION: Into the Cardinal's Labyrinth

Introduction	3
Chapter 1	7
Chapter 2	16
Chapter 3	27
Chapter 4	39

Part 2
APPROACH: Tracking Down Hyperpolyglots

Chapter 5	67
Chapter 6	73
Chapter 7	94
Chapter 8	106
Chapter 9	111

Part 3
REVELATION: The Brain Whispers

Chapter 10   147

Chapter 11   156

Chapter 12   161

Chapter 13   170

Chapter 14   176

Part 4
ELABORATION: The Brains of Babel

Chapter 15   187

Chapter 16   214

Chapter 17   231

Part 5
ARRIVAL: The Hyperpolyglot of Flanders

Chapter 18   247

Chapter 19   259

Acknowledgments   271

Appendix   274

Notes   277

Index   295

Catch a young swallow.
Roast her in honey.
Eat her up.
Then you will understand all languages.

—Folk magic incantation

When we wonder, we do not yet know
if we love or hate the object at which
we are marveling; we do not yet know
if we should embrace it or flee from it.

—Stephen Greenblatt,
Marvelous Possessions

Mezzofanti's Gift

Part 1

QUESTION:

Into the Cardinal's Labyrinth

Introduction

To sea-going travelers of 1803, pirates in the Mediterranean posed a terrifyingly reliable threat. So when an Italian priest, Felix Caronni, set out from the Sicilian port of Palermo, it was conceivable that neither he nor the ship's cargo of oranges would ever see their destination. Indeed, Caronni's boat was captured, and for a year he was jailed on the northern coast of Africa, headed for certain slavery, until French diplomats secured his release.

When the priest returned to Italy, he set out to write an account of his narrow escape. Appearing in 1806, it was the first published mention of a certain professor of Oriental languages at the University of Bologna who had helped Caronni translate a document from Arabic. This twenty-nine-year-old professor, Giuseppe Mezzofanti, a priest and the son of a local Bolognese carpenter, was reputed to know twenty-four languages.

More than thirty years later, a group of English tourists visiting Rome sought out Mezzofanti and asked him how many languages he spoke. By then he was the Vatican librarian and would soon be elevated to cardinal. "I have heard many different accounts," one tourist asked the prelate, "but will you tell me yourself?"

Mezzofanti hesitated. "Well, if you must know, I speak forty-five languages."

"Forty-five!" the tourist exclaimed. "How, sir, have you possibly contrived to acquire so many?"

"I cannot explain it," said Mezzofanti. "Of course God has given me this peculiar power: but if you wish to know how I preserve these languages, I can only say, that, when once I hear the meaning of a word in any language, I never forget it."

Engraving of Giuseppe Mezzofanti.

At other times, when asked how many languages he spoke, Mezzofanti liked to quip that he knew "fifty languages and Bolognese." During his lifetime, he put enough of those fifty on display—among them Arabic and Hebrew (biblical and Rabbinic), Chaldean, Coptic, Persian, Turkish, Albanian, Maltese, certainly Latin and Bolognese, but also Spanish, Portuguese, French, German, Dutch, and English, as well as Polish, Hungarian, Chinese, Syrian, Amharic, Hindustani, Gujarati, Basque, and Romanian—that he frequently appeared in rapturous accounts of visitors to Bologna and Rome. Some compared him to Mithridates, the ancient Persian king who could speak the language of each of the twenty-two territories he governed. The poet Lord Byron, who once lost a multilingual cursing contest with Mezzofanti, called him "a monster of languages, the Briareus of parts of speech, a walking polyglott, and more,—who ought to have existed at the time of the Tower of Babel, as universal interpreter." Newspapers described him as "the distinguished linguist," "the most learned linguist now living," "the most accomplished linguist ever seen," "the greatest linguist of modern Europe." He was continually referred to as the pinnacle of human achievement with languages. A British civil servant who directed a survey of all the languages of India between 1894 and 1928 summed up the linguistic situation in the province of Assam, where eighty-one languages were spoken, by writing that "Mezzofanti himself, who spoke fifty-eight languages, would have been puzzled here."

In 1820, Hungarian astronomer Baron Franz Xaver von Zach visited Mezzofanti, who addressed him in Hungarian so excellent, the surprised Baron said he felt "stupefied." Then (as he wrote later), "he afterwards spoke to me in German, at first in good Saxon, and then in the Austrian and Swabian dialects, with a correctness of accent that amazed me to the last degree." Mezzofanti went on to speak English in conversation with a visiting Englishman, and Russian and Polish with a visiting Russian prince. He did all of this, wrote Zach, "not stuttering and stammering, but with the same volubility as if he had been speaking his mother tongue."

Despite this adoration, Mezzofanti was also the target of sarcastic barbs. Irish writer Charles Lever wrote that Mezzofanti "was a most inferior man. . . . An old dictionary would have been to the full as companionable." Baron Bunsen, a German philologist, said that in all the countless languages which Mezzofanti spoke he "never said anything." He "has not five ideas," said a Roman priest quoted in a memoir. A German student who met him in the Vatican remembered, "There is something about him that reminds me of a parrot—he does not seem to abound in ideas."

A Hungarian woman visiting him in 1841 asked how many languages he spoke.

"Not many," Mezzofanti replied. "For I only speak forty or fifty."

"Amazing incomprehensible faculty!" the woman, Mrs. Polyxena Paget, wrote in a recollection, "but not one that I should in the least be tempted to envy; for the empty unreflecting word-knowledge, and the innocently exhibited small vanity with which he was filled, reminded me rather of a monkey or a parrot, a talking machine, or a sort of organ wound up for the performance of certain tunes, than of a being endowed with reason."

Yet many others were unburdened of their skepticism when they encountered the man in the flesh. Scholars, philologists, and classicists trooped off to test or trap Mezzofanti and were, one by one, bested and charmed. In 1813, a scholar from the University of Turin, Carlo Boucheron, met Mezzofanti at the Library of Pisa, armed with hard questions about Latin. Expecting that Mezzofanti had spread himself too thin to know anything substantial about the arcana of Latin's history, Boucheron had called him a "mere literary charlatan."

"Well," Boucheron was asked several hours later, "what do you think of Mezzofanti?"

"By Bacchus!" Boucheron exclaimed. "He is the Devil!"

Mezzofanti himself, humble about his gifts, said that God had given him a good memory and a quick ear. "What am I," he used to say, "but an ill-bound dictionary."

On one occasion, Pope Gregory XVI (1765–1846), a friend of Mezzofanti, arranged for dozens of international students to surprise him. When the signal was given, the students knelt before Mezzofanti and then rose quickly, talking to him "each in his own tongue, with such an abundance of words and such a volubility of tone, that, in the jargon of dialects, it was almost impossible to hear, much less to understand them." Mezzofanti didn't flinch but "took them up singly, and replied to each in his own language." The pope declared the cardinal to be victorious. Mezzofanti could not be bested.

All that was left was for Mezzofanti to ascend to heaven, where the angels might discover, to their glittering surprise, that he spoke the angelic tongue, too.

Chapter 1

A typical midtown Manhattan lunch crowd was packed into the Japanese restaurant around me. Behind the counter were the cooks who had produced the fragrant bowl of noodles I was now eating.

The boss, an older Japanese man, read from waiters' slips and shouted orders to his crew in Japanese. Two heavy-set, young Hispanic men, with tattooed arms and baseball hats worn backward, moved from pot to pot through the steam-filled space, ladling this, mixing that, all so smoothly I couldn't tell when they had finished one order and started another. In the quieter moments, they filled containers with chopped herbs and wiped down counters, talking to one another in Spanish and addressing a third cook, another Japanese man, in the pidgin English of the restaurant kitchen.

Three languages, two of which weren't native to the people speaking them, and the rhythm of their immaculate noodle ballet never stuck or slowed.

It's amazing that the world runs so well, given that people use languages that they didn't grow up using, haven't studied in schools, and in which they've never been tested or certified. Yet it does. The noodle scene was probably reflected that same day hundreds of millions of times all over the world, in markets, restaurants, taxis, airports, shops, docks, classrooms, and streets, where men, women, and children of all skin colors and nationalities met with, ate with, bought and sold with, flirted with, boarded with, worked next to, served, introduced, greeted, cursed at, and asked directions from others who didn't speak their language. They did all this successfully, even though they might have spoken with accents, used simple words, made mistakes, paraphrased, and done other things that marked them as linguistic outsiders. Such encounters between non-native speakers have always textured human experience. In our era, these encounters are peaking, as the ties between language and geography have been weakened by migration, global business, cheap travel, cell phones, satellite TV, and the Internet.

You may be familiar with the stories of languages, such as English or French or Latin, that are (or were) valuable cultural capital. This book tells another story, about a kind of cognitive capital, the stuff you bring to learning a new language.

We once lived in bubbles, disconnected from the hubbub of the world. But more of these bubbles, where one or only a few languages used to be spoken, are connected each day, and more and more of us are passing between them. It is clear that multilingual niches are proliferating, and that monolinguals (such as myself) need to live and act multilingually. But that's not what I'm writing about.

Something else is happening as well: we've begun to want to naturally move among these bubbles unimpeded. Maybe you're a Dagestani woman living in Sharjah, one of the United Arab Emirates, who speaks Russian to your husband while he speaks Arabic to you. Maybe you're an American project manager leading phone meetings, in English, with engineers from China, India, Vietnam, and Nigeria. Maybe you're a Japanese speaker working next to two Hondurans in a noodle shop. Maybe you're a Beijinger finally realizing your dream to see the Grand Canyon. Ideas, information, goods, and people are flowing more easily through space, and this is creating a sensibility about language learning that's rooted more in the trajectories of an individual's life than in one's citizenship or nationality. It's embedded in economic demands, not the standards of schools and governments. That means that our brains also have to flow, to remain plastic and open to new skills and information. One of these skills is learning new ways to communicate.

If you could alleviate people's anxieties about language learning, you'd solve what has shaped up to be the core linguistic challenge of the twenty-first century: How can I learn a language quickly? How well do I have to speak or write it for it to be useful? Whose standards will I have to meet? Will I ever be taken as native? And are my economic status, my identity, and my brain going to be changed?

How adults learn languages is central to the emergence of English as a global lingua franca. In fact, the spread of English is the signal example of the reconsideration of "native-like" abilities in a language. In the coming decades, as many as two billion people will learn English as a second language. Some large fraction of them will be adults who are attracted by the prestige and utility that has made it the most popular language to learn over the past five decades. In China, the size of the English market has been valued at $3.5 billion, with as many as thirty thousand companies offering English classes. It's said that on a daily basis, as many as 70 percent of all interactions in English around the world occur between non-native speakers. This means that native English speakers have less control over determining the "proper" pronunciation and grammar of English. Some experts in China and Europe now advocate teaching standardized foreign Englishes that wouldn't fly in the language's home countries.

English may be the only global language with more non-native speakers than native ones. However, it isn't the only additional language that people are learning in the $83 billion worldwide language-learning market—a figure that doesn't include spending on schools, teachers, and textbooks in educational systems. In the United States, 70 percent of college students in foreign-language classes study Spanish, French, and German, though Arabic, Chinese, and Korean are increasing in popularity. If you live in Brazil, you'll learn Spanish, now compulsory in schools. If you live in East Asia, it's Mandarin Chinese. In Europe, thanks to the European Union, it's French and German. Hindi in India. Swahili in East Africa. Tok Pisin in Papua New Guinea. But speaking like a native, at a moment when people need extra languages to make a living, is a standard to which adult speakers literally cannot afford to be held.

Also, pumping new life into endangered or extinct languages depends on teaching them to people who have lost the moldable brains of youth.

And when ancestral tongues die out, their communities don't become mute—children and adults learn to speak something else, often a language connected to the demise of their ancestral one. I say this not to glibly dismiss the issue but to point out the full scope of the problem. Also, exciting new technologies for translating speech and text between languages don't eliminate the need for people to learn languages. But they might enable multilingual transactions—for instance, by using free machine translation tools, I can get a rough gist of a web page in a language I don't know.

The fragmentary, improvised, simultaneous use of several languages all at once that I witnessed in the noodle kitchen doesn't occur only in New York City, London (named in 1999 as the most multilingual city in the world), Mumbai, Rio de Janeiro, and other major world cities. No longer are borders, universities, and transportation hubs the only linguistic crossroads: this morning, my Twitter feed featured updates in French, Spanish, Korean, Mandarin, Italian, and English. That same feed reported fraudulent email scams, called 419s, that have begun to circulate in Welsh, German, and Swedish.

Anyplace on the globe, you can surf through television channels in many languages; on the news channels, you'll see political protesters half a world away carrying signs written in English. Pop stars learn other languages in which to sing songs, to win ears in more markets. And it's not just in the flow of digital information that we're encountering more languages. Signs on the streets in your city are appearing in more languages than they used to, and on any given day, your local hotel might be home to a trade delegation from Kazakhstan, Brazil, or Bulgaria.

With so many languages to learn and so many reasons to learn them, it's easy to miss the sheer humanity of the undertaking, which is evident in the biological equipment—brains, eyes, tongues, and hands— that every adult brings to the task. And if you've ever tried to learn a language, you already know that adult brains have limits (though not absolute ones) that constrain their efforts. As a result, people will speak their new languages with a lot of variety. They won't sound like native speakers. And yet they may need to speak new languages and dialects in order to survive in this economy. What should they do?

cleaner hoses. Because we know how hard it is to learn even one foreign language, we receive the tales with awe. Then we repeat them with a skepticism or wonder that we save for stories about saints, healers, and prodigious lovers.

At the outset, all I had were such stories, the tantalizing tales told over the centuries about people with remarkable linguistic gifts. Most of the stories are legends, unreliable as wholes. Yet hidden in them are kernels of truth that are subject to discovery, assessment, and testing, which in turn can guide further exploration. Do such language super-learners really exist? How many are out there, and what are they like? What could this gift for learning languages amount to, if it's real? And what are the upper limits of our ability to learn, remember, and speak languages?

Mezzofanti's Gift is an account of my search for solid answers to these and other questions. I decided to write as a curious adventurer rather than as a scholar, seeking the freedom to move across intellectual borders. Because this journey had no predestined end, I couldn't write as if I knew what I'd find. I drew on published research literature, my interviews with scientists, my investigation in historical archives, memoirs by—and, of course, my interviews with—hyperpolyglots. An invaluable amount of information was gathered via an online survey of people who say they know six languages or more. All this was necessary to see why these souls have escaped the curse of the gods—and what the gods might have demanded of them in return. Would the secret of speaking many languages provide a key to the secret of speaking any language at all?

During my explorations, I grappled with the question of how best to make sense of what hyperpolyglots do in their lives with their languages. Whose standards would I use to judge their abilities, if indeed those need to be judged? I also had to confront why language scientists have refused to consider hyperpolyglots, talented language learners, and language accumulators as anything more than curiosities or freaks. For instance, Carol Myers-Scotton, a linguist who is an expert on bilingualism, recommended in one of her books, "When you meet people who tell you they speak four or five languages, give them a smile to show you're impressed, but don't take this claim very seriously." I'm not exaggerating when I say that no one has critically looked at people who have learned as many languages as hyperpolyglots claim, though scientists have studied people who have learned one or two "second" or "foreign" languages very well. They prefer one kind of talent over another because of an obsession with native-likeness as the sole goal of language learning and an assumption that the native speaker is the sole model of success as a linguistic insider. Over and over I was told, sure, someone could learn the vocabularies of many languages, but no one could learn many languages at a native level. But, I wondered, could they be fluent in many languages? How fluent? What are the limits? These are questions that motivated me.

On my way, I'd have my own brain scanned. I'd make a fool of myself—and have fun doing it—in Hindi, Italian, Spanish, and some other languages. I'd also travel the world, from Europe to the United States to India to Mexico, talking to people who, one way or another, are making their way through Babel. Tracking down experts and rooting out facts and theories from scientific publications didn't prepare me for the amazing specimens I'd meet. Some hyperpolyglots are human sponges, able to absorb or inhale languages unbelievably quickly. Others are human cranes who can lift many languages at once. Still others are human slingshots, using their experience in a few languages to fling them further.

These aren't geniuses, but they do possess unusual neurological resources. They have a penchant for conspicuous consumption of time and brainpower that appears to be linked to the brains they possess. What makes them who they are is not merely genetic; they're influenced by the same trends as the rest of us. They're choosing the same languages most people would. And they're using them for the same purposes. Their personalities defy generalization—I didn't find it necessary to mistrust them as crippled egos who require the salve of attention. Nor did I dance too often with their veracity. A healthy skepticism got me through, in particular because I didn't profile in depth anyone with a financial interest in hyping their abilities.

By the end of my journey, I realized that hyperpolyglots are avatars of what I call the "will to plasticity." This is the belief that we can, if we so wish, reshape our brains—and that the world impels us to do so.

Two quick examples of the impetus for high-intensity language learning should suffice. "I want to be a polyglot," someone posted on Twitter; I asked him why. "Because I want to be able to go anywhere and be able to communicate with anyone," he replied. Then there was a news story extolling ten-year-old Arpan Sharma, a British boy who supposedly speaks eleven languages, who explained that "When I'm an adult . . . I want to be a surgeon who can work in all the hospitals of the world and speak the language of the country I'm in." Whether you have learned one additional language or a dozen, you have emulated this same desire. I hope I'm not glorifying them too much by saying that the hyperpolyglot makes visible the myriad strands of our linguistic destinies, whether we speak only one language or many.

Some of these strands and destinies take shape in the group of people who form what I call a neural tribe. They've developed along neurological paths distinct from the rest of us, journeys that have given them a sense of mission and personal identity as language learners.

Linguistically, they're out of time, place, and scale. Could they be an advanced specimen of the species? It's tempting to think so. They are not born; they are not made; but they are born to be made. We'd need more advanced neuroscience to explore the nuances of the linguistic brain. I hope to be around to see it.

It's an odd tribe—there is no unified voice, no leaders, and no rules. In many ways, it's a lost tribe, belonging to no nation. Yet, their dislocations seem reminiscent of everyone else's. They have something to tell us about what our brains can do and what we must do to make our peace with Babel.

Chapter 2

W hen the topic of hyperpolyglots comes up, the historical character Giuseppe Mezzofanti inevitably does, too, so it made sense for my quest to begin with him. I headed to Bologna, Italy, where I hoped to uncover, with 150 years of linguistic and neurological research to my advantage, evidence that his admirers and biographers had overlooked. It wasn't just the number of languages ascribed to Mezzofanti that impressed me; it was the speed at which he was said to learn them, and his ability to switch between them. How could he do that? *Could* he really do that? Did he know languages rather than facts about languages, and could he use them in a specialized, substantial way? The answers would anchor a deeper investigation into the nature of linguistic talents.

There was also the open question about his methods. When, in 1840, the Russian scholar A. V. Starchevsky met Mezzofanti in Rome, he successfully puzzled the language genius by speaking to him in Ukrainian.

Mezzofanti seemed surprised. "What language is that?" he asked, in Italian.

"Little Russian," Starchevsky replied, using a term of his day.

"Well, come to see me again in two weeks," Mezzofanti said.

Starchevsky returned to find the cardinal able to speak to him, very fluently, in Ukrainian. They chatted for hours. Understandably, the Russian was amazed. How had Mezzofanti done it?

The simple answer was that Russian and Ukrainian are related languages, both belonging to the East Slavic subgroup of the Slavic language family. "I had known Russian already," Mezzofanti explained.

This didn't satisfy Starchevsky. "One knowing Latin can easily learn Italian," he said, "but not within a fortnight." After the visit, he became obsessed with the notion that Mezzofanti possessed some esoteric key, perhaps a verbal elixir. For forty years, he read everything about the polyglot cardinal that he could find, but an answer eluded him.

"I was about giving up my task," he recalled, "when suddenly I struck the hidden secret of Mezzofanti." He passed this secret along only to his students, which allowed them to master a new language in three to four weeks, he said. A new "polyglot college" would be founded in St. Petersburg, headed by Starchevsky, who would use the technique to teach the seventy languages of the Russian czar's domain.

"Every man of average capability can learn any foreign language within a month," Starchevsky proclaimed, "and whoever fails is a lazy or a stupid fellow." Plans for the college were lost in the tumult of the Russian Revolution. But what had the Russian found?

With minutes to spare in Geneva, Switzerland, I found my overnight train to Italy. On the platform, I checked my ticket with the conductor, hauled my suitcase down the sleeper car's narrow hallway into its tiny, tidy compartment, and unpacked a sandwich and a bottle of beer. I took out *Moby-Dick* and kicked off my shoes. After a hectic day of travel, I was looking forward to a quiet evening. I also needed to be rested so I could hit Bologna's libraries and archives first thing in the morning.

A couple of minutes later, the conductor came by, a grandfatherly Italian with a thick black moustache and forbearing eyes, gesturing for my ticket. Aha. He shook his finger, said something in Italian, and pointed to the ticket's date, by which I grasped: the ticket is for today's date, but for a month later. Fortunately, the conductor can tell me where I can go, I thought. No, wait, I realized, he can't speak English. And I don't speak Italian. I can speak Spanish, I said. (At least enough to understand what needs to happen here, I thought to myself.) Oh, so can I, he said, and, switching to Spanish, he explained what he was going to do. The suitcase was unstowed; the sandwich, beer, and book packed up; and I was squeezed past two backpackers who were waiting for what turned out to be their compartment.

The train had started out, and now I needed a berth. Until he could secure me a permanent spot for the night, the conductor put me in a compartment with a man who spoke only Italian. In preparation for my trip, I'd been reading a new book about Mezzofanti that had been written in Italian—or, rather, I'd been placing Italian words into grammatical patterns from Spanish. Whenever I'd gotten stuck or wanted to check an intuition (or, let's face it, a flat-out guess), I'd made liberal use of Google's language tools. Now I found myself with someone to speak to, but my lips were welded shut. Ashamed that something more Spanishified than Italian would come out of my mouth (especially since it had been primed talking with the conductor), I let the welds hold, and the opportunity flashed by like the Swiss countryside.

I spent the night in a compartment with a youth from South Korea who spoke a bit of English and a Peruvian guy living in Geneva who spoke English, Spanish, French, German, and Portuguese. Not all equally well, he admitted, and he'd once known Italian, but as soon as he'd studied Portuguese as an adult, he lost his Italian *completely*. His English was far from impeccable—his accent thick and his sentences simple—but would I say he spoke English? We talked about educational philosophies for a while, all in English, and I didn't choose easier words on his behalf. Sure, I'd say he spoke English.

And let me tell you, there's nothing like a trip on a European train to make a white American fellow realize that English, his cradle and his throne, has also been his prison. Sitting with a guy who speaks five languages (four of which he wasn't native to) was intimidating. I started to feel defensive: to be fair, if Americans lived near or traveled across as many borders as Europeans do, they might be multilingual, too. It's all about context and need, and those together engender a cultural confidence about learning languages that's hard to replicate. Once monolingualism is in the genome of a culture, it's hard to breed out.

I told him I was going to Bologna to research a nineteenth-century cardinal, Giuseppe Mezzofanti, who spoke a huge number of languages, seventy-two of them, or so it was said. I felt compelled to include that last caveat—I didn't want him to think I accepted the claim uncritically. Had Mezzofanti actually been able to speak that many? I didn't know for sure, though all the accounts of his life had confirmed a very high number.

"Seventy-two languages," my new friend said. "That's incredible."

I know, I thought, it's *incredible,* isn't it? If there were no traces, or if the stories could be proved false, I would at least be able to feel the grim satisfaction of the devil's advocate: to have dispelled a fraudulent reputation, to have discredited a miracle.

But if clues to his genius could be found, then this trip would count as a pilgrimage. As a kid, I had fantasized about learning many languages, too. To be able to talk and read in something other than English seemed proof that a gawky pubescent dreamer could shed his gawkiness and achieve his dreams of escaping to far-off places. But the dream sagged to the ground like a kite on a windless day. At the start of every summer vacation, my mother made me list what I wanted to accomplish by August. The top of the list: "Learn French." (My family's ethnically French.) And there it stayed, year after year; I never learned French. *I never even began.* Without anyone to help me, I didn't know where to start. High school Spanish beckoned, but the dullness of the classes bleached my passion and the language along with it.

In college, an academic advisor noted Spanish on my transcript. "What about studying abroad in South America?" she asked. My reluctance was brief. Soon enough, I found myself sitting in a kitchen in Bogotá, Colombia, attempting small talk with Zoraida, my host mother. A desperate search for chitchat, not my strong suit even in English, had me squeaking *"Me gusta tu perro"* about the small white dog licking my hand.

"You already said that," Zoraida remarked in Spanish.

Understanding that much was luck. Eventually I grew to say, read, and comprehend much more, surprising myself. Traveling made it easier to hang on to the language. I understood entire lectures delivered in the pure accent of the Colombian *altiplano* without registering that I was doing so. A girlfriend, an American, who had acquired French and Spanish during what appeared (to my dreamer's eye) to be an exotic childhood, spurred me to get language experiences of my own. Which is why, after college, I lived in Taiwan teaching English, studying Mandarin Chinese, picking up a bit of Taiwanese (a bar trick that proved as useful in the classroom), and testing the folk wisdom that lovers make the best language teachers. Days went by when I spoke no English outside of the classroom. I wondered: If this keeps up, will I recognize myself?

At my best moments in these languages, I felt comfortable speaking and listening, and I always improved, though not unceasingly—the plateaus could be as long and unbroken as Kansas. Back in the States, with English full-time, my fluencies collapsed, perhaps because I hadn't reached a high enough level, or because I didn't do the right things to keep up my skills. Floating in the back of my mind was the thought that if I couldn't gain a native's fluency, pursuing these languages was inconsequential.

The truth is, I'm neither a language superhero nor a hyperpolyglot. I consider myself a *monolingual with benefits*: more than a monoglot, much less than a polyglot. Fantasies of restoring some bit of that fluency in Spanish and Chinese rise up now and then, but I might as well hope to grow feathers and fly. I loved using those languages, but finding opportunities to do so where I live takes effort. I can be lazy and haphazard. My forty-three-year-old memory is more sieve than steel trap. And I bear the emotional legacy of teachers and textbook writers who made me submit to pedagogical contraptions that made language learning cumbersome and absurd. One goal of adulthood is to avoid all the irrelevant and absurd things imposed on us in childhood, so the path clearly leads away from the language classroom. Life is Sisyphean enough as it is.

Yet, in speaking another language, I've also experienced some of the thrillingest thrills in my life, when the sunlight of sense shone on gobbledygook; when the smooth and effortless Spanish or Chinese conversations of my dream life happen when I'm awake. When I piece together a sentence in Hindi to the delight of my hosts. When I overhear Beijing merchants discuss the price of some merchandise in Mandarin, and then tell them, in Mandarin, that I know the true price after they've quoted me a higher one. When I glimpse, even for a split second, a different way to be, and begin to accrue more self—an uncanny me emerging from a strange syntax. These are feelings I love, and would love to have again. That much I share with the hyperpolyglots I describe in this book.

But I don't know why the hard part of learning languages was so hard, or why the easy parts were easy. All I know is that I don't want to speak seventy-two or even twelve languages. I really just want more of the easy and less of the hard.

The next day, I arrived in Bologna. I wanted to find the truth, but if it eluded me, I wouldn't be surprised.

Before embarking for Bologna, I had contacted a few experts for some perspective on what I hoped to find. One was a linguist at the University of California at Berkeley, Claire Kramsch, who had published and written a lot about multilingualism, so I looked forward to her sympathetic insights. Yes, she told me, there are people who learn many languages. Then she paused. "Not only Europeans, I mean, but in Africa children grow up knowing, speaking, parts or elements of eight or nine different languages at the drop of a hat because they live in regions where villages have their own languages, and people intermarry and learn each other's ways of speaking, and so forth.

"But I wouldn't say that they *speak* different languages," she added, in a charming British accent of her own. "They speak many different languages, but they don't necessarily know how to read or write in them, which often don't have a written form. And those languages are used in very specific contexts—you need to know the language of the tribe that you're going to meet at the water pump, but you won't necessarily know how to order meat from them at the market. So each language is restricted to a particular domain.

"I don't know how to call these people," she admitted. "I suppose you call them multilinguals, but in another sense from people who have the full range of competencies in the spoken and written language. You've got to qualify what it means to speak a language."

That knot of a question stayed with me. *What does it mean to speak a language?* In Ann Patchett's novel *Bel Canto,* the multilingual interpreter, Gen, must ask for a doctor in the many languages spoken by the people with whom he's been kidnapped. Gen knows a bunch of words and how to pronounce them; he knows how the words are put together; he knows how to construct sentences. These three areas—lexicon, morphology, and syntax—make up what linguists call the "code." Maybe you could call knowing the code speaking the language. Yet Gen also judges how he puts the code to work. This is called "pragmatics." He's constantly weighing word choices, worrying that he's said the wrong thing to the wrong person. Now, the tricky part about the subtleties of pragmatics is that you have to learn them firsthand. Say you're in Japan, leaving a country inn after a meal, and the owner, a woman, says to you, *"Arigato gozaimashita"*—"Thank you (for what you did eating in my restaurant)." How do you respond? Though you know *Doiteshimashite*—"You're welcome"—this would be wholly inappropriate. Properly and politely, you might bow. You may also say, *"Domo,"* or "Thanks," as in "Thank *you* very much." Interestingly, to act most like a linguistic insider, you would be right to say nothing at all.

Maybe the right question was not about *speaking* a language, it was about *knowing* a language—which had several definitions, Kramsch acknowledged. By her definition, knowing a language means that someone has to have the code and its pragmatics, and be able to make literate use of the code. They also have to possess a strongly felt, deeply held combination of language, identity, and culture that makes up the intangible but visceral quality called an "attachment" to language. Only those people who feel that attachment powerfully enough to defend it can "know" a language.

According to Kramsch, to know a language means that you know the culture of its native speakers. You carry the language's cultural baggage—which would mean, among other things, that you know the significance of what you choose to say in this or that language. "If you talk to Latinos in the United States, that's why their attachment to the language is more than just about their ability to use different labels for the same object," she said. "It's an attachment to an emotional kind of world of experience that is indissociable from the use of the language in particular contexts."

"So those people who simply master the linguistic system, should they be limited from saying that they speak that language?" I asked.

"No," she said. "They speak the language, but they have no cultural attachment to it."

"Does that disqualify them from being able to claim that they're multilingual?"

"One has to bear in mind," she said, "that there are these kinds of people, who don't associate any particular cultural baggage with any of the languages that they speak. One can play terrific scales on the piano and have a dazzling mastery of scales and notes, but that doesn't mean to say that you understand Mozart or that you are a gifted musician. It's one thing to master the code. It's another thing to understand what people mean, or why speakers of that code don't use it interchangeably."

"What's the most languages you've felt someone personally engaged with?" I asked her.

"Oh, I don't know," she said. "Testimonies of multilinguals show that they resonate personally and culturally in a different manner with maybe three or four languages. Five is stretching it already, and that includes your own, the one you grew up with." Most of these people grew up with three languages and then added a fourth, she added. They were personally engaged with the culture and what she called "the frame of mind of the speakers of the language."

"One of my sons," she said, "he grew up in three languages and added a fourth, but even though he learned languages on the side, I can't say [of] his sixth or seventh languages that he resonated with them. . . . In my case, I resonate culturally to three. Even though I had Russian, Greek, Latin, et cetera. But . . . these are butterflies," she said, laughing, "that I add to my collection."

Of course, one can legitimately set the bar for knowing a language in any number of places, and the limits that one employs will reflect one's experiences and investments. By her definition, six-year-olds who can't yet read can't be said to know even their native language. The same is true for people who, no matter how proficient, haven't grown up acquiring the cultural baggage of a language. Later, I wondered why anyone would want to tackle learning a language if one were always to be held to a native speaker's knowledge as the target to shoot for.

The point she made in closing was a valuable one. "You know, the languages we speak are so much a part of the experiential fabric of our lives, so asking how many languages you know is only asking half the question," she said. "You should also ask, *In how many languages do you live?* Of course, the more languages you have in your life, the more enriched your experiences are, but keeping them all up requires more travel and contact than most people can do. So I would say that people could do, at the utmost, four or five languages."

I also asked Robert DeKeyser, an expert in language acquisition at the University of Maryland, what he thought about the stories of Mezzofanti.

"If you have a good memory and you're motivated, then learning enough vocabulary in a dozen languages is not a feat at all. The reason more people don't do so is that very few people are motivated to do so," DeKeyser said.

"What is much harder," he said, "and what you *do* need a special aptitude for, is that you need to be fluent, and not only fast and fluent, but accurate in a wide variety of languages. There, you're not just talking about vocabulary, you're talking about grammar. And you're not just using grammar, but doing it very quickly, like native speakers do, using a number of rules at an amazingly high rate of speed. So you need a lot of practice.

"In turn," he continued, "that implies two other things: first, a much larger amount of time than is needed for memorizing vocabulary, and also what I would call a capacity for monitoring in your speech what you know about grammar. So, even if you know all the basic grammar, it still takes a lot of effort to use it at normal speed in spoken language. I think that if you do find someone who is exceptionally good at speaking a fairly high number of languages quite fluently and accurately, what you're going to find is really typical of them is that they are so good at doing this monitoring.

"It's not like we only have eighteen compartments for language in the brain and then we're done," DeKeyser said. "But in order to learn so many languages so well, and to keep them up after learning them, you need an amount of time that nobody has, even if you spent all your time speaking and practicing languages.

"So when we hear these stories about cardinals one hundred or two hundred years ago, I'm very, very, very, very skeptical," he said, "because most people who are not linguists don't even realize what it really means to learn a language. They also don't realize that—even if you can speak a language fairly fluently—how incredibly far away you are from native proficiency by any real standards."

He'd brought up native proficiency as a standard of comparison without any prompting from me. Was that the best criterion to use for someone like Mezzofanti?

DeKeyser was born and raised in Belgium, a country that's officially multilingual yet so politically fractious, it's often held up as a case study for why political systems can't function smoothly with more than one official language. Dutch is spoken in the north; French in the southwest; German in a small southeastern area; and everyone studies English. (DeKeyser speaks all four.) Added to the stew is the polyglot bureaucracy of the European Commission, based in Brussels, a city where you're most likely to hear French, though Dutch is an official language, too.

Belgians' multilingualism stems from economics—the country depends on imports and exports—and from the tiny size of the Dutch-speaking population, about 22 million worldwide. Taking on a number of languages is a social expectation, something that children are taught to believe in—and not, I was interested to find, something they magically imbibe in the Belgian tap water. Taking language courses is a recreational pastime that's subsidized by the government. The happy outward face that Belgians put on their many languages masks the economic tensions between regions of the country. I once heard someone call Belgium a "nice laboratory for multilingualism." Someone else called it "a low-grade linguistic Serbia." That sounded more realistic.

Before we parted, DeKeyser shared a dim memory from the late 1980s, in which a Belgian bank, now defunct, had sponsored a contest to find the most multilingual Belgian. A sort of language game, with rules. Hundreds of people had applied. Contestants were tested in brief conversations with native speakers from universities and embassies.

"Of course, a lot of people claimed a lot more languages, but they couldn't do very much in these languages," he said. "One of my colleagues was involved in testing one person in Hindi, and this person knew a lot about Hindi and could converse a bit. But could you say this person *knew* Hindi?"

He couldn't remember the bank or the name of the winner or how multilingual he or she proved to be. Of course, the number of languages would have to be very small. Maybe, DeKeyser said, only eight?

A real, living hyperpolyglot whose oral skills have been assessed by experts? Hmm, I thought. Now, that's definitely someone I'd like to meet.

Chapter 3

Seen from the window of my penthouse bed-and-breakfast, the red roofs and orange walls of Bologna's buildings glowed like embers. Down there, somewhere, was Mezzofanti's secret, waiting to be unearthed. Each morning, I woke early to look at the sun pouring over the roofs, the cathedral, and the two tall, leaning towers, the Due Torri, rising from the spreading light. An elevator cage rattled up the shaft to greet me and delivered me to the first floor. I walked through the cool porticos of the narrow, jumbled streets as single scooters buzzing down the cobblestones scuffed the morning quiet.

Along the way to the library that housed Mezzofanti's archive, I'd stop at a bar for espresso and a pastry. My first morning, I could only ask for *un espresso*, point, and shrug. Does anyone care how well a visiting foreign writer talks in the local tongue? By the end of the week, I was better at shrugging, was pointing less, and had mastered *Per favore, un espresso e un dolce*; *Come pagare*; and *Come si dice*. I had also learned the essential phrase *Non posso parlare italiano*, which will always be true.

Under a statue of Luigi Galvani, the eighteenth-century physician who discovered how electricity moves muscles, I read the newspaper, in English, until the gates to the Archiginnasio public library opened. Built between 1562 and 1563, the Archiginnasio housed the university until 1803; part of this large public facility became the municipal library in 1838, and now its courtyards and grand lecture halls offer a miniature history of Bologna. During World War II, Allied bombs damaged most of it—though, luckily for me, the Mezzofanti papers stored there had been spirited to the hills. One day, I drifted into the anatomical theater, a large wood-paneled room lined with wooden statues of ancient scientists and doctors. Destroyed in the bombing, these statues rested high on the walls and had been reconstructed to look down, as they had during the Renaissance, on a central marble dissection table. There, in the name of medical science, the bodies of executed criminals had been cut apart, sectioned, labeled, and compared. Never, though, the bodies of hyperpolyglots. Or their brains.

I'd painted a nice picture for myself of how my first day in the rare manuscript room would go. I'd come in and introduce myself with magical Italian fluency, then blow the dust off a box lid and find—oh, confessions, boasts, poems, or perhaps the parchment on which a pact with Mephistopheles was signed in blood, promising a lifetime of unlimited linguistic capacity and an eternity in the Dark One's company. Evidence of Mezzofanti's prowess would be so irrefutable, the truth about the cardinal could now be revealed.

What did happen was more like this: I stumbled up the stairs, following signs I could barely decipher. *Biblioteca* and *manoscritti*, easy enough. The woman at the guard desk stopped me with a stream of Italian before I could make the common signal for *I don't speak your language*. I shrugged my shoulders—she kept talking. Then I tried the universal gesture for *I'd like to look at the manuscripts. Manuscritti*, I said. *Manoscritti? Sì.* She pointed down the hall. I turned to walk. No, no, no, she said. Exasperated with my stupidity, she gestured to my laptop, then handed me a slip of paper to fill out: *nome, indirizzo, telefono.* Fine; I filled it out. The paper stamped, where to go now? She pointed. Down the hall.

The room that housed rare manuscripts was long and high-ceilinged with tall bookshelves behind glass doors. In the archival-quality silence, librarian heads swiveled when I entered. *"Buongiorno,"* I said. *"Buongiorno,"* said one librarian, a middle-aged woman with a decidedly curdled attitude. I knew only the name of the librarian I'd emailed a few weeks before—me writing in English, her replying in Italian, me putting her replies into online translation tools. Paola Foschi? I asked, pronouncing it *foshee*. The uptight librarian added an expression of puzzlement. Ah, she said, *foskee,* then she asked me to wait.

Another woman with narrow glasses and pursed lips approached me, and I introduced myself. Her eyes lit up with recognition, and a flood of Italian came out of her mouth, the only recognizable word being *Mezzofanti.* We'd communicated so well by email. Now we faced each other like sailors from two distant nations with a sail to raise or a whale to harpoon and no shared words for getting it done except Mezzofanti. *Sì, Mezzofanti,* I said. She went off, bustled at one of the bookshelves, and presented me with a bound ledger, about two feet long and fourteen inches wide, a handwritten catalog of every single item in the ninety-odd boxes of Mezzofanti's collection.

This was the *inventario.* Paging through it for a minute, I felt my heart sink. Each entry had been written with a light quill pen, the handwriting ornate and illegible. I mentally kicked myself: I should have practiced reading nineteenth-century handwriting before I came, and now I've wasted a trip. I fought through a few more pages. If there's information here, I won't recognize it, I realized. Forget secrets.

At that moment, Paula Foschi interrupted me, pushing another massive volume across the table's dark wood and gesturing for me to open it. It was a duplicate *inventario* volume, devoted to Mezzofanti and written in a modern, readable hand. I wanted to kneel in thanks.

Immediately the dizzying polyglot nature of the *inventario* was revealed. Of all ninety boxes of his papers, which were filled with writing in Latin, Italian, and other languages, I was most interested in the first half-dozen boxes, devoted to his linguistic acquisitions. The contents were arranged alphabetically, by language: *Angolana, Armena, Birmana, Bolognese, Catalan, Cinese, Inglese.* On and on they went. Eventually I counted fifty-six languages, all sporting their Italian names. It was like a map of a desert as vast and forbidding as the desert itself.

The *inventario* described the contents of each box, down to the individual item: family letters, official correspondence, official documents. Some just said "miscellaneous." How these had been identified and by whom, I didn't know, but it had been a polyglot someone. I was jealous of that someone, who could have told me what those documents actually said. The entries described each one, and when relevant, cited its first few lines—in Italian or Latin, German, French, English, Spanish, Portuguese, Russian, Chinese, Arabic, Armenian. Often entries said, "a letter in German," "a letter in Dutch." Sometimes the cataloger, stumped, maybe overwhelmed, tagged it merely as a *"Componimento di _____."*

The relics of the hyperpolyglot saint. Mezzofanti. He's real, I thought, absolutely real. By the end of the day, my head swam with fragments of languages and alphabets, and I couldn't wait to continue my search. I was tapping, tapping, tapping: listening for something hollow and hoping to find something big.

My second morning in Bologna, when the bartender asked me for *due euro,* instead of handing over five and hoping the breakfast cost less, I gave him the two he asked for. In the manuscript room, the librarians smiled when I arrived. *"Buongiorno,"* they said, which meant *Welcome!* And also, *We're sure you'll read flawlessly in Italian today! We're happy to bring you boxes, but only two before lunch!*

Yesterday, I had looked only at the *inventario*'s listings. Today I planned to dig into the boxes themselves, which arrived on a wheeled cart, one by one. Constructed out of cardboard to look like books, they were antiqued with a patina of dust. Opening the lid released a musty smell—some hadn't been cracked for decades. (The scrupulous librarians pantomimed how I should add my signature to a list of others on a sheet inside the boxes.)

First box, first file. In "Angolana," whatever that was, were four items of *versi*. One a poem about Bethlehem, another about the Three Kings. Dated 1844, 1845, 1847, and 1848. Between the sentences was a Latin translation of each. Had my cardinal written these? If he knew Angolana, why did he need the Latin translation, too? I was tapping, tapping, and here was a hollow sound, which I ignored in order to move on.

The next file, labeled Coptic, contained two poems about the Three Kings, another about Bethlehem, with Latin translations. This repetition of themes would make sense to me only later. Many letters, but not in the twiggy scrawl that I would come to recognize as Mezzofanti's. On and on it came, on stiff, browned paper, cut in all sorts of irregular sizes. Time had reduced some of it to the texture of a butterfly's wing.

The next box. Albanian (a poem, a list of verbs, and some sentences); Algonquin (a grammar, a dictionary, and a catechism, none written in Mezzofanti's hand, but the first part of a translation of the Book of Genesis, which was his); Amharic; Arabic (a long lecture by Mezzofanti about the history of Arabic); Basque (a collection of words); Burmese (some prose); Bohemian (some language exercises); "Californian" (a grammatical sketch of Luiseño, an indigenous American language, which wasn't done by Mezzofanti); Quechua, a native South American language (a list of words, not in Mezzofanti's hand); Persian (a poem by Mezzofanti about a Persian poet); and other assorted items in Chinese; Coptic (Egyptian written with an adapted Greek alphabet); Danish; Hebrew; Ethiopian (a translated letter); French; Greek; English; Italian; Latin; "Livonese" (possibly Livonian, a nearly extinct language once spoken in what is now Latvia and Estonia); Maltese; and Dutch. Already I was finding evidence that Mezzofanti, indeed, knew parts of many languages. But how well did he know Algonquin or Burmese? That was less clear.

The *inventario* listed many *versi*. I looked up *versi* in my dictionary. The first meaning was what I'd expected: "verse, poetry."

The less literal meanings surprised me. Second was "sound, noise, cry," as an animal might. Third was "silly noise." Next was "direction, way." Next was "way," as in method: *Per un verso o per un altro.*

If you know Italian well, this cluster of *verse, sound, animal cry, silly noise, way,* and *method* might seem perfectly natural, like a snail in its shell, like a leaf on a tree. Some would say these meanings are the surfaced tips of submerged metaphors whose linkages, though very real, aren't visible. Perhaps the mark of knowing a language is an ability to grasp what's submerged as surely as you or I can recognize in a glance three connected lines as a triangle. Certainly Mezzofanti knew his native Bolognese this way, maybe a few other languages, too. But did he know all fifty-eight or seventy-two or one hundred fourteen of them like this? For that miracle alone, Mezzofanti might have been canonized, back in the days when people believed that a person could really be in two locations at once (as Saint Catherine could do) or levitate (as Saint Joseph of Copertino could do). Today this claim would garner only skepticism.

Sitting at that long table in the Archiginnasio, looking through the contents of the first box, I realized I was so intent on the voices of doubters and believers going back and forth in my head that I had stopped paying attention to the boxes and their contents. Stop, I told myself. You just got here. Stop and look. Revelations will come.

That afternoon, I wandered up Via Malcontenti, the street where Mezzofanti was born. A narrow side street, its only storefronts now are a tanning salon, a small grocery, and a sex shop. You'd have to tow the parked cars, drag away the trash bins, and clean the graffiti from the walls to capture a ghost of Malcontenti as it was when Giuseppe Mezzofanti lived there. Opposite the sex shop, about twenty feet high on a cracked wall, is a plaque that reads, in Latin:

> Here was born Mezzofanti, who by a miracle was uniquely able
> to learn the speech of every country.

Under it sits another plaque, this one in Italian, that reads:

> Here there was a carpenter shop
> where Giuseppe Mezzofanti
> the most supreme of polyglots
> in 1781 at the age of 7
> with Francis his father
> worked with a plane and a saw.

You couldn't pick a better way to emanate a powerfully miraculous vibe in Catholic Bologna than by being the unusually talented son of a carpenter. It was said that young Giuseppe worked on a bench in the street, before a building where a priest, Father Respighi, tutored rich boys in Greek and Latin. Overhearing the recitations from the window, the carpenter's son soaked them up. When Respighi discovered this, he pleaded with Giuseppe's reluctant father to let the boy go to school.

It's true that Mezzofanti was born, raised, and lived on Via Malcontenti until 1831, when he moved to Rome, where he died and was buried in 1849. But his early education likely began with less drama than this tale would imply. According to family sources, he attended a basic school from the age of three, at first merely to keep him out of mischief while his parents worked, but it was soon discovered that he knew the lessons, too. There began his study of Latin, ancient Greek, and French. A hundred years earlier, a Bolognese boy who displayed intellectual promise could have become a scholar or an artist, gone into business, or become a military man, but in a declining city tightly controlled by the Church, the best path for a bright boy born in the latter half of the eighteenth century was the priesthood. At twelve, Giuseppe entered the seminary.

No matter which story you believe, Mezzofanti's work with languages seems to have begun when he was very young. This gave him important early experiences with many sorts of sounds and ways to structure words and sentences. Once he was in the seminary, his language studies intensified—Hebrew, Arabic, Coptic, more German, more French—and this early exposure clearly gave him an advantage later on.

Now we'd say that the young student's brain was plastic, and that he was taking advantage of his youth, when the neural circuits in his brain that control the physical and mental actions involved in language were still very flexible. In time, this plasticity dwindles. Around the age of six is said to be the cutoff for acquiring a native-like pronunciation, because the brain's connections between sounds you perceive and the motor commands for reproducing them harden early.

However, even among bilingual children, the second language, no matter how early it's learned, may be accented, especially if it's spoken less than the first. By around twelve, very few are likely to ever *sound* native, as a rule. (Though some individuals can, especially if the language they're learning is similar to their first.) By fifteen, a person will not easily have a native-like grammar. (Though a few people do, especially if the languages are similar.) After that time, adults can learn words and what they mean fairly well—it's something we do in our native languages for our entire lives. And though picking up new grammatical rules is harder, adults are literate and have longer attention spans, both of which benefit them as learners.

Maybe Mezzofanti had other advantages. What could they have been? Take a look at the pedagogical techniques of his day. Imagine a small room crammed with desks, boys hunched over worn-out books, reading in hypnotic unison sentences they didn't comprehend, then one by one translating aloud into Latin or Italian when the teacher prompted. Containing few everyday words, the sentences are long, round, and come from poetry, the Bible, or classical works. Grammatical patterns, lists of verbs or noun cases, are recited, but novel sentences are never created. No, these methods probably weren't so special, actually.

Is this a credible beginning for a hyperpolyglot? A modern person would think, *To communicate, one must communicate*. To talk meaningfully, one must have explicit lessons in doing so, you might suppose. But Mezzofanti did no role plays, no skits; had no phone apps; didn't Skype with his native-speaking tutor. The language lab was an invention two hundred years away. As I later found, hyperpolyglots tend to succeed no matter the type of specific teaching methods. Some are devoted autodidacts; others happily study in classrooms; others learn what they need from other speakers. One can also pinpoint the benefits of the kind of schooling that Mezzofanti did receive. Studying Latin and ancient Greek gave him a good start in Romance-language vocabulary and the structure of Indo-European languages, as well as broad experience with two alphabets. (He'd go on to read and maybe write in a total of six.) And though the educational tradition suffers compared to what we do today, it gave him two important tools for his linguistic enterprise: an accomplished memory and confidence.

Not many advantages came from his broader environment, which wasn't particularly multilingual. Had he been immersed in a setting with many languages, he might have picked them up, at home and in the streets. Yet Giuseppe didn't live in a border town or a capital city. His family didn't migrate; both parents were Bolognese. Giuseppe himself didn't travel outside of northern Italy until the middle of his life, so he probably never encountered the other Italian languages in the places where they had originated. Had he been able to surmount the mores of his family's laborer class in order to travel, he might have found that up and down the Italian peninsula, so many different varieties of languages were used that Italy was, as one scholar puts it, "a riot of linguistic variation." Most people were probably monolingual, speaking only the local dialect. In 1860, when an independent, stable Italian republic was finally established, only 10 percent of the population spoke the prestigious Florentine dialect we now call the Italian language.

On the other hand, history conspired to bring the languages of the world closer to Mezzofanti. Beginning at a fairly young age, he had three teachers, all of them Jesuit missionaries who had been expelled in 1767 from parts of the Spanish empire. They probably exposed Giuseppe to Spanish, Swedish, German, and French. They might have given him lessons in Tagalog and some indigenous American languages. Even more powerful than the language lessons would have been an introduction to the Jesuits' scientific approach, which recognized the power of language, not only for converting savages but as a tool to export the West's learning. To cite but one example among many, it was a Jesuit, Matteo Ricci (1552–1610), who translated Euclid into Chinese.

At fifteen years old, after long nights in the library preparing for an exam, Mezzofanti collapsed. Afterward, he dropped out of school, and what occupied him for the next several years is unknown—perhaps he planed wood in his father's workshop on Via Malcontenti. After recuperating, he finished school and in 1797, at the age of twenty-three, was ordained and appointed a professor of Arabic at the University of Bologna. He'd been making the trek up and down the Archiginnasio steps for barely half a year when European politics intervened. After refusing to swear an oath to the (short-lived) Cispadane Republic that Napoleón had carved out of northern Italy's papal states in 1796, the young professor was cruelly stripped of his post.

I mention this political history to show how far-ranging and unpredictable the factors that make a hyperpolyglot can be. Had he kept his job, the young Mezzofanti would never have landed in the geographic and social spaces where multiple languages cross and congregate. From 1796 to 1800, the armies of Napoleón and the Austrian dynasty battled over the strategic and political prize of Bologna, where hospitals filled up with wounded men from all over the linguistically diverse Austrian empire, men who needed Mezzofanti's priestly services. As nurse and confessor, Mezzofanti improved his German, and also picked up Hungarian, Czech, Polish, Russian, Flemish, and perhaps Romani. He claimed he could acquaint himself with a language in fourteen days. He did this, it was said, by asking the patient to say the ordinary prayers, from which he could discern words and patterns.

"In such cases," Mezzofanti told Augustin Manavit, who wrote a biography in French of the cardinal, "accordingly, I used to apply myself, with all my energy, to the study of the language of the patients, until I knew enough of them to make myself understood." He added: "Through the grace of God, assisted by my private studies, and by a retentive memory, I came to know, not merely the generic languages of the nations to which the several invalids belonged, but even the peculiar dialects of their various provinces."

In his archives, I found records from this stretch of his life. He received a certificate, dated 1798, which commended him (in Italian) for helping "every time someone sick came to us speaking in a language unknown to us." The next year, he received another certificate applauding him for his "tireless zeal" interpreting in various languages for the sick. So there's a record of his learning languages from people, not from books, and from people with whom he may have shared no other language. This in itself isn't a feat. Traders, explorers, and missionaries have always ventured among people who don't speak their language, and either constructed a common one (a pidgin) or learned one another's. Yet there's no record of anyone else with the resources to acquire as many languages as Mezzofanti apparently did.

After losing his professorship, Mezzofanti supported his parents, his sister, and her family by teaching languages to foreigners and to children of rich families, who then hired him as a librarian for their private collections. He worked on languages mainly by seeking out travelers coming through Bologna. "The hotel keepers were in the habit of apprising me of the arrival of all strangers in Bologna," Mezzofanti told Manavit. "I made no difficulty when anything was to be learned, about calling on them, interrogating them, making notes of their communications, and taking instructions from them in the pronunciation of their respective languages."

Was Mezzofanti gifted? He seemed to possess an indigenous talent for some aspect of languages, and he matches some of the descriptions of other brilliant youths: he excelled despite training of variable quality (when he had it at all) and handled a great deal of linguistic material at a very young age. Also, he evidently had drive and a very long attention span.

"I made it a rule to learn every new grammar, and to apply myself to every strange dictionary that came within my reach," he said. "I was constantly filling my head with new words; and, whenever any new strangers, whether of high or low degree, passed through Bologna, I endeavored to turn them to account, using the one for the purpose of perfecting my pronunciation, and the other for that of learning the familiar words and turns of expression."

For most of his life, the Bolognese scholar priest was thin and pale. "His whole appearance," noted one writer, "indicates delicacy." In his later years he was described as a "cheerful old man." Mrs. Polyxena Paget remembered him as "small in stature, dry, and of a pale unhealthy look. His whole person was in monkey-like restless motion." His eyelids twitched. Reactions to this tic were varied. Some said it made him look weak.

He ate little, never drank wine, and slept only three hours a night. "During the long nights which he devoted to study he never, even in the coldest weather, permitted himself the indulgence of a fire," wrote one of his biographers. He could not be persuaded to use the small portable brazier called a *scaldino* (or *scaldén* in Bolognese) favored by Italian students, to warm his hands or feet. Humble, he would not let people kiss his ring, the usual greeting that cardinals receive. Three times in his life he fell desperately ill, and each time, he admitted to a "confusion of languages." After one illness, he temporarily forgot all his language acquisitions but Bolognese. There's no record of how he got them back.

Among his jobs, he worked as *confessore dei forestieri,* the priest who heard the confessions of foreigners. Once the authorities called him to the jail cell of two prisoners who were to be executed the next morning. No one could hear their confessions. They were going to die sinners— because no one else could speak their language. That night, back in his room, Mezzofanti learned to speak it well enough by morning that he could confer God's forgiveness before they went to the gallows.

Or that's how the story goes.

Another time, a woman came to see Mezzofanti with a problem: her maid, who spoke only Sardinian (which no other priest in Bologna knew), wanted to confess her sins for Easter. Give me two weeks, Mezzofanti said, I'll learn Sardinian. Laughing, the woman agreed, and every day for an hour, the maid visited with Mezzofanti. By Easter, it's said, he could speak enough Sardinian to hear the maid's confession.

On my first dive into Mezzofanti's papers, I was impressed by the profusion of languages—how this frail fellow had scoured clean the world's grammatical stables. Yet, as I went along, I became more disappointed with such mundane relics. Something was missing—the remnants of a process, even a miraculous one, for *learning*. If he'd had a method, I couldn't find the instructions, or the word lists, or grammar exercises, or scraps of relevant notes. Maybe they'd been destroyed or weren't worth saving. Maybe, with such a prodigious memory, he'd gotten most of it into his head at the first pass, where it stuck.

Then I discovered something that made me wonder what Mezzofanti had *really* been up to.

Chapter 4

After several days, my ability to read Mezzofanti's ABCs had improved, even though his alephs and betas were nervous squiggles and his Chinese characters misshapen lumps. What bogged me down was the handwriting of his contemporaries—the letters he received had evidently been scrawled with tree branches and chicken feet, dipped in ink.

In this correspondence, I found evidence for the case I was hoping would not be disproved. Dating from the 1820s to the 1840s, he received letters in Latin, Modern Greek, Italian, English, German, Spanish, French, Portuguese, Russian, Polish, and Arabic. It's safe to say he could read all of these—none that I saw came with versions translated into Italian or Latin. He also wrote and read in Dutch, Turkish, Hungarian, and Catalan. Here was someone carrying on correspondence in fifteen languages, using four different alphabets!

Yet doubts started to creep in. Maybe it didn't mean much—maybe he needed a dictionary to read and write. Did he do this? There was no way to tell. Experts say it's easier to remember a word you're going to recognize in speech or writing than if you have to speak or write it. On the other hand, being literate means you have less wiggle room for errors. The profusion was certainly impressive—Mezzofanti could

function in as many languages as he needed to. But how well? What
levels of proficiency had he attained?

With this question in mind, I pondered the Algonquin file. As an
American, this made me smile: part of the first wave of American popular culture to hit Europe in Mezzofanti's time was James Fenimore Cooper's *Leatherstocking Tales,* and Mezzofanti spoke warmly of *L'ultimo dei
Mohicani.* I wondered if Mezzofanti had brought these associations to
his study of the language. In the file I found a sixty-page description
of Algonquin grammar, not in Mezzofanti's hand, along with scraps of
paper with Algonquin words and phrases, translated into Italian or other
languages, written in many styles. Perhaps they reflected the styles of
his teachers.

Working through boxes, I'd been looking at a polyglot stew. I could
be said to be "reading" only in English and the Romance languages,
though I recognized many of the others. At one point, switching
between descriptions in Italian and letters in Portuguese, I came upon
the Algonquin grammar and then a set of conversational phrases, written on a page with Algonquin on one side and French on the other. *Je te
salue, mon fils. Te portes-tu bien? As-tu fait un bon voyage? As-tu fait une bonne
traversée?* I read along happily—oh, these are conversation starters, questions that Mezzofanti learned to ask in Algonquin. Perhaps he asked
them of Native American converts he met in his office.

This struck me as funny. Did he learn such questions in other languages, too? If so, he could use them like a script. Meet a native speaker,
pull out the pertinent questions. You'd seem polite—and in control of
the conversation. *Are you going to Naples? What's the name of your town?*
Learn to pronounce it the right way, and you'd be highly regarded. You
wouldn't even have to understand the answers—you'd move on to the
next question. *How old are you?*

One of Mezzofanti's biographers claimed that Mezzofanti was "completely master" of Algonquin (though it's not among the thirty languages
he supposedly knew best). Mezzofanti claimed to have learned it from a
longtime missionary in America. Based on what I saw in the archives, he
might only have mastered Algonquin chitchat with Algonquin-speaking
guests. Not Algonquin. Not jokes in Algonquin. Not politenesses. But a
formula for performing in Algonquin.

How limited would Mezzofanti's Algonquin have to be for us to cross it off his list of languages? Was this enough evidence to remove it from his list? And if it were removed, what other languages would have to be crossed off, too?

Before I could really consider the implications of this, I doubled back to check what language I'd been reading with such ease. French. I'd been reading in French as effortlessly as if it were English.

My first thought: *But I don't read French.*

Next: *What else have I been reading without knowing it?*

And then: *How much does a bit of language matter?*

What you're ultimately going to make of "bits of language" matters when you start to wrestle with the question of how many languages Mezzofanti knew and used. He left no definitive list of them; the resulting vacuum has long attracted controversy. Perhaps the first person to raise the issue in publication was Thomas Watts, a member of London's Philological Society and an important figure in the expert dissection of Mezzofanti. An intermediary between the period of Romanticism, to which Mezzofanti belonged, and the rise of empirical science and the age of brain studies, Watts himself was said to read fifty languages, including Chinese. Watts's essay "On the Extraordinary Powers of Cardinal Mezzofanti as a Linguist," which he read to the Society in 1852, diligently assembled, for the first time in English, disparate accounts of the Bolognese lion of languages.

The other important figure was Charles William Russell, an Irish priest, scholar, and president of what was then called St. Patrick's College, Maynooth (also known as Maynooth College), who'd met Mezzofanti in Rome twice and later, in 1858, wrote a clarifying biography, *The Life of Cardinal Mezzofanti,* which opened the cabinet of curiosities where Mezzofanti had been abandoned by science. Russell's goal was to separate the facts from fantasy, the reality from the myth.

His book is an absolute treasure, studded with the names of royals and intellectuals, with fascinating whispered asides on every page. At the beginning, Russell devotes 120 pages to describing a menagerie of polyglot scholars, monarchs, missionaries, explorers, and warriors who knew many languages. Most came from European countries. Mithridates makes an appearance. So does Sir William Jones (1746–1794), a British judge in India and a philologist who said that he knew twenty-eight languages. Part of a chapter discusses infant prodigies and unschooled polyglots, such as the British traveler Tom Coryat (1577–1617), who walked all over Europe and eastern Mediterranean countries, accumulating Italian, Turkish, Arabic, Persian, Hindustani, and probably a dozen other languages he had no use for at home.

Against this backdrop, Russell sets Mezzofanti's monumentalism: "Cardinal Mezzofanti will be found to stand so immeasurably above even the highest of these names . . . that, at least for the purposes of comparison with him, its minor celebrities can possess little claim for consideration," he wrote.

An enemy of Mezzofanti's skeptics, Russell contributed to a concrete case for his skill by creating a list of languages that Mezzofanti knew. More important, he lent a sense of order to the reports of firsthand observations. He borrowed a basic framework from William Jones, who had sorted his own twenty-eight languages according to his abilities in each.* The result produced something like the following.

Russell placed fourteen of Mezzofanti's languages at the lowest level, which meant that he'd studied the grammar and vocabulary but had never been observed using the languages: Sanskrit, Malay, "Tonquinese," Cochin-Chinese, Tibetan, Japanese, Icelandic, Lappish, "Ruthenian," Frisian, Lettish, Cornish, Quechua, and Bimbarra. In seven other languages, he could begin a conversation and knew conversational phrases: Sinhalese, Burmese, Japanese, Irish, Gaelic, Chippewa, Delaware, and "some of the languages of Oceanica." Such linguistic adventuring may be impressive, though one has to note that this calculation means that Mezzofanti possessed only bits of language in a third of the seventy-two languages with which Russell credits him.

According to Russell's best evidence, Mezzofanti had only the rudi-

---

*Eight he studied critically, eight he could read with a dictionary's help, and twelve others he considered "attainable." The eight he could speak he supposedly did so as perfectly as he did his native English.

ments in two more sets of languages. He could converse in eleven more, though there were too few eyewitness reports of his Kurdish, Georgian, Serbian, Bulgarian, "Gipsy language," Peguan, Welsh, Angolese, "Mexican," "Chilian," and "Peruvian" to really pin down his abilities. (Which puts the modern observer in the peculiar position of having to suppose that Mezzofanti might have had greater abilities in some languages than anyone knew.) However, in nine languages (Syriac, Ethiopian, "Amarinna," Hindustani, Gujarati, Basque, Wallachian, "Californian," and Algonquin) he "spoke less perfectly . . . in all of which, however, his pronunciation, at least, is described as quite perfect," Russell wrote.

Yet there were thirty languages that Russell and Watts agreed, more or less, that Mezzofanti had *mastered*. "These he spoke with freedom," Russell wrote, "and with a purity of accent, of vocabulary, and of idiom, rarely attained by foreigners." He defined Mezzofanti's "fluency" as an ability to talk without interruption (regardless of content) and with grammatical accuracy. "Above all," Russell wrote, a man could be truly said to know a language thoroughly "if he be admitted by intelligent and educated natives to speak it correctly and idiomatically."

For his part, Watts defined "mastery" as being "able to speak [a language] with perfect fluency and correctness," which would match "in the knowledge of it, on a level with the majority of the natives." In addition to perfect pronunciation, Watts also noted that the cardinal "conversed" in his languages, greeting people with "great spirit and precision." In his reckoning, the real measure of a rare ability would lie in conversation.

The thirty (as listed by Russell) were Hebrew, Rabbinical Hebrew, Arabic, Chaldean, Coptic, Ancient Armenian, Modern Armenian, Persian, Turkish, Albanian, Maltese, Greek, Romaic, Latin, Italian, Spanish, Portuguese, French, German, Swedish, Danish, Dutch, Flemish,* English, Illyrian, Russian, Polish, Czech (which Russell calls Bohemian), Hungarian, and Chinese.

Interestingly, these were the thirty languages he'd learned before he was thirty years old, according to reports. They represented a whopping

---

*Dutch and Flemish, of course, are widely acknowledged now to be the same language.

eleven linguistic families,* five of which (Romance, Germanic, Slavic, Hellenic, and Semitic) gave him the bulk of his acquisitions. With that much learning experience, each language would have become a small variation on a broader theme, providing a learning boost for each subsequent one. If he read these languages, he would have grappled with six different alphabets (I knew that he didn't read Chinese—trying to do so caused him some sort of breakdown—so I don't count it here).

On a total language count, Watts and Russell would eventually disagree. Russell said Mezzofanti had seventy-two languages, a number with some religious significance: it was the number of languages that was said to have resulted from the Tower of Babel's fall. Watts disputed some of Russell's sources, eliminated duplications, and without mentioning Russell's overlay of religious symbolism, reduced the overall repertoire to sixty or sixty-one.

But their fractiousness is superficial. Neither scholar doubted Mezzofanti's achievement or its glory, and, interestingly, neither one invoked the divine (angels, tongues of fire) to explain his gifts, not even Russell, for whom Mezzofanti's figure carried a religious charge. More significant, they both agreed that Mezzofanti had mastered thirty languages. *Mastered them.*

Despite Russell's careful accounting and Watts's surgical follow-up, disentangling Mezzofanti from folk legend and the preoccupations of his contemporaries is far from straightforward. It's not only a matter of how you define what it means to speak a language; it also matters who does the listening.

We commonly assume that native speakers are qualified to judge how well someone uses their language. But their opinions of another's mastery can take a cultural coloring. In Bologna, Italians welcomed my small attempts with praise, as have Mexicans and Colombians with Spanish. In Taiwan and China, people responded to my elementary abilities with polite enthusiasm: "Oh, you speak Chinese very well!" "Really,

---

*Semitic, Hurro-Urartian, Afroasiatic, Hellenic, Indo-Iranian, Turkic, Romance, Germanic, Slavic, Uralic, and Sino-Tibetan.

you don't have to be so polite," I'd reply in Chinese. I took the titters of shocked delight to mean that the sophistication of the reply (which I'd learned from a friend) had outstripped their true opinion of my skill.

By contrast, the French are vehemently uninterested in having a foreigner mangle their language—in stereotype, anyway. Theoretically, French natives would rate you lower in French than Spaniards would in Spanish. In Japan and Korea, a lower-skilled non-native will be highly regarded and praised, while someone with better skills will be viewed as a threat. Former US ambassador William Rugh, who was posted to Yemen and the United Arab Emirates, once counseled that if you're a non-native Arabic speaker appearing on Arabic-language media, it's better to keep a conversation going than to worry about being grammatically correct; the effort, which is appreciated by Arab audiences, looks good diplomatically. For cultural reasons, Arab audiences also prefer truthful speech, so they are more tolerant of imperfect Arabic than of an interpreter, who may alter what a person means. So various are all these responses that you'd have to conclude that a native speaker's opinion isn't necessarily a legitimate criterion.

An even bigger problem is that one person's "nativeness" in language X isn't necessarily the same as another's. Any close look at a speech community demonstrates that pronunciations, vocabularies, and grammars are heterogeneous across social divides, genders, and geographical areas. Two speakers of two dialects would both be considered native speakers, even though they might not be able to describe how their version differs from the standard—and though they might judge the other speaker's variety as somehow wrong or incorrect. In sign languages, the problem is profound. If you define a native speaker as someone who uses a language from birth at home, then there are hardly any native signers, since the majority of deaf children are born to hearing, nonsigning parents. (I'm speculating, but perhaps this is why sign language courses are so popular in the United States, where college enrollments went up more than 16 percent from 2006 to 2009: though there's a robust deaf culture, there's no native signing community to which one, by definition, can't ever belong.) Russell, the biographer of Mezzofanti, never says what sort of native speaker he's gathering evidence from.

Even if you could presume that each native speaker knows the same things that other natives know, it is a shallow standard, because one can pronounce words like a native speaker and also lack linguistic creativity. Confused with a real speaker, the mere mimic gets labeled as a "master" simply because she's able to string together words uninterruptedly as if she knows what she's doing. What's often called "fluency" might be no more than confidence (or blitheness). It's possible that Mezzofanti only ever aspired to "passing" in most of his languages. One piece of evidence for this is his clear phonetic enthusiasm, which Russell stingingly noted when describing Mezzofanti's English (the italics are his): "If I were disposed to criticize it very strictly," the Irishman wrote, "I might say (paradoxical as this may seem,) that, *compared with the enunciation of a native,* it was almost *too correct to appear completely natural.*"

Less obviously, Mezzofanti's social rank would have restricted an accurate read of his abilities. His meetings were probably fairly formal, which would have reduced unexpected or intimate topics. He could have controlled the meetings, too, so that none of them would endanger his linguistic reputation. Who would dare report that a person of such status couldn't actually do what he claimed?

And the Mezzofanti of legend grew in other directions. Travelers to Italy who embarked on the so-called Grand Tour sought out Catholic excesses that fascinated and disgusted them. Their accounts would have drawn Mezzofanti as a Romantic figure, a symbol of Catholicism's vivacious ruin. In response, the Church would have asserted the opposite. Mezzofanti represented the Church's ideal view of itself—conservative, theologically pure, and world-encircling—an image embedded in hagiographies like Russell's.

It's also easy to overlook the fact that judgments of "mastery" vary from era to era and to assume that the "fluency" and "mastery" of the eighteenth century would mean the same now that they meant then. Only a small bit of digging turns this on its head. In 1875, for instance, knowing French to the satisfaction of Harvard College meant you could translate at sight "easy" French prose. You didn't have to orate or converse in it or demonstrate your understanding with a French speaker.

Another example comes from the life of the adventuring hyperpoly glot Sir Richard Francis Burton (1821–1890). To show his British military superiors that he knew Hindustani, he had to translate two Hindustani books into English, translate a handwritten text, write a short essay, and have a conversation.* (He passed.) Nevertheless, over his lifetime, many of his linguistic achievements were in the spoken mode—in 1853 he became one of only a dozen Christians to have sneaked into the holy city of Mecca by passing as an Indian Muslim—one possessing fluent, though accented, Arabic. Yet to his military superiors, "knowing" a language was likely to mean knowing its grammatical particulars and its life in texts.

If time gets in the way of really knowing what someone like Mezzofanti or Burton was capable of, it also helps to explain why the hyperpolyglots of yesteryear seem to be bursting with languages while a modern educated person with a grasp of more than four is a rarity. One can talk about active language skills (talking, writing) and receptive skills (reading, listening); the receptive ones—which even monolinguals may have surprisingly a lot of in other languages—are generally easier to acquire and use. In the era of Mezzofanti and Burton, scholars spent far more time reading and translating texts—in receptive activities, in other words—than they spent communicating with people. I'm not saying that no one talked to other people in foreign languages; I'm

---

*Hindustani was the eighth language Burton learned in his life, after Latin, Greek, French, Italian, Provençal, Spanish, and Béarnais. He would go on to learn Gujarati, Persian, Sanskrit, Marathi, Arabic, Sindhi, and Punjabi—all by the age of twenty-four. By 1848 he passed official exams in six languages and had prepared for two others. He also learned Telugu, Toda, Somali, and Swahili—all told, twenty-nine languages and eleven dialects. "In those days," Burton wrote, referring to the days of the East India Company, "sensible men who went out to India took one of two lines—they either shot, or they studied languages." Learning languages was made easier via the habit of assigning local women to soldiers as "temporary wives." A "walking dictionary," such a wife would be called. Burton also took up with local prostitutes; that was how he learned Somali. Burton would go on to surpass another soldier, Christopher Palmer Rigby, who was considered to be the most outstanding speaker of languages in the Indian Army; for this reason Rigby later became an enemy. Burton never seems to have claimed that he spoke twenty-nine languages concurrently but learned them in blocks or spurts, and when he returned to Arabia after several years in England he had to refresh his Arabic. He probably was never using more than three to five languages at a time—not a lot for an adventurer, more than your average armchair explorer, yet a far cry from the twenty-nine attributed to him.

saying that for the people who were going to go around saying they knew language X or Y, one could assume that their legitimate language activities were reading and translating, which are less taxing and stressful to the brain. You can get a lot of support for reading and translating through dictionaries and grammars. To converse without embarrassing yourself, you have to monitor what you hear and what you say in real time, and not only that, but voices in real life come with accents (which add social information) and environmental noises (which require focus); it's also a very pragmatics-heavy activity. Thus, in Mezzofanti's time, it would have been relatively easier to rack up languages, and to do so legitimately, than it would be today, when we seem to treat oral communication as the hallmark of "knowing" a language.

Given the variety of historical lenses through which one can view the criteria for speaking or knowing a language, it's simply impossible to assess definitively the claims about Mezzofanti's ability in all of his, based on the evidence that Russell provides, anyway.

An unavoidable conclusion is that a count of one's languages is, at best, an imperfect convenience for talking about someone's capabilities in them. A language isn't a unit of measure like a kilo or an inch. What is the thing that one has when one has more than one language? Six languages with closely shared vocabulary and grammar don't burden one's memory or mental processing as much as six unrelated languages would. Likewise, six languages in which one can speak, read, and write don't represent the same sort of cognitive investment for an adult learner as six languages in which one has varying degrees of proficiency across a variety of tasks.

So what's another way for us to grasp the scope of someone's "cognitive investment"? Here are some possibilities.

A folk notion is that when you dream in a language, you've crossed some threshold on a path to fluency. In the 1980s, Canadian psychologist Joseph De Koninck found that students of French who made the fastest progress were those who reported speaking French in their dreams sooner than fellow students. Among another group of students studying French, those who had more REM (rapid eye movement) sleep over the course of a six-week immersion program improved the most. For people who have more experience in their languages, perhaps this isn't a workable measurement alternative, since bilinguals report that they speak, think, and hear in both of their languages. Often, what determines their dream language is the one they used right before they slept, not the one they know the best.

A related notion is that when you really know a language, you think in it. In fact, the brain doesn't think in any language. What people refer to as "thinking in a language" comes from being able to speak more immediately in a language without rehearsing it or translating it from a language one might know better; the spoken thought feels as if it's closer to its source in the brain.

Does speaking in a different language alter one's perception? Can the structure of a language and the way its vocabulary maps meanings make the world more colorful, your friends more friendly, the trees wilder? The "linguistic relativity hypothesis," or Sapir-Whorf hypothesis, as it's alternately called, proposes that the language you speak actually molds your perception of the world. Quite literally, if two languages have a different range of color words, the person speaking both languages fluently will assign his perception of colors to two different names and perhaps categories. If that's true, then the hyperpolyglot's world must appear kaleidoscopic. Indeed, scientists have observed monolingual speakers of Korean using a term, *paran sekj,* or "blue," to refer to a greener, less purple color than Korean-English bilinguals think of as "blue." Other scientists have since seen how bilinguals categorize common containers and even conceptualize time differently from monolinguals. But this evidence is controversial, and the effects of language on cognition haven't been isolated precisely.

One question that polyglots don't get asked is, "When you go crazy, what language do you go crazy in?" Which is too bad, because it's been demonstrated that psychotic polyglots, it turns out, aren't equally disordered in each of their languages. In one case recorded by British psychiatrist Felicity de Zulueta, her psychotic patient, a native English speaker, switched into Spanish because he knew that Zulueta also spoke the language. Both were then surprised that his hallucinations and disordered thoughts disappeared. "In Spanish . . . he felt he was 'sane,' but when he spoke in English, he went 'mad,'" Zulueta wrote. In three other cases, Zulueta's patients had disordered thoughts or heard voices in the language they had learned first and used most. Using a language that they spoke less frequently overall and learned later dismissed their delusions. In another case, a patient was equally psychotic in Italian and English, but heard voices only in Italian, her mother tongue. Not only that—in English she denied that she heard voices at all, whereas in Italian, she readily admitted hearing them. Other patients hear friendly voices in their native languages, hostile ones in their second languages. A subsequent researcher quipped that the more competent an insane person was in a language, the higher their degree of psychosis.

Some scientists have suggested that the extra effort of using a second language jolts people out of a deluded state into reality. Others suggest that the deeper relationship to your first language makes you less inhibited, and so more likely to express what's troubling you. In a language learned later, you can hide from your true self.

People are unlikely to tell potential employers that they can be mentally unbalanced in two languages and unstable in a third, or that they dream in three languages but never in a fourth. Which underscores the convenience, in comparison, of counting hyperpolyglots' languages and what they can actually use them for.

Your opinion of Mezzofanti may also depend on how valuable you think a less-than-complete knowledge of a language is. I'm talking about more than a snippet or a bit, more than an exchange of pleasantries or asking for bus directions. A good working knowledge of the core of the language, one that allows you to have real interactions to achieve some purpose, albeit in a limited domain, is what's at issue here.

In the Western conception of what it means to know a language, these circumscribed abilities don't seem to count for much. The dominant view seems to be that language is a discrete object out in the world. Learning it involves shuttling its pieces into your body; once you know it, it's inside you. In the 1960s, linguists developed a twist on this by arguing that children became so good at language so quickly because when they were born, they already had pieces of language inside them.

Just as you know you aren't hungry anymore by some digestive instinct, you know a language when it reaches some predetermined mark inside you, nourishing and enlightening you. If you've gathered only a few pieces of a language, a snack, it can't change you. It doesn't count. Call this the "all or nothing" view.

Nor does a bit of language matter as long as possessing a sole language is the political foundation of the nation-state, "a community imagined by language," as Benedict Anderson has written. This notion emerged in Europe during Mezzofanti's day. In the nationalist's view, a citizen demonstrates her affiliations to the homeland by speaking and writing the national language fully. She preserves her affiliations by eschewing other languages, regional dialects, and nonstandard ways of speaking and writing. In this way, "nativeness" becomes as much a political project as a linguistic one. Speak like a citizen, speak like a native—it amounted to basically the same thing. In France, for instance, spoken and regional dialects were looked down upon in favor of the cultivated Parisian dialect; the French Revolution brought with it the unification of the language. Until the 1960s, very few Indonesians spoke *bahasa Indonesia* as a first or mother tongue; now millions of them speak what is, in fact, the country's official language. Schools taught the standard language and governments created exams to test ability in that language. Soon, private companies began accepting the results of those exams for their own determinations of a person's proficiency, his ability to serve an institution's goals.

Things get trickier when more than one language is involved. Here, to "know" a language means—at least in the folk view of languages—that you keep it separate from the others you might know. For a long time, bilinguals were criticized for speaking sentences that contained both their languages. This "code switching" is very rule-governed. Yet it was viewed as a person's inability to keep things straight, and marked, therefore, their failure to know either language. Bilinguals were seen as abundantly imperfect or overburdened, another unfortunate implication of the "all or nothing" view.

A bit of language matters more in parts of the world where language isn't viewed as a discrete object, but something more diffuse and external, like clothes. You don't put it *inside* yourself. Instead, you wrap yourself in it. Neither does it create some lens by which the essences of things take different forms. It's a tool. A tool you use when you need it and as often as you need to—as I needed French and Italian in the Archiginnasio. Call this the "something and something" model.

A bit of language matters in places where the language isn't written down, or where not many people are literate, where fewer resources for making language a fixed, bounded thing exist. Also, a bit of language matters more in countries that have built nationhood around many languages than in those whose national identity is founded on just one. In southern India, for instance, languages appear to be more like uniforms or badges; you wear them to tell people your social identity—the class or caste you belong to, the region you come from, your religion, family, profession, and significantly, your gender. When they treat you like someone who speaks that language, then that's who you are. But Mezzofanti didn't come from any places like these. So what was he doing?

One way to resolve these views is through the idea of "multicompetence." This has gained some traction in the twenty years since British linguist Vivian Cook proposed it to describe the "language supersystem" or the "total language system" that multilinguals possess. Cook's goal was to help to see second-language speakers as "successful multicompetent speakers, not failed native speakers," as he wrote. He meant to replace the "all or nothing" view with the "something and something" view. This means that a multilingual person doesn't carry two or three monolingual speakers' worth of language in his or her head. And not only that, you can't say they know "less than" monolinguals or any other comparisons that make them seem like half-empty glasses. It's not correct—and it's unfair—to compare language learners to native speakers who know only their one language; it's an apples to oranges comparison. The persistent mark of one's status as a linguistic outsider is not a *failure,* but a *difference.* Take a native Mandarin speaker with no other languages and a businessman learning Chinese at the age of fifty. The native speaker can't be more "successful" in her language, because she never set out to achieve it, while the businessman can't be less "successful" than she is. He's bitten off a harder task than she has.

Certainly, Cook wrote to me in an email, humans tend to leave their multicompetence unexplored. "I think that the human ability to learn languages in natural environments is mostly untapped," he wrote. But what are the upper limits of multicompetence, however you want to define that? He was unable to say.

Without being able to observe Mezzofanti directly, it's hard to nail down the scope or depth of his multicompetence. You can, if you indulge in a bit of anachronism, imagine what he (or anyone) would have to do to gain the same accolades now. For instance, according to the current European Commission standard for language proficiency, a person at the highest rating—someone we would say had "mastered" a language—has to "have a good command of idiomatic expressions and colloquialisms," "convey finer shades of meaning precisely," and "backtrack and restructure around a difficulty so smoothly the interlocutor is hardly aware of it." I can't say in how many languages Mezzofanti really had such abilities.

To be sure, there's a big difference between a truly multicompetent person and someone with lots of "bits of language," who would have a hard time succeeding, for instance, at a set of language competitions that the German government has held since 1985 for students between seventeen and nineteen years old. They undergo a yearlong battery of tests, including discussing a cartoon and a text; submitting a written exam that involves translating, writing, and summarizing; writing a 3,000-word essay; and participating in oral exams as well as a multilingual debating session. Faking abilities, much less in the required minimum of two languages (they can work in as many as four), would be impossible.

Several years ago, I interviewed a member of the US intelligence community who went to job fairs recruiting foreign-language experts and, every so often, met a person who claimed to speak forty languages. Inevitably, the claim was accompanied with the word "fluently."

He greeted these with exasperated disbelief. I'm a non-native learner of six languages, he told me. I know what I need to do to learn a language, I know what I need to do to get good at it. Not only are the claims implausible, they're unsupported. No one who says he or she has forty languages has ever tested out in all of them.

He then described to me what he hired people to do. They'd have to know how to distinguish a prayer from a coded transmission. How to parse the speech of a non-native speaker, mispronunciations, errors, and all—someone who may or may not be nervous, who may be speaking in a dialect, who might be using a cell phone connection with lots of static and environmental noise. You don't get skills like that by watching a few movies. It takes hundreds of hours of practice. It takes firsthand experience in the culture. Given the stakes, analysts should have them.

Could anyone do this in thirty languages? Probably not. But one's ultra competence in one language could certainly be informed by a sizable multicompetence in dozens. Indeed, my contact said he works with people who are very good in ten to fifteen languages, people who say, I've got to go learn Georgian, and off they go, and then return and say, I'm going to Estonian school, all while they're studying Turkish at home. In multilingual environments like this, amazing feats of language prowess are everyday affairs. He told me about a former colleague who wanted to learn languages well enough to quote proverbs in them. It became a game between him and his hosts to sit and quote obscure proverbs to each other. "This guy was *untouchable* as far as languages go," my contact marveled.

Even for a person with a good working knowledge of a language that falls short of nativeness, not all professional avenues are closed. Mezzofanti might fare better by the standards of the aviation industry and its expectations for English proficiency among pilots and air traffic controllers. In 2008, the International Civil Aviation Organization (or ICAO, a United Nations–mandated agency) introduced requirements that they be able to speak and understand English to a certain level of proficiency by March 2011. The goal was to make the Babel of the skies clearer and safer.

Implementing the standards butted against some linguistic realities, though. One was the diversity of accented Englishes that pilots and controllers encounter every single day. In one nine-hour observation, Turkish air traffic controllers interacted with 160 pilots from Turkish airlines, 14 from German airlines, and 104 pilots from airlines from 26 other countries—all speaking English. Yet only 2 of the 104 pilots worked for airlines based in an English-speaking country and presumably were native English speakers.

Rather than focus on producing native-like English speakers, ICAO focused on flying and landing airplanes safely. You didn't need to discourse about squids or default swaps or the existence of God, as you might have to do in other tests of language proficiency. Instrumentation and weather terminology are more relevant topics. You don't need to speak English like an American or a Brit; you have to be intelligible. This is no easy feat, but it's one that, unlike native pronunciation, is achievable by adults. And you don't have to be error-free. After all, even native speakers make errors.

Most important was the ability to manage a conversation by asking for clarification, communicating understanding, and rephrasing one's request or description, among other things. A surprisingly large amount of talk between pilots and controllers is about the talk itself; one study in France concluded that only about one-quarter of what they say concerns the actual flying of the plane. Everything else is asking for repetition and clarification, and managing who's speaking when. Such skills are also achievable by adults as a part of their linguistic multicompetence.

These new standards are meant to complement the stock of set phrases used by pilots and air traffic controllers. Using only well-practiced set phrases, a pilot could sound perfectly fluent and fly the plane safely. This is true—provided that systems are working and conditions are normal. If they're not, and extra discussion is required, the consequences can be fatal.

In 1993, a McDonnell Douglas MD-82 jet crashed in China, killing twelve and injuring twenty-four, after coming in to land too low. "Pull up, pull up," the airplane's automatic controls warned. The Chinese pilot's last words: "What does 'pull up, pull up' mean?" In 1995, an American Airlines Boeing 757 on its way from Miami to Cali, Colombia, crashed in the mountains when the plane went off course. The pilots' own confusion was a major cause of the accident. American Airlines investigators also speculated that the pilots and the air traffic controller had run out of phraseology—they didn't share the stock of phrases to help with problem-solving. The pilots didn't speak Spanish; the controller later said that because his command of English was limited, he couldn't convey his misgivings to the crew. The annals of aviation tragedies and near-disasters are filled with stories about language failures—something that ICAO desperately wants to change.

If these institutional standards seem too loose or too restrictive, you could let hyperpolyglots themselves define the standards of their multicompetence. Because there's no community in which those standards grow, no hyperpolyglot police, this can be tricky. Yet it's worth inquiring what polyglots expect themselves to be able to do.

In the online survey I opened up to people who know six or more languages, I asked what it meant to "know" a language. Most people replied that you had to do be able to do things in that language: talk to natives, express oneself, consume media. No one described the relevance of immediacy. To this crew, to say you "know" a language, the ability to call it up and use it without preparation, is not required—which is something like saying, "Yes, I have a screwdriver," and yet having to walk back to your house to get it. Also, not a single one of the seventeen hyperpolyglots who claimed to know eleven or more languages said that sounding like a native speaker was important at all. In fact, doing *anything* like a native was not, for them, a sign of success. This included knowing anything about the culture. Only one person listed knowing the culture as important, then added that your average person doesn't even know his or her mother tongue's culture completely. Instead, they focused on comfort at functional abilities: one must know how to speak, read, and write "intelligently," "without major difficulty," and "without feeling that I have to avoid any theme or activity."

"I reach a point," one person wrote, "where the grammar clicks in my head where the structure—any structure—is there to create sentences. It's a matter of knowing the vocabulary and how to use that vocabulary to fill in the structure."

You don't want to "get lost in the community where the language is spoken"—knowing a language isn't about blending in, it's about moving through communities, and indeed moving from one community to another with no obligation to stay. Flowing through languages, flowing through the world. In my travels among polyglots, it would become a consistent theme.

From my perspective in Bologna, it looked as if Mezzofanti had had a very rich linguistic life. Claire Kramsch had compared this to someone practicing musical scales, someone merely mastering a code. What I saw, combined with what I knew about Mezzofanti's life from others, didn't look like scale practicing. Okay, so maybe Mezzofanti wasn't a virtuoso at harpsichord, guitar, and flute. But he'd be that much more entertaining on each instrument because you knew he could play the others—his flexibility in itself was a sort of virtuosity.

Take his poetry, for example. Scattered in the files, it's mediocre at best—rote verse for ceremonial occasions. He wrote little scraps in English for visitors like Miss Hunter, Miss Haiselden, and Miss Lanveur. One read:

Dear god, hate sin
the world despise
then you begin
to be divinely wise.

Another one went like this:

Let mind be right, and heart be pure;
This, will good works ensure.
Good fruits come forth from a good tree:
God! give me such to be.

Prize-winning *versi* these weren't; more eloquence comes out of fortune cookies. But he had to have a more than passing familiarity with the English code to be able to rhyme (despise / wise, pure / ensure) and keep sentences so brief. And to write in a style, and on appropriate topics, that resembled the edifying verse of the early Victorians, he'd have to know enough about English cultural sensibilities to key his poems to visitors' upper-class tastes. Of course, he didn't have the same sensibilities available to him in Chinese or Armenian, but must we cut them from his list of languages because they didn't improve his poetry?

The next morning, I went to visit Franco Pasti, a Bolognese librarian and scholar who wrote *A Polyglot in the Library* (in Italian, *Un poliglotta in biblioteca*), about the period of Mezzofanti's life between 1812 and 1831, when he worked as the librarian in the University of Bologna, until he was called to Rome. I was excited to meet Pasti—surely he must have insights into our shared obsession. He was a trim man sporting a gold bracelet and a crisp dress shirt, with the sly elegance of a ballroom dance instructor. *"Molto piacere,"* I said. He looked surprised: *"Piacere,"* he replied. It was no great feat; I'd looked up the phrase that morning.

Do you want to see Mezzofanti's library? he asked. Of course I did. Pasti escorted me to a long room with high vaulted ceilings and walls of books behind glass doors. At the head of the main hall sat a massive, dark wooden desk under a huge window, set like a shining eye overlooking the polished tables and chairs. At the time, Pasti whispered, they built libraries as temples for books. I could easily imagine Mezzofanti seated at his high altar, translating the heart of some text in snatched bits of time—he'd managed the library and its thirty thousand books with only one or two helpers. This work must have suited him—the library, famous for its collection of Arabic and Persian manuscripts, left him time to work on his languages.

By this point in his life, his reputation as a hyperpolyglot had taken on a life of its own. In 1817, the same year that Lord Byron stopped by, a Russian princess and a countess visited; so did a Croat, a Scotsman, French, Italians, scores of Americans and British people. Some wrote requesting his autograph. It was not as undignified as feeding the geek in a carnival sideshow, but this time in his life has the air of performance and spectacle—he was an entertaining freak. His biographies made much of his celebrity, which became concrete to me only when I saw the stacks of paper slips with the names and titles of his visitors. Born at a historical moment that put Bologna at a linguistic crossroads, Mezzofanti benefited from that access, then grew a reputation that amplified the effect. He *became* the crossroads.

As Pasti describes in his book, Mezzofanti also worked as theological enforcer. In the 1820s he translated Scripture from local vernaculars back into Latin, searching for the sources of heresies buried in the language. In one such translation, he'd read a translation of the New Testament in Persian that had been produced in Calcutta, read the Greek from which the Persian version was translated, compared the Persian to the Vulgate Latin original, then written an analysis in Latin and Italian.* I also found a note in English from an American woman, Deborah Emlen, who had rejected her Quaker beliefs and accepted the Roman Catholic creed; Mezzofanti translated this into Italian, probably for the sake of her Catholic fiancé's family.

During the same period, he also patrolled customs to intercept books brought into the papal states and reviewed the wares of booksellers in the market. Unapproved or banned books with licentious or politically liberal ideas were confiscated and destroyed. This puts his attachment to Bologna and the Pope in a different light. Did he stay in Bologna because he loved it so much? Or was it because his conservatism might, in other parts of Europe, endanger his life? By 1831 he was in Rome, as much pushed there by political enemies in Bologna as beckoned by the needs of the Church.

Standing in the darkened temple to books, Pasti explained how little known Mezzofanti was in his hometown. True, there were well-placed mentions in travel memoirs. But in his own city, he had little renown beyond what he was awarded by high-ranking Church officials and the aristocratic families in whose libraries he had served. Pietro Giordani, the political revolutionary, acknowledged the oversight. Mezzofanti, he wrote, "deserves a wider fame than he enjoys, for the number of languages which he knows most perfectly, although this is the least part of his learning." Even today, Pasti says, Mezzofanti is rarely acknowledged. There are the plaques on Via Malcontenti, and a street far from the city's center named after him, but none of his anniversaries was ever celebrated.

In the archival manuscript room off the main reading room, a librarian sat at a desk while two researchers pored over books. Pasti pulled out the inventory of Mezzofanti's library, which had been drawn up by a bookseller after his death. (Later I would find the original handwritten ledger that listed the cardinal's estate at his death.) It's famous, Pasti said, and it made some stupid mistakes identifying languages. But it helped the cardinal's family get quite a sum of money from Pope Pio (Pius) IX, who then donated it to the University of

---

*The issue concerned what it meant to say someone was baptized "in" water.

Bologna library. The researchers scowled at us as we whispered to each other.

He also showed me a reproduction of the Codex Cospi, a parchment text made in pre-Columbian Mexico and transported to Bologna well before Mezzofanti's time. The codex contains hundreds of glyphs that probably mark auspicious dates of the calendar. I had already seen Mezzofanti's handwritten analysis of the codex, one of the first attempts to decipher it. Pasti said that until Mezzofanti correctly identified it as Mexican, it was called the "Chinese book." Along with the codex analysis, I found in his papers a history of Arabic, a comparison of Swedish and German, and an attempt to translate the book of Genesis into Algonquin. The hyperpolyglot may not have published much, but it's not completely accurate to call him a mindless church functionary or a mere parrot.

In the archives, I found *versi* that hinted at Mezzofanti's experiences as a hyperpolyglot, offering a glimpse of a mind as human as it was powerful. Some of the *versi* were epigrams obviously written for various visitors. Most often they were blessings, prayers, or some exhortation to holiness, yet a few talked about languages, fame, and God. Because the man wasn't given to writing raw expressions of emotion, these *versi* are as close as one can come to actually seeing life from his point of view.

In some, he chides himself to be modest (and to the degree that he was perceived this way, he succeeded). As he reminded those who put him on a linguistic pedestal, speaking many languages wasn't as impressive as holiness, service to God, and going to heaven. I like the notion of Mezzofanti telling his visitors not to focus on his polyglottism—even though that was likely the reason they'd come to see him in the first place. His humility about fame has a chaste appeal:

> *Why do you ask my name?*
> *Why will you have it here*
> *Where many names appear*
> *illustrious, known to Fame.*
> *But since you are so kind,*
> *I write it, and remind:*
> *what World offers is vain*
> *Oh let us Heaven gain!*

There was also this poem, which Mezzofanti wrote in Italian:

Of all the thousands of voices in various accents
that come from human breasts in hundreds of languages
the one that's dearest to a virtuous and modest heart
is the voice that praises and extols the Creator.

Perhaps because he'd staked his sense of self on languages, his ego, vulnerable to accolades and attention, needed dampening.

As I was leaving the library's main doors, Pasti turned to me to say that he doubted Mezzofanti's skills. This surprised me. In his book, he hadn't probed Mezzofanti's reputation with any skepticism. Now he was telling me that back then, the standards for what it meant to speak or know a language were "very low." "I don't think he actually spoke Persian or Arabic."

"How do you know?" I asked, hoping he'd uncovered some damning evidence.

He shrugged. "Just a feeling," he said.

Knowing I might never visit the archives again, I had hit on a solution to get at Mezzofanti's proficiency: I'd count the letters he received in each language. If he got many, he must have been writing a lot, and that, maybe, pointed to a great deal of practice, then to a high degree of proficiency. It was a fair social science hypothesis.

I told Pasti about my plan. The librarian smirked at me.

"You are a positivist, I think," he said. A positivist is someone who believes you can get at truths only through what can be counted, measured, and observed. I was shocked—I've been called names before, but never *that*. Pasti had interpreted Mezzofanti's life, leaving tabulation to people like me. With a grin, the librarian punched my arm lightly.

"I have to leave Bologna with some hard facts about Mezzofanti," I said. "People are going to expect me to come up with a hard answer. I just can't give them more anecdotes."

Pasti's smile was unforgiving. "That proves it," he said. "You are a positivist."

Back in the Archiginnasio, I slumped at the table with an unopened box and the *inventario* in front of me. Pasti wasn't the first person to discourage me about Mezzofanti's true nature. And he wouldn't be the last. Maybe he didn't quite understand my desperate desire for a visual encounter with the hyperpolyglot, if not in flesh, then in fact.

One thing was clear: I could stay in Bologna until my Italian was *molto perfetto,* and the truth about the hyperpolyglot would elude me.

I departed Bologna with one intact conclusion: Mezzofanti learned and used numerous languages in a range of ways.

Given the rich purpose evident in those boxes, I was entirely willing to extend to his legacy the notion that those uses were real and meaningful. Even if many of them were narrow, they were *his,* no less legitimate for being idiosyncratic. I also felt certain that the languages weren't objects of beauty that he displayed like butterflies in a collection. Though I couldn't read most of the languages, the artifacts indicated that he *used* them. Maybe not all at the same time—some he might have kept on the back burner. To my eye, at least, they looked like tools. Some of what he used languages for clearly involved high-stakes communications. Some of it was the equivalent of a verbal *amuse-bouche.* Some of it was memorized chitchat ("Will you visit the Pope in Rome?") for social lubrication. His abilities may have been less than perfect or fluent or native-like. That patchwork quality was something I would find to be common among hyperpolyglots.

My skepticism eroded on another front, as well. Without some kind of mental gift, Mezzofanti couldn't have made so much—even half as much as was claimed—of the language encounters that he sought. After all, many people live at linguistic crossroads where they can be immersed in many languages; some may even love languages. Yet very few become hyperpolyglots. Moving forward, one crucial dimension of my search had to be to characterize, as best I could, the mental powers that he and other hyperpolyglots brought to bear on language learning.

I also recognized that his linguistic patchwork reflected a level of brainwork that wouldn't be captured in a single number representing the languages he spoke, read, or translated. One skepticism I was willing to jettison: disqualifying someone solely because they had a large number of languages associated with their name. Other things could disqualify them, I vowed. Not the number of languages. (Nor could it *qualify* them, but more about that later.) I also vowed that I wouldn't look at people with an "all or nothing" eye but only a "something and something" one. Among other things, this meant that individuals could be interesting even if they weren't native-like in all their languages.

I left with the belief that Mezzofanti did things with languages that the people who speak them natively would never do. Topping the list was his ability to rapidly analyze languages and his prodigious memory (as evidenced by performance and his own claims); an apparent ability to mimic speech sounds that weren't native to him; and an ability to switch among his languages without interference. These are unique skills; monolingual native speakers don't necessarily have them, and, except for the language switching, neither do bilinguals. The native speaker wasn't the hyperpolyglot's twin, joined in comparisons; some-one else would have to take that role.

Mezzofanti's time and place seemed distant and inaccessible. But was he truly one of a kind, the only member of his species? Or could others like him be living among us now?

Part 2

APPROACH:
Tracking Down
Hyperpolyglots

Chapter 5

earing retirement, Dick Hudson, a linguist at University College, London, took up an overlooked query: Who had learned the most languages ever? In the mid-1990s, he sent this question to LINGUIST List, a popular forum with language scientists. A flurry of postings listed the names of well-known hyperpolyglots of yesteryear, including Giuseppe Mezzofanti. Others cast doubts that the upper limit for languages would be very high. For all purposes, it remained an open question, a natural experiment whose results had never been analyzed.

A couple of years later, he received an email that began like this: "Sir, First, let me apologize for bothering you, but I saw an article you wrote and had to write." The writer, N., had found Hudson's posting and wanted to describe how his grandfather, a Sicilian with no formal schooling, had learned languages with such remarkable ease that by the end of his life he could speak seventy, as well as read and write in fifty-six.* This grandfather was twenty when he moved to New York in the 1910s. There he found a job as a railroad porter, which brought him into contact with travelers who spoke many different languages. N. said

*To preserve the writer's anonymity and that of his family, N. is not his real initial.

he once watched his grandfather translate a newspaper into three languages on the spot.

When N. was ten years old, in the 1950s, he accompanied his grandfather on a six-month world cruise. Whatever port they called at, N. said his grandfather knew the local language. Their trip took them to Venezuela, Argentina, Norway, the United Kingdom, Portugal, Italy, Greece, Turkey, Syria, Egypt, Libya, Morocco, South Africa, Pakistan, India, Thailand, Malaysia, Indonesia, Australia, the Philippines, Hong Kong, and Japan. Assuming the grandfather spoke the local language at each port, one can figure that he knew some of at least seventeen (including English)—though there was no mention of what he could accomplish in each.

Even more amazingly, N. claimed that this talent ran in his family. "Every three or four generations there is a member of my family who has the ability to learn many languages," he wrote. His grandfather once told N. that his own father and great-uncle could speak more than one hundred languages.

When Hudson read this, its significance was crystal clear. Studying the genetic basis of abilities in language, especially the heritability of language disorders, is cutting-edge territory. In the 1990s, exciting work was performed on a family with developmental language problems who had the same mutated gene. Could there be a genetic link for exceptional abilities? Perhaps a hyperpolyglot gene?

With N.'s permission, Hudson passed the mail on to LINGUIST. Seeing a need for a better label for people who learn lots of languages, Hudson chose *hyperpolyglot*. *Multilingual* didn't cut it; *polyglot* felt too pedestrian. A hyperpolyglot, in Hudson's terms, was a person who could speak six or more languages. Hudson had found that community-based multilingualism, where everyone, not just special individuals, spoke many languages, had a ceiling of five languages. So someone who spoke six or more had to be exceptional, Hudson reasoned. They weren't just polyglots, they were *hyper*polyglots.

Hyperpolyglots caught Hudson's attention because they were beyond the pale of linguistic theory. With only one exception that he knew of—the study of a severely mentally impaired man named Christopher who knew twenty languages—no one had ever addressed the issue. No longer a professor affiliated with an institution, Hudson had nothing to lose by following up a fascinating but ignored phenomenon, though N. disappeared shortly after his letter was published.

If you believe that language is innate and uniquely human, then the question about how many languages a person can learn would seem trivial. Learning one language is itself an evolutionary marvel; learning many of them, well, that's gilding the lily. A language superlearner deserves about the same attention as an ultramarathon runner—accolades and respect for pushing basic human equipment to an extreme, but not the scientific interest you'd give to, say, a human who could breathe underwater or flap his arms and fly.

If pushed to explain the hyperpolyglot phenomenon, an innatist might say that every baby's brain comes equipped with a primordial universal grammar, a sort of periodic table that contains the basic properties of all the world's languages and all the dimensions along which they differ. Coming into contact with a real language (or several) triggers some properties from that table. The ones left untriggered disappear. Because all the languages on the planet differ along a finite number of dimensions, even an adult should be able to retrigger these properties and their permutations, given enough time. Theoretically, there should be no limits on how many languages a person could learn. If most people don't, it's because they'd rather carve whalebone, grow the perfect orchid, or sit on the beach.

Those of an opposing theoretical bent, the emergentists, see language not as inborn but as a behavior that grows out of a set of simpler, overlapping cognitive skills. At certain moments in a child's development, such skills are enhanced by experiences that bootstrap them to a higher level of complexity. In this account, protogrammars don't have to exist in babies' brains—as expert learners, humans can fill in gaps from their environment. Accordingly, an emergentist's explanation of the hyperpolyglot goes something like this: people with a gift for learning languages must recognize and parse patterns extremely well. Surely this makes a kind of intuitive sense. But here the account stalls. At what point does parsing patterns become knowing a language? And how can you escape the influence of your earliest language—or harness your knowledge of it—to become fluent in later ones?

Meanwhile, the applied side of linguistics, which deals with foreign-language education and literacy, developed the notion of language-learning "aptitude." It was really a measure of how quickly a student could achieve proficiency in an extra language in an allotted time period. As the concept was first developed in the 1950s, aptitude had four dimensions—how well a person can recall sounds; how sensitive she is to grammatical patterns; how well she can produce new sentences based on what she analyzes; and how well she learns how words in the first and second languages connect. Later, the notion evolved, adding new understandings of how memory works.

But aptitude was never applied to hyperpolyglottery. The bulk of research on aptitude had been done by the bureaucrats of the foreign-language education establishment in Washington, D.C. (and other capitals), where the typical learner of interest was an adult who'd mastered one language well enough for spycraft and diplomacy. The massively multilingual person? Barely interesting.

Even if hyperpolyglots had been examined through the lens of aptitude, the concept had shortcomings. For instance, standardized tests of aptitude tend to predict a student's grades in certain kinds of classrooms better than they predict real-world language use. They also don't predict how adept a person could ultimately become in a language—high aptitude is no guarantee that abilities won't peak quickly. More important, there's no agreement on what aptitude is made of, how much it can be cultivated, and how much is inborn. Aptitude could make for a potent political time bomb in many educational settings. Holding out high aptitude implies low aptitude, which, in turn, implies the promise of handing out educational resources on an unequal basis. If the aptitudes you find striking happen to correspond with certain genders, races, or classes, then you'd look as if you were cementing old privileges. It's safer to assume that all students possess a generic cognitive profile and teach them with fitting uniformity.

Hudson was stymied. Even if the feats of successful language learners are no longer explained through mystical sources—whether visits from angels or pacts with demons—we can't ignore how some people are faster learners and better users of their languages. Perhaps they can read shades of meaning more acutely, even mimicking sounds more exactly. Some of these people, who are on the high end of a normal curve, count as experts. Yet others go far, far beyond this. How to explain this?

As he told me in a series of exchanges by email and phone, Hudson himself worked hard to learn various languages before traveling to the places they were spoken. He'd put in the required time on task. Yet after coming home, he found that his abilities rapidly and inevitably dwindled. Others learned faster and kept their knowledge longer than he did. How did hyperpolyglots retain their skills? Could average language learners do the same?

Hudson was also alarmed by a negative trend in foreign-language education in Britain. Politicians lectured Britons on learning languages so they could get jobs in the European Union, while universities removed foreign-language requirements and shut down language departments when enrollments dropped. Further, the government was constantly exporting English teachers, textbooks, courses, and programs, helping the country to earn £1.3 billion a year. In other words, learning languages was for citizens of other countries—who would then compete with Britons for jobs. The irony was underscored by the fact that by 2005, immigrants had transformed London into a place where at least 307 languages are spoken, making the capital of one of the most monolingual countries in the European Union the most multilingual city on the planet. A new approach to foreign-language education was direly needed.

Meanwhile, in the United States, a long-documented shortage of language analysts in US intelligence agencies meant that evidence of an imminent terrorist attack on September 11, 2001, sat undiscovered in a queue until much too late. As it plotted its counterterrorism strategy, the US government was in a bind: unwilling to trust intelligence work to recent immigrants (especially ones from the same cultural groups that al-Qaeda drew from), the national fear of anything foreign had long snuffed out the immigrant-family languages it now desperately needed for a range of government functions. Coupled with a peacetime vacuum of political will to build a linguistically expert workforce, these trends, some of which dated back decades, ruined some of the country's greatest human resources: linguistic fluency and cultural knowledge. Experts had long warned of such a shortage; in 1980, Senator Paul Simon published a searing jeremiad, *The Tongue-Tied American: Confronting the Foreign Language Crisis*. Yet the necessary funding for something as intangible as language could be mobilized only by a crisis.

The problems ran much deeper, though. Failing to produce enough language experts for government and business was considered the fault of the educational system. Yet success in language learning, whenever it occurred, was seen as the product of intense self-fashioning; it was, by and large, an individual's project. Such a view threw up barriers to connecting teachers and learners in ways that would make their efforts sustainable and promote brain plasticity. It also voided any legitimate role for government, which would be the prime beneficiary of expanded linguistic skills. The result was a profound inability to go about building more cognitive capital in the society around foreign-language learning.

As Hudson saw it, cultural blindness, social inertia, and political inaction stood in the way of the language learning that the British and the Americans needed to do. Perhaps the way forward could be found in the methods or gifts of high-performing language learners, Hudson thought. They're the Olympic athletes of languages. "If we understood how the gold medalists got their talent," he told me, "then we might know better how to teach ordinary people to speak more languages."

Was this true? He'd have to meet some gold medalists to find out.

Chapter 6

Every so often over the next several years, Hudson emailed me the name of another hyperpolyglot. *Have you ever heard of Harold Williams?* I'd write him back: *I have* (Williams was a New Zealand journalist, said to know fifty-eight languages.) *What about George Campbell?* Yes, he was a scholar from Scotland who could "speak and write fluently in at least 44 languages and had a working knowledge of perhaps 20 others," read his *Washington Post* obituary.

One drawback loomed: Hudson couldn't hook me up with a real, living hyperpolyglot—he'd never met one. And in that, we were equal. At the time, little information about them had shown up online. Now you can easily go to YouTube and find videos of people rattling off messages in eight or ten languages, but when I began my research, I could only hope that such virtual communities existed, and the Wikipedia entries on famous polyglots hadn't yet been written, squabbled over, or removed.

A recurring frustration was that the modern scientific literature was nearly silent on the topic, except in decades-old studies about how trauma or disease in the brain damages a person's ability in one or more of their spoken languages. The best example, an article by an A. Leischner from 1948, originally in German, references Georg

Sauerwein (1831–1904), a German who apparently could speak and write twenty-six languages (though "otherwise he was rather untalented," Leischner quipped). Others Leischner called "very talented." He was trying to understand the principles that ordered languages in a person's brain by seeing which languages were affected by strokes. It seemed hyperpolyglots were most interesting when they were no longer so.

The trail of apocrypha about language-learning talents can most reliably be picked up in newspapers, especially in the obituaries. In a newspaper archive, I discovered the tale of Elizabeth Kulman, a girl born in St. Petersburg in 1809, who resolved to become the Russian Mezzofanti. Before she reached the age of sixteen, she spoke Greek, Spanish, Portuguese, "Salamanic," German, and Russian. All told, she "mastered" eleven languages; she spoke fluently in eight, it was said. But Elizabeth never had the chance to scale the Mezzofantian heights she desired. From the time she was eleven years old, she'd slept no more than six hours a night to allow for more time to study. The lack of sleep made her frail, and at seventeen, she died.

In the same archive was the tale of Ira T. O'Brien, an American blacksmith in Rome, Georgia, who was nicknamed "Rome's Learned Vulcan." According to the 1898 report, O'Brien spoke Greek, German, French, Spanish, Italian, Latin, and other languages. A quiet, unassuming man, he was described as having "gigantic stature" and "prodigious strength." But the writer questioned "why a man of his unquestioned learning and talents should be content to serve the humble role of a blacksmith."

One answer was that, some sixty years earlier, the humble role of blacksmith had been a ticket to the big time. In 1838, the governor of Massachusetts, William Everett, in a speech to a group of educators, mentioned a "learned blacksmith" from Connecticut named Elihu Burritt (1810–1879) who had taught himself fifty languages. Burritt, then twenty-eight years old, had a compulsion for only two things, manual labor and reading foreign languages. He always told people that he hadn't sought any of the attention or accolades that resulted from Everett's speech. During the decade he spent teaching himself to read a number of foreign languages, in what appeared to be an attempt to surpass the scholarly achievements of his dead older brother, he supported himself by forging garden hoes and cowbells. He was proud to say (and probably said more than was necessary) that he carried his Greek and Latin grammars to work in his hat and studied them during breaks. But languages and garden hoes didn't pay. Burritt, seeking translation work, wrote to a prominent Worcester citizen; the letter was published in the newspaper, where it caught Governor Everett's eye. The poet Henry Wadsworth Longfellow arranged for him to study at Harvard, but Burritt declined, saying that if he didn't work at the forge, he'd get ill. Before Paul Bunyan and Johnny Appleseed, Burritt was a shining example of American self-making and the faith in self-improvement, all in service of what would later seem a very un-American pursuit.

Predictably, his linguistic achievement has been mostly forgotten. When I went to the New Britain, Connecticut, public library to look at the Burritt collection, the librarians said that no one came to research what he did (or claimed to do) with languages; the scholars who came were mostly interested in his later work advocating the abolition of the military. After I asked to look in the bookcases lining the small special collections room, the librarians were surprised to find, behind the smeary glass of the doors, his language books: a Hindustani New Testament, a Tamil grammar, a Portuguese dictionary, a tiny, brittle-paged copy of *The Odyssey* in Greek, wrapped in oilcloth and tied with stiff red cord. Burritt had delved into Portuguese, Flemish, Danish, Swedish, Norwegian, Icelandic, Welsh, Gaelic, and Celtic. Russian and other Slavic languages followed, then Syriac, Chaldaic, Samaritan, and Ethiopic. One of his biographers, Peter Tolis, granted Burritt thirty languages; *Knight's Cyclopedia of Biography* gave him nineteen.* When I visited the American Antiquarian Society in Worcester, which Burritt used as a resource, I found that it had had grammars and dictionaries in far fewer exotic languages than he claimed. In 1837, the collection contained books in thirty-one languages; in eight languages, the holdings consisted solely of copies of the New

---

*English, Latin, Greek, Hebrew, Syriac, Samaritan, Arabic, Turkish, Persian, Ethiopic, Italian, French, Spanish, German, Danish, "Irelandic" (perhaps Gaelic), Estonian, Bohemian, and Polish.

Testament. Interestingly, the society's library also contained a number of books in Native American languages such as Massachusett and Narraganset. Burritt never bothered to learn these—to a Yankee barely out of the backwoods himself, the languages of New World natives wouldn't have been as exotic, or have conferred on him as much stature, as Chaldean or Samaritan. "His compulsive and erratic study of languages was not an end in itself," wrote Peter Tolis, "but a means of social escalation, a kind of intellectual stunt he used to emancipate himself from the blacksmith shop."

Elihu Burritt.

Burritt never claimed to speak his languages—only to read them. During his most intense decade of study, he spent four hours a day (one at lunch, three in the evening) studying and marked his progress in a ledger like so:

> June 9.—68 lines of Hebrew; 50 lines of Celtic; 40 pages of
> French; 3 hours studying Syriac; 9 hours of forging.

or:

> June 10.—100 lines of Hebrew; 85 pages of French;
> 4 services at church; Bible-class at noon.

When Burritt was thirty-three years old, he abruptly quit his languages and his tools, realizing, as he told a hometown crowd once, that "there was something to live for besides the mere gratification of a desire to learn, that there were words to be spoken with the living tongue and earnest heart for great principles of truth and righteousness."

Leveraging his improbable linguistic celebrity, he became a reformer for peace, abolition, and cheaper postage for transatlantic letters and eventually wrote thirty books. It's said he was so famous, he never paid for a hotel room or riverboat passage. Later in life, he returned to languages, promoting the wonders of Sanskrit to young women in New Britain. How I would have loved to peek in on Mr. Burritt's Sanskrit Lessons for Young Yankee Ladies, the petticoats and scrimshaw in the glow of Burritt's enthusiasm. After he died in 1879, friends praised him for his "child-like and beautiful personality."

In 1841, a plaster cast of Burritt's skull was taken by prominent phrenologist Lorenzo Niles Fowler. This was perhaps the first instance in which a polyglot's abilities were given a specific location in the head, albeit by phrenology, which was fashionable for a time but eventually was lambasted as a pseudoscience. Phrenologists regarded the surface of a person's skull as a map to his or her intelligence, personality, and character. The phrenologist's job was to decode the relative size and shape of the brain's discrete areas, thirty-seven in all, with names like "veneration" and "agreeableness," stretching from the nape of the neck up to the nose, and down the temples around the eyes to the nose.

Here's the drawing of Burritt's head from Fowler's publication:

No. 43. Side View

Elihu Burritt in profile.

On the phrenological map, the "Language" organ makes up part of the territory around the eyes, though this wasn't notably prominent on Burritt. But the author apparently knew that the blacksmith didn't *speak* fifty languages and could only read them, so he credited the organ of Form with the blacksmith's gifts. In his write-up for a phrenological journal, the phrenologist (who may or may not have been Lorenzo Fowler himself) reported his astonishment at the shape of Burritt's Form, "and the power it confers of retaining the shapes of letters and words constitutes his principal aid in his lingual pursuits," he wrote. According to phrenologists, Form is where memory of figures, like shapes and faces, spellings, and images were contained. To remember the words, Burritt relied on the faculty of Eventuality, which was "immense." In Burritt, it "confers a retentiveness of historical and literary memory, probably unequaled in the world," Fowler wrote. "He apparently knows EVERY thing." I was never able to track down Burritt's skull cast, which has, I imagine, suffered the same fate as Burritt himself.

In an Australian newspaper archive, I also found this appraisal of the American Jeremiah Curtin, Mezzofanti, and other polyglots. I love the way these accounts make each one sound more accomplished than the previous.

Here and there in my library explorations I found hyped, exploited children, one of the most colorful of whom was Winifred Sackville Stoner Jr. (1902–1983). In 1928, *Time* magazine reported that Cherie (her nickname) had mastered thirteen languages by the age of nine, the same year she passed the entrance examination for

SPEAKING SEVENTY TONGUES.

Has there ever lived a linguist who was acquainted with more languages than the late Mr. Jeremiah Curtin, the translator of "Quo Vadis," who died the other day?

Probably not. Even he himself did not know, within a dozen or so, how many different and distinct tongues he really spoke. It is certain, however, that he had mastered in his time no fewer than seventy different speeches and dialects.

Perhaps his nearest rival was Giuseppe Mezzofanti, the great Italian cardinal and keeper of the Vatican library, who died at Rome in 1849. Mezzofanti spoke and wrote fifty-eight living languages with ease and fluency, and had at least a partial knowledge of most of the dead ones. Altogether he knew 114 speeches or dialects. On one occasion he received in audience a Magyar noble, a Hindu pundit, a Chinese mandarin, and a Berber chieftain from Kordofan, and conversed with them, each in his own speech.

Barthold Niebuhr, again, knew twenty languages by his 30th birthday, and mastered many more in later life, his knowledge extending to such rare dialects as Jazygian, Finnic, Biscayan, and Tartarian. But even this record was eclipsed by the marvellous Johann Baratier, who at the age of 5 knew Greek, Latin, and French, besides his native German. He compiled a Hebrew dictionary at 12, and published a French translation of the Itinerary of Benjamin of Tudela at 13. At 19, when he died, he spoke and wrote thirty-three languages.

Then there was Conon Gabelentz, and his even more talented son, Georg Gabelentz, who between them mastered over one hundred languages.

Newspaper article about polyglots.

Stanford University.* Her only rival for the public's fascination with child prodigies was William James Sidis (1898–1944), whose admission to Harvard at twelve as a math and philosophy prodigy made him a prime example of nurture by pushy parenting. (Sidis died at the age of forty-four, having lived the second half of his life doing menial jobs.†) Cherie was a product of the same.

Her mother, the strong-willed Winifred Sackville Stoner, touted the "natural education" that developed her daughter's genius: putting colorful pictures over the baby's crib, dispensing with nursery rhymes she called "silly," and reading her the Bible, mythology, and Latin classics. Baby Cherie was also given a typewriter to create stories and poems (which Sidis was also doing at the age of four), on which she composed the nineteen-couplet historical poem that starts, "In fourteen hundred ninety-two, Columbus sailed the ocean blue / And found this land, land of the Free, beloved by you, beloved by me."

In 1921, Mother Stoner (as she was called) would attempt to hush the news that her sixteen-year-old genius offspring had met the older globe-trotting French count Charles Philippe de Bruche and married him thirteen days later. By all appearances, the count was the perfect man for the teen prodigy—a swashbuckling adventurer who searched for lost manuscripts and spoke seventeen languages. Sadly, he died in Mexico City in 1922, soon after Cherie and probably her parents had discovered that he wasn't an aristocrat but rather a penniless con artist named Charles Philip Christian Bruch—and to top off his deception, he probably didn't speak those seventeen languages either.

A couple of years later, the two Winifreds embarked on a world tour to "find geniuses." They were accompanied by six-year-old New Yorker

---

*Naturally, one asks, who certified her abilities, and by what standards? In Mother Stoner's lectures on natural education, she brought small children onstage and asked them to repeat "cow" and "pig" in Chinese, "good-bye" and "good morning" in Japanese, and "Twinkle, Twinkle, Little Star" in Latin. After the children repeated the words, Mother Stoner announced, "There you see, they speak Japanese." "If Miss Winifred Stoner, the accomplished daughter, speaks her twelve languages only on that basis, she has not added much to the world's stock of knowledge," wrote one E. X. Porter to the *New York Times* on May 4, 1915.

†Sidis was also said to be a prodigious language learner, though the myths perpetuated about him make this difficult to determine.

Lorraine Jaillet, a "genius" who spoke six languages. (No word on how many geniuses they found.) Cherie married and divorced again and was on the verge of yet another engagement in 1930, when a mysteriously resurrected Bruch showed up. Cherie dismissed him, and to be safe, had her marriage annulled. After one last media splash in 1931, occasioned by her lawsuit against a lover, Cherie lived quietly in New York City for the rest of her days. One joke after her third marriage was that she could speak eighteen languages but couldn't say "no" in any of them.

Through my connections to linguists, I knew about the less dramatic life of Ken Hale, a highly regarded linguist at MIT and a champion of minority languages around the world, who died in 2001. His colleagues attribute fifty languages to him. He began learning them as a boarding school student in Arizona, first picking up Spanish, then Jemez and Hopi (two indigenous languages of the Southwest) from his roommates. After college, he and the woman who became his wife, Sally, went to tuberculosis sanitariums in Arizona to tape-record messages from members of tribes who couldn't write letters to their distant families.

Hale wasn't the only linguist with a facility for being able to rapidly find a way to say a lot of things in very many unrelated languages. He does, however, seem to be unique in the number of tales told about his feats. Everyone I speak to at linguistic conferences seems to have a Ken Hale story, or to know someone who did. Once, he spoke Irish to a clerk at the Irish embassy until she begged him to stop; her Irish wasn't as good as his. After watching the television miniseries *Shogun* with subtitles, he was able to speak Japanese. While doing fieldwork in Australia, he and an Aboriginal collaborator named George Robertson Jampijinpa would show up in a village at 10 a.m. to begin working on the local language, and by lunchtime Hale (who'd never heard the language before) would be conversing fluently. This kind of admiring lore was matched by his colleagues' regard for his scholarly work, "which almost certainly could not have been carried out by a fieldworker who was not a natural polyglot," wrote Victor Golla, another linguist, or "by someone who was not virtually a native speaker himself." The linguists didn't seem to care that Hale himself hated the myth. "Here we go again," he was known to say when it came up.

One useful way to think about what a hyperpolyglot can do is to see which languages he "speaks" and which ones he "talks in." Hale would say he could speak only three (English, Spanish, and Warlpiri, an aboriginal Australian language). The others, he only talked in—he could say a few things in a few topics—but he didn't know how to communicate in all of life's relevant situations, like walking through a doorway with someone. The bits of language he possessed didn't include bits like "After you, Alphonse" or "Age before beauty." In some languages it was hard to know how to say something as seemingly simple as "yes." These were some of his hallmarks for "speaking" a language, and Hale claimed he didn't possess them. What about the time he took a *Teach Yourself Finnish* book on a plane flight and landed in Helsinki using Finnish? That was just "talking in" the language. (The same story is told about Hale and his use of Norwegian.)

One of his sons, Ezra, explains that his father used languages in a few ways. It made mundane things exciting; it broke the ice in new situations; and it insulated him and helped him overcome his shyness. "I remember one time I decided to do a video of him and said we should go down to the audiovisual department and get a video recorder," Ezra told me. "His reaction was something like 'Are you crazy? We can't just go down there, you can't just do that.' But when we got there, there were three people standing around all excited to hear about our planned project. Dad just stood around quietly and somewhat awkwardly.

"Yet if the video equipment had been at the Chinese embassy he would have taken the lead, gone in there, spoken Mandarin or preferably some obscure dialect, and walked out with the AV equipment without thinking twice about it. But because there was no obvious common ground with whoever was working at the MIT AV department, he was comically afraid of going down there."

As in the case of Mezzofanti, Hale was caught in a self-reinforcing spiral of being legendary, such that the reality of his "something and something" abilities in dozens of languages became an "all or nothing" reputation through the alchemy of awe (or envy). His gift became a professional asset, which led to increasingly public performances of his virtuosity at a high-profile university; then his scholarly reputation and his friendly generosity pulled more and more languages, speakers, and learning opportunities his way, creating more opportunities for performances to be seen and heard by more people, who lent their exaggerations to the reports. Underneath the reputation, though, Hale was shy and modest, which former colleagues cited to explain why he denied the genius myth. To them, he just didn't want to own up to it. More likely, the refusal was real, and he probably didn't want to be seen as a freak. Still, people wanted to believe—so much so that his denials were rejected to his face, as in a 1996 interview.

Hale was asked: "You know that you are some sort of a legend, when it comes to learning languages—the number of languages you know, the speed with which you learn new ones. Can you give us some tips as to how to go about learning a new language?"

"A legend! It's a complete myth!" Hale said. "Let me take this opportunity to dispel that myth! I am going to tell you the truth. Don't delete this part!"

"Promise," said the interviewer.

"The truth is, I only know three languages and one of them is English. So all I really learned was two languages: Warlpiri and Spanish. Those are the only two that I feel like I know."

"How about Navajo?"

"I know a lot about Navajo, but I can't converse in Navajo."

"That is not true."

"It *is* true. I can't converse in Navajo. I can say a lot of things that make people think I can converse, but when somebody talks back, I can't respond to them in an adequate way. Saying things is totally different from conversing. I can say many things in different languages, but conversing is a different thing. Talking a language is really different from knowing something about a language."

Then he shared some of the tips and tricks he'd honed for building his linguistic patchwork. First, he said, you want to get a handle on the sounds, so get a native speaker and go through words for body parts, animals, trees, things in the environment. Fifty words would give you the basics, more if it was a tone language. Then ask for nouns and verbs, and start building sentences. Learn how to build a noun phrase. Elicit items actively; don't rely on a textbook's prechewed material. "I learn ten times more by just doing what I just told you, because then I can hear it. I have to hear it. I can't just look at it," Hale said.

He also recommended that one learn how to construct complex sentences early. In school these are usually taught late, but because they're regularly patterned, they can be easy. So, he said, learn how to make relative clauses right away, because with a relative clause, you can say "the thing that you hit a baseball with" if you don't know the word for *bat*. I've never taken this advice, but if I were ever to try to learn a foreign language again, I know I would find this construction handy. Of course, speaking in more complex sentences also sounds impressive.

As far as I could tell, no one had ever assessed his language abilities or measured his cognitive skills. "Think of Ken's ability to learn languages the way you might think of Mozart's ability," Samuel Jay Keyser, another MIT linguist, wrote me in an email. "Ken's ability to learn language was much like that, an amazing gift the neurological basis of which is a mystery."

I found hyperpolyglots fascinating icons of a cultural desire to feel connected in the modern world through foreign languages. An Austrian-born, New York–based artist named Rainer Ganahl has helped me understand how these desires arise and the shape they take.

Ganahl is a gangly-limbed man with wild dark hair, which I know from watching the videos he's made; the emails he's sent me are so extravagantly misspelled that I suppose he's either constantly in a rush or typing from a bicycle. Since 1992, he's created various installation pieces and video projects based on his learning of Japanese, Greek, Arabic, Korean, Chinese, and other languages. He has videotaped himself reading Arabic and Chinese and once put his Japanese study materials, including a desk, on display. He called the boxes of videotape, five hundred hours of it, a sculpture. At first, I was surprised to find that he wasn't trying to become fluent in any of these languages. And that he admitted this. Rather, Ganahl's art puts his experiences of becoming a linguistic outsider into a concrete form that can be inspected and critiqued. This was crucial. Until 1992, he was interested in language acquisition and could speak five languages, then made language learning itself his artwork, once he faced the fact that he wouldn't be fully perfect in every language. He considers himself a "semiprofessionaldilettante." "I can say *I am not a terrorist* in eleven languages," he quips in one video. (He stands by his misspellings, too. "It s in fact often poetic," he wrote to me once. "And often a bit of a walk on the wild provocative line.")

His 1995 essay, "Travelling Linguistics," might serve as something of a manifesto for many hyperpolyglots and high-intensity language learners someday. In it, Ganahl puts a larger historical frame around his own attempts to move away from his mother tongue. "There are many reasons why somebody ends up speaking or learning a 'foreign language' voluntarily or involuntarily," he wrote. "I would like to look at some reasons that may in fact be interrelated: educational, political, colonial, migrational and psychological reasons."

Ganahl lays out how, in the medieval period, people learned other languages, such as Latin, Ancient Greek, and Arabic, in order to access culturally powerful religious and scientific texts. (This reading and translating paradigm would have guided Giuseppe Mezzofanti in the outset of his career.) In the nationalist era in Europe, the languages dissected and offered in schools were ones that reflected national consciousness. Later, during the age of exploration, colonization, and empire building, some Europeans learned and studied the languages of distant places in service of subjugating them, at the same time that colonial subjects were learning the languages of their rulers.

Today, Ganahl argues, it's all about tourism, migration, and in particular, shopping—language learning has been brought to the nexus of the consumer and the consumed, where the strength of one's abilities in a language are verified by how convincingly you can portray a tourist, a shopkeeper, hotel owner, or day laborer. Leave behind the smooth politenesses of the diplomat, the invisibility of the spy, or the abstruse etymological tricks of the Orientalist; those model performances aren't relevant any longer. In touristic, commercial contexts, native speakers of those languages get used to non-native speakers' accents and grammar, changing (if not lowering) the bar for their visitors' language performances. The irony, Ganahl says, is that the instant gratification of shopping is antagonistic to the persistence required for language learning. Buying a shiny new dictionary or downloading a podcast for language X may feel good. It's not language acquisition, though.

Rainer's history has a European frame, but statistics show that migration and tourism trends will continue worldwide as he laid them out. Between 1960 and 2005, the number of worldwide migrants doubled, from 75 million in 1960 to 191 million in 2005. World Bank statistics from 2005 show that of the top ten migration corridors (not including Russia), six of them involved movement between countries with different national languages.* The bulk moved within Europe/Central Asia, South Asia, and sub-Saharan Africa, which means that people from predominantly multilingual countries headed to other multilingual countries. One can speculate that they added to their linguistic repertoires as they went. As for tourism, in 2008, there were 924 million international tourists, but the World Tourism Organization anticipates 1.6 billion a year by 2020. (Only 25 million tourists traveled in 1960—a 3,596 percent increase between then and now!) Any growth in tourism creates a surge in language learning, as more vendors and workers will want to speak the language of their customers. The emergence of global English is part of this trend as well. To native English speakers, the story is about the popularity of English, which reaffirms the centrality of American economic and military power (and provides for the Brits a glimpse of bygone glory). For the rest of the world, it's about trying to reduce linguistic friction, enabling one to move wherever, talk to whomever, and sell to whomever.

Hovering in the background of Ganahl's essay is the necessity of brain plasticity.† I call this relentless linguistic adaptation the "will to plasticity." This phrase deliberately echoes German philosopher Friedrich Nietzsche's famous phrase "will to power," the underlying force that drives human individuals, societies, and even the natural world away from static states of existence. In the twenty-first century, our version of

---

*These were no. 1 Mexico–US, no. 3 Turkey–Germany, no. 4 India–United Arab Emirates (UAE), no. 5 Philippines–US, no. 7 Germany–US, no. 9 India–Saudi Arabia. Migrants between Afghanistan and Iran, Algeria and France, and Egypt and Saudi Arabia wouldn't need to learn new languages. In 2010, no. 5 was China–US, no. 6 was Philippines–US, and no. 10 was India–UAE.

†Neurobiologist Marcus Jacobson defined "plasticity" as the adjustments of the nervous system to changes in the internal and external "milieu." Changes to the internal milieu come from trauma and disease. Changes to the external milieu occur through input through the senses. These two milieus also interact with each other in ways that scientists are trying to understand. I use "plasticity" in the second sense, as well as in these interactions.

this appears to be the "will to plasticity," where "plasticity" is decidedly neurological. The will to plasticity is the "incessant augmentation" of circuits in the brain—among them, language circuits. "Plasticity is an intrinsic property of the human brain," wrote Harvard neuroscientist Alvaro Pascual-Leone, "and represents evolution's invention to enable the nervous system" to adapt to new environments.

You can see the will to plasticity all over the language realm. Bestselling self-help guru Tim Ferriss published "language hacking" guides on his website that promise to help you learn a language in three months. A New York–based writer, Ellen Jovin, has a blog that describes her project to study thirteen languages in three years and to write a book about it. In relatively quick succession, two memoirs of foreign-language learning by American women were published, *Dreaming in Hindi* by Katherine Russell Rich and *Dreaming in Chinese* by Deborah Fallows.

Less visible but highly fascinating is an international language-learning club I stumbled across called the Hippo Family Club, which was founded in 1981 by an iconoclastic Japanese educator named Yo Sakakibara. His fascination with language-learning methods and his devotion to global harmony were summed up in a motto: "Anyone can speak seven languages." In my brief sojourn among the Hippos, I didn't meet anyone who speaks seven languages, but the friendly, fun social atmosphere makes members think they could achieve that.

Reading up on Hippo (as it's known in Japan, South Korea, and Mexico; in the States, it's called the Lex Language Project), I found an enthusiasm for duplicating a child's linguistic experience. "Our research shows that anyone, at any age, can acquire new languages. Unfortunately, the way most people usually attempt to learn a language, in a traditional classroom, does not provide a conducive setting for language acquisition. Infants don't learn their native language by breaking the language down into little pieces of grammar and vocabulary, or by looking in a dictionary, so why should a child or adult learn other languages that way either?"*

---

*Whether or not children are better language learners, and in what way, is a frequent topic among foreign-language learners and language acquisition scientists. I like what Rainer Ganahl told me: "Kids do not necessarily learn better, but their feeling for time and success is different." Which the Hippos also embrace.

Hippos—as members call themselves—attend weekly sessions where they sing songs, play games, and recite stories in a core set of languages. At home, they're supposed to keep their language CDs playing constantly in the background; on the CD, one story after another is told in a rotating set of languages, including your own.* These broad associations are known as the "big waves," in which you get the intonation of sentences. Eventually, they say, you'll get the "small waves," which are the individual sounds, as well as meanings.

Intrigued by the approach, I decided to visit the Hippo Club in Chihuahua, Mexico, where I stayed with a family and met a number of people in their club. Some adults told me that they'd been listening to French or Japanese stories on their CDs, when suddenly they realized, "I know what that means!" They felt the transformation to be so remarkable because they hadn't done any active study—they'd learned "naturally." Hippos are adamant that the club doesn't "teach" them. Whenever I used the word *teach,* people bristled. We don't "teach" language, they'd say; they prefer to say they "encourage." The method, which is resolutely antischool, bills itself as not having tests, grades, or teachers. Likewise, Hippos don't "learn" language, they "acquire" language. We become like babies, we absorb language the way babies absorb it.

One wants to know, does it work? Elizabeth Victor, Lex Language Project's executive director, says that she can speak "about" five languages. She explained: "I can do business in Japanese, I can find lost luggage in Spanish and French, I can make friends in Chinese, and beyond that I can say 'I'm hungry' or 'I'm tired' and maybe understand things that people say to me." To her, "speaking" a language means she can converse and communicate—not that she's fluent or "near-native." Unfortunately, because Hippos are adamantly opposed to testing, the organization has no evidence how well this environment works.

One goal in Chihuahua was to look for these outcomes. I spent some time talking to a pretty Japanese teenager, Tomoko Suzuki, who should

---

*Hippo's official seven languages are Mandarin, English, French, German, Japanese, Korean, and Spanish; they have since added Arabic, Cantonese, Hindi, Indonesian, Italian, Malay, Portuguese, Russian, Swahili, Swedish, Taiwanese, Thai, Turkish, and Vietnamese.

be a model example of what Hippo membership can produce. Because her father, Kenshi Suzuki, is the head of the Japanese Hippo organization and Yo Sakakibara's successor, she's grown up at Hippo Club meetings, CDs playing in the background all the time with a steady stream of foreign visitors in her house. Her parents even met each other at a Hippo meeting.

"How many languages did you grow up with?" I asked her.

"I grew up with nineteen languages," she replied. "Basically Japanese, but basically nineteen languages." Her abilities in about a dozen of these (including Russian, Malaysian, French, and Mandarin) are limited to reciting the Hippo creed. Yet several years of living in the United States have made her English nearly accentless. I met her in Mexico because she happened to be three months into a yearlong exchange program. The Mexican Hippos all praised her Spanish; she sounds just like a Chihuahuan, they said (for instance, she can say the *ch* sound like *sh*). Nevertheless, the Hippo method couldn't prevent a mishap that often befalls learners of third languages: her languages kept intruding on one another. The first time she'd called her parents on the phone, she couldn't remember any Japanese, and when I interviewed her in a coffee shop, her Spanish kept popping out.

"Would you say that you can speak Russian?" I asked.

"No, I only know how to introduce myself," she said. "But I'm still speaking one different language and for me, is *muy*, uh, very special."

Later that night, I was able to see the Hippo scene close up. In Chihuahua, in the meeting was held in a long, concrete room with an iPod plugged into a public address system at the front. About a half-dozen families filtered in and greeted each other, the kids breaking off immediately to play with each other, the adults introducing themselves to me in English, and when they discovered that I knew some Spanish, switching back and forth. The meeting began with the club leader, a man named Miguel Duran, punching in songs in German, Chinese, English, and Japanese, each of which incited arm waving, hip swinging, and fast stepping. Unaccustomed to this behavior, I followed the other adults, who hokey-pokeyed with as much abandon as the kids. Then we sat in a circle and passed around a microphone to individuals who had memorized specific speeches or stories in various languages. Children boldly grabbed the microphone first, sometimes sitting on their parents' laps, and recited their speeches unabashed. When the microphone came to me, I thought I'd show off a bit and introduced myself in both Spanish (which had been warmed up already) and Mandarin. At the end, everyone clapped.

We were doing something part language karaoke, part Romper Room, part linguistics crossroads. Standing in the circle, everyone's bits of languages were made relevant, even honored. The positive feedback from the group would presumably encourage individuals to do more. From what I could hear of pronunciations, they didn't sound precise. I'm not sure this mattered. Here were linguistic outsiders creating a convivial social inside for themselves.

After the meeting was a tamale dinner in my honor, which gave me a chance to talk to the parents. One father was a systems engineer; another was a pharmaceutical salesman; another was an industrial engineer. The economics of their pursuit turned out to be more relevant than the psychology of it. These were middle-class Mexicans who belong to churches but who don't have social ties that give them outlets for their aspirations, which are only tangentially about language. If they were richer, they'd send their kids abroad to camps and schools; if they were poorer, they'd be too busy to come to class.

They come because they want their kids to have more languages than just English, to be more than bilingual. Their parents want them to be economically competitive, and they realize that everyone else in the world speaks English, too. Miguel Duran told me that people do join Hippo because they think it'll benefit their English, but *poco a poco* it becomes less about English, and more about other languages. As one of the fathers said to me, "I don't want to learn seven languages—I want to grow the ones I have. But the idea is that someone can't know where they're going, or what languages they're going to encounter." As an anthropologist named Chad Nilep who has studied the Hippos told me, not everyone is able to think of themselves as multilingual. But what the club does, through its openhearted pseudo-immersion, is to license people as multilingual—and therefore as citizens of the world.

The motivation to be cosmopolitan, not just an English-flavored version but a polyglot version of it, has a spot on the time line of multilingualism's political evolution. Go back to prehistory, a time of linguistic wildness, when we can imagine that each roving band of humans grunted its own dialect, and uncountable versions of half-congealed speech codes could be overheard at every cave and watering hole. Any one of these codes had a range, not a center nor an edge; not until bands clashed, merged, or partnered and settled into villages did they acquire a physical place, a homeland. Over thousands of years, these became city-building empires that swept many languages away. On borders and in cities, people spoke several languages; so did those moving through cities—merchants, explorers, officials, and religious itinerants; so did women who were married to men in other groups; so did elites; so did everyone in geographically isolated places where trading and navigating required knowing the languages of one's equally isolated neighbors.

All this was endangered, thousands of years later, in the era of the nation. For a period of about 250 years, monolingualism became the standard model in most places, because the boundaries of the nation were drawn to include all the people who spoke alike. This unity was threatened by multilingualism and its taint of barbarity, impurity, and unnatural mixing.

Fast-forward to the end of the cold war, when the primacy of the nation-state had broken down. Money, information, and labor were seeking ways to flow unimpeded through national boundaries. The melting pot—the social crucible that created monolinguals and sorted multilinguals—no longer resembled the ideal image of progress and harmony. Linguistic heterogeneity had blossomed anew. Along with a newfound pride in various ethnic identities came an awareness of the historic cost of speaking only one's mother tongue. It looked as if the linguistic future for humanity was one in which language could slip the ties of place as in the primordial past. Even after moving from their homelands, families stayed in touch using phones and computers and remained connected to the cultural products of home through satellite television. This increased their willingness to migrate and blunted the force of assimilation. For those who lived far from borders, those same tools imported cultural and linguistic diversity and the cultural capital promised by such diversity.

On the street and in the ether, Babel grew. Governments began to acknowledge that multilingualism was a major feature of the geopolitical future. In 2002, the European Union advocated a "mother tongue plus two" educational policy.* In the last five to ten years, countries as diverse as Colombia, Mongolia, Chile, South Korea, and Taiwan have embarked on ambitious plans to make their countries bilingual—and English isn't always the second language.

The hyperpolyglot embodies both of these poles: the linguistic wildness of our primordial past and the multilingualism of the looming technotopia. That's why stories circulate about this or that person who can speak an astounding number of languages—such people are holy freaks. Touch one, you touch his power. That's why Mezzofanti was challenged to a tournament by Pope Gregory XVI, and why Russell and Watts argued about how many languages he knew. It's why the governor of Massachusetts hailed Elihu Burritt, and why Ken Hale became a myth despite his protests. Once you say you speak ten languages, you'll soon hear the gossip that you speak twenty or forty. That's why people who speak several languages have been mistrusted as spies; people wonder where their loyalties truly lie.

That's why someone could want to be a polyglot.

I've gotten a bit ahead of my story, because at the point that Dick Hudson and I were swapping names of deceased language superlearners, I was still looking for a living specimen. I learned about a Swedish language enthusiast, Erik Gunnemark, and mailed him the article I'd written about language superlearners. A few weeks later, his neatly typed reply (he didn't use email or computers) arrived. He had been working

---

*Progress, however, has been slow. Only half of EU citizens polled in 2005 said they could hold a conversation in at least one language other than their mother tongue, which makes for the unexpectedly high number of 250 million European monolinguals. The highest rates of bilingualism were in Luxembourg, Latvia, Malta, and Lithuania; the lowest were Hungary, the UK, Portugal, Italy, and Spain. See the results of the 2005 Eurobarometer poll at http://ec .europa.eu/public_opinion/archives/ebs/ebs_237.en.pdf.

on his own book, *Polyglottery Today,* but his collaborators had moved on, and now he was too frail to continue. A dedicated traveler, Gunnemark was no linguistic slouch himself, noting that he speaks six languages fluently, seven languages fairly well, and fifteen at a "mini level" (or for simple everyday conversation). He also said he could translate from a total of forty-seven languages, though for twenty of them he needed dictionaries.

Erik Gunnemark. (*Courtesy of Dan Gunnemark*)

His theory of hyperpolyglot abilities was a simple guess: they must have photographic memories. "This seems to be the only explanation why some superpolyglots 'know' more than fifty languages although they can't speak more than half of them (or less)," he wrote.

This was before I'd learned enough about hyperpolyglots to generalize about them, so his statement seemed rather bold to me at the time. It was more sensible to assume that they popped up randomly in the population, at the same frequency as other types of eccentrics. I thought, he knows more than I do. Maybe he's right.

Something else he wrote stopped me cold.

"On the whole one should concentrate on *modern* polyglots, usually born after 1900," he wrote. "That means that Mezzofanti must never be mentioned; he has nothing to do with polyglottery as a science—may be regarded as a mythical person."

A mythical person? This didn't make sense. I'd seen Mezzofanti's handwriting, his papers, his letters. Did Gunnemark know something about Mezzofanti that I didn't?

I would never get an answer. By the time I wrote him back to ask, the Swede had passed away after an extended illness.

Chapter 7

The one language accumulator that Dick Hudson knew about, Christopher, isn't someone you can call up for an interview. His answers tend to be monosyllabic, and he's not known as much of a conversationalist, whether in English (his mother tongue), or in his twenty or so other languages.* Brain-damaged, Christopher can't do simple self-care tasks; he could never hold a job. His performance IQ is very low (he's never scored higher than 76) and has a mental age of nine. Remarkably, though, he has a knack for learning languages.

He spends much less time at languages than one would think. "He spends most of his waking hours digging in the garden, working in the [wool] carding shop, reading newspapers, listening to music and indulging in a variety of other occupations," wrote University of College London linguist Neil Smith and collaborator Ianthi-Maria Tsimpli, at the Aristotle University of Thessaloniki, in *The Mind of a Savant: Language Learning and Modularity*, their first book about Christopher's language abilities.

---

*Christopher can translate from and communicate in Danish, Dutch, Finnish, French, German, Modern Greek, Hindi, Italian, Norwegian, Polish, Portuguese, Russian, Spanish, Swedish, Turkish, and Welsh.

Perhaps it was Christopher's mother's bout with German measles early in her pregnancy. Perhaps it was the bad fall she had. Perhaps it was her long labor, during which the nurses sent for oxygen. But in February 1962, six weeks after he was born, Christopher was diagnosed as brain-damaged. At six or seven years old, his fascination with foreign languages was triggered by watching the 1968 Mexico Olympics. He often pretended to be from a foreign country, wearing a towel as a turban or a matador's cape. "He had a precocious talent, but he was also afflicted with a minor speech defect, poor eyesight, and a degree of clumsiness that seemed to confirm the diagnosis of mental handicap," wrote Smith and Tsimpli.

Though he's never been formally diagnosed with autism, he displays many autistic traits. From the documentary films and photographs I've seen, he's a short, very sweet-looking, shambling man with thick eyebrows and a dark moustache. Smith and Tsimpli describe him as "socially unforthcoming" and "emotionally opaque." He is uninterested in social formalities and unable to perceive what other people might be thinking.

Another trait of the autist is an obsessive interest in one topic: in Christopher's case, it's languages. In French and Spanish, Smith says that Christopher is fluent, and "quite fluent" in Greek. German is easy for him, as is Dutch. Before his appearance on a Dutch television show, someone suggested that he might improve his "rudimentary" Dutch, so after a few days with a grammar and a dictionary, he was able to converse with people before and after the program, performing as so many linguistic virtuosos before him had. In his other languages, he's accumulated huge amounts of vocabulary, which he learns with what appears to be a voracious, bottomless memory. One time Smith and Tsimpli gave him an hour-long grammar lesson in Berber and left him some basic books. A month later, he remembered everything about the Berber lesson.

What's also amazing is that Christopher can also switch among all of his languages quite deftly and translate to and from English with ease. (Going between other languages is harder for him.) The point is, he's not simply a memory prodigy. Yet when you read more deeply about what he can and can't do, it's not clear that he contributes to an understanding of what language-learning talent might look like.

It depends in part on how you define *talent*. If it means that some-one learns new languages quickly, and also pays attention to the declen-sions and inflections of words and making the elements in noun and verb phrases agree, then Christopher has a talent. On the other hand, if by "talent" you mean performing anywhere close to what native speak-ers do, he doesn't qualify. In many of his languages, much of what he says is repetitive; his translations are imperfect, particularly in languages that are further from Romance and Germanic. As Smith and Tsimpli acknowledge, though he's fluent in just a few of his languages, Christo-pher doesn't know any of them to a native-like degree.

Others have noted that his English, though that's his mother tongue, isn't native-like, if you consider understanding metaphors to be part of a native's skill set. Phrases like "standing on the shoulders of giants" con-found him. Some scientists have suggested that in order to comprehend a metaphor, you have to know that someone intends a meaning other than a literal reference to giants' shoulders.

Christopher also doesn't learn new grammars completely. After four years of Greek lessons, for instance, he grew his vocabulary, became more fluent, and reduced his errors. Yet he didn't get better at dis-tinguishing syntactically good from bad sentences. Normal second-language learners have a harder time with the structure of words than with the structure of sentences; Christopher was the opposite. He's gen-uinely obsessed—and genuinely excellent at—the mechanisms of con-structing words, especially their spellings. He can also use four writing systems. Given a newspaper in one of his languages, he selects words and identifies parts of speech and other properties.

The biggest limitation—and the one that may provide the true mea-sure of what he can do—is that in most of his foreign languages, his English grammar influences what he says or translates. When asked to translate, "Who can speak German?" he answered with *"Wer kann spre-chen Deutsch?"* not *"Wer kann Deutsch sprechen?"* It's as if his English is just ventriloquizing in other languages.

As Smith and Tsimpli put it, "It is not too inaccurate to suggest that Christopher's syntax is basically English with a range of alternative veneers." The technical word is a *calque*—a word-for-word translation from one language to another. (One well-known example is the English calque "long time no see" of the Mandarin *hao jiu bu jian*.) In languages like Dutch and German (with a syntax and a word order very close to that of English), the learner can calque away and remain intelligible; the further a language's word order gets from English, the bigger impediment calquing becomes to being understood (and not sounding absurd). This echoes a folk sentiment about polyglots in Norwegian that someone told me: *Hvis en nordman hævder at han snakker syv språk, så er seks af dem norsk.* (If a Norwegian claims to be able to speak seven languages, six of them are Norwegian.)

Recently Smith, Tsimpli, and some colleagues gave Christopher another kind of linguistic workout by teaching him British Sign Language (BSL), an experiment they document in their second book about him, *The Signs of a Savant: Language Against the Odds*. A sign language is an intriguing challenge. Where a speaker produces a strict string of sounds, a signer often assembles multiple bits of meaning in the same moment of time. This makes calquing of the sort that Christopher does in other languages more obvious. Also, a system requiring manual dexterity and eye gaze was a challenge for a man with limits in each.

Christopher's abilities were compared to those to a group of university language students who had tested well on a written test of grammar in foreign languages. His understanding of BSL was good. Yet he had difficulty bringing his talents, whatever they are, to BSL. He had difficulty learning to use grammatical functions that required precise hand control. He developed eye contact with his teacher, but because he doesn't generally look at faces, he misses the facial movements that BSL uses to signal negation or ask questions like "What?" or "Where?" The normal learners were about as good as Christopher was in BSL.

From the beginning, Smith and Tsimpli hadn't been interested in hyperpolyglottism itself, so they didn't nail down in what way Christopher might be talented (at least in spoken and written languages). The theoretical fish they looked to fry concerned "modularity"—the idea that language is a separate function in the brain. It is thought to be so separate that someone with asymmetric cognitive faculties (like Christopher) could have mostly intact language. Modularity was interesting in itself; so was the nature of thought, and whether or not language could be unique to humans or not. Such claims about modularity were a red flag for critics, who dove at Smith and Tsimpli's conclusions about Christopher in the earlier book. Debunking the analysis of Christopher would take down the argument about modularity, too.

Some weren't convinced that Christopher had, in fact, an intact language faculty, because he was so limited in English. (Smith argues that the structures of English in Christopher's head were intact, which meant he is still a good example of modularity. His communication failures aren't governed by what Smith locates in the "language faculty.") Other critics disputed that Christopher qualified as a savant, or that his fascination with languages was so remarkable. A survey of autistic savants from the 1970s showed that 19 out of 119 children were similarly obsessed with language forms. The survey turned up one child who sounded like Christopher, described by his parents as someone with "a working knowledge of French, Spanish, Japanese, and Russian—knows at least the alphabet and pronunciation of Arabic, Hebrew, and several others." (Many more people on the autistic spectrum are fascinated by machines, however, than by languages.)

Others commented that Christopher didn't have a linguistic ability as much as a powerful talent for recognizing patterns. Only coincidentally was this proficiency attuned to language, specifically words. He was also boosted by a powerful rote memory, considered one hallmark of autistic savants (said to be true because they remember what they see or hear without consciously thinking about what they're taking in. Overall, Christopher's memory profile, especially in working memory, is very strange). Both together give him analytic ability as well as recall and performance. Yet, because he makes so many mistakes and can't break away from English sentence patterns, "it would appear that Christopher is not so much a successful learner of languages [in the strict sense] as he is an obsessive accumulator of minutiae that happen to be linguistic in nature," wrote one reviewer of *The Mind of a Savant*.

In the second book about Christopher's BSL, Smith and his coauthors appeared to agree with that assessment. They now wrote that his abilities "are only partly linguistic" and that his case "provides no relevant evidence" for language talents. Inexplicably, they continued to describe him as "mastering spoken languages" and as "supremely gifted at learning new languages." They disputed the notion that Christopher is merely a good pattern recognizer—he fails to recognize them in music and games. And he got stumped when trying to learn an artificial language with a word whose meaning depended on where it was placed in a sentence.

What does this remarkable man have to do with the rest of us? To Smith and Tsimpli, his case means that language learning doesn't require some traits we take for granted, such as good general learning abilities, average cognition, and a theory of mind. Critics suggest that the only people who would want to perform like Christopher would be those who'd be satisfied with calquing their mother tongues—even though many language learners would happily accept his memory and skills at parsing and assembling words. This shows why language learning isn't purely a memory feat: you have to make word orders more automatic than you can consciously retrieve through, say, a mnemonic.

With such profound asymmetries, Christopher couldn't be the exemplar of a talented language learner. Certainly not the hyperpolyglot. Yet his case forecast a lot about what I should expect to find at the upper limits of language learning: superior abilities in one area accompanied by deficits in others, mainly. That imbalance might be in intellectual skills. It could also be in areas of language itself—good with words and word forms, Christopher was relatively bad at syntax. Yet it also showed that eroded social and pragmatic skills would be a bigger handicap than poor syntax. A foreign-language speaker who calques all the time can bridge communication gaps in other ways. Even if your pronunciation isn't perfect, if it's good enough to clarify and repair, then you're communicating.

I could not escape the notion there was someone Mezzofanti-like out there. My search had to continue.

Erik Gunnemark, who was eighty-nine when he died, had written *The Art and Science of Learning Languages,* a very nearly complete handbook about how to become a polyglot. In the foreword he even quotes a black magic spell to learn many languages: "Catch a young swallow. Roast her in honey. Eat her up. Then you will understand all languages." Did Gunnemark roast swallows? Probably not. He seemed like someone who took his own practical advice, which was to build activities for learning around concentration, repetition, and practice. He called these the "three pillars" of language learning.

Many people have an aptitude for doing this that may not emerge until adulthood, Gunnemark wrote. That's just as well: he considered them better language students than children, because they're more disciplined and make better use of time. "A child has to learn about the world and a language, an adult only has to learn about a language," he wrote. Children have the advantage of living in a world mainly composed of concrete objects that can be named by caretaking adults who are also patient listeners. Adults, who dwell in realms of abstractions, could compensate by observing languages in the environment.

Intriguing ideas. Sensible, even familiar. However, they provided no clue as to why he had told me that Mezzofanti was a myth. Had he read Russell or Watts? Had he found them overdazzled by thin shreds of evidence? Their judgment stretched too thin?

Gunnemark's rejection was overprudent, I thought. As packaged in spectacular display as Mezzofanti was, there was some genuine feat there. The cardinal *did* accumulate many languages, I would have said to Gunnemark, and a good number to a very high standard, and all to the degree that he needed them in the sphere he worked in, even if he couldn't, in many of them, match what a native speaker could do.

But, okay, say I ignore Mezzofanti. Who was the best candidate for the world's most accomplished hyperpolyglot? Gunnemark's letter to me contained a pantheon of polyglottery, a list of "modern superpolyglots":

Eugen M. Czerniawski (b. 1912)
Ziad Fazah (b. 1954)
Arvo Juutilainen (b. 1949)
Donald Kenrick (b. 1929)
Emil Krebs (1867–1930)
Lomb Kató (1909–2003)
Pent Nurmekund (1905–97)

Why these seven? Why only one woman, Lomb Kató*? Gunnemark didn't explain.†

I'd first encountered Lomb Kató, a Hungarian hyperpolyglot, in a 1996 article by Stephen Krashen, a University of Southern California linguist and an expert on language acquisition. In 1995, Krashen had been teaching in Hungary, where Lomb lived and was locally famous. She'd also written a memoir, *Így tanulok nyelveket,* or *How I Learn Languages,* which was first published in 1970—only in Hungarian. When Krashen interviewed the eighty-six-year-old, she was learning her seventeenth language, Hebrew.

Lomb Kató. (*Courtesy of Lomb János*)

"What Lomb Kató had was a heroic drive to get comprehensible input and to retain it," Krashen told me, holding her up as a triumph

---

* Hungarian surnames appear before given names.

† In general, famous language learners, language accumulators, and language geeks tend to be men, though lack of real evidence has to leave this an open question—a link between gender and language-learning ability hasn't been explored, not surprisingly; researchers haven't looked at the links between language aptitude and socioeconomic class, race, ethnicity, or sexual preference, either. In my online survey of those speaking six or more languages, 69 percent were male. This doesn't mean that men are better than women at learning languages—it may simply mean that men are more likely to fill out online surveys that are designed to appreciate their intellectual prowess. Indeed, boasting about the languages one has studied or can speak is a display of geek machismo. On the other hand, professions that require high-level linguistic skills, such as interpreting, have more women practitioners than men; one suggestion is that interpreters must be invisible and nonegotistic, a role that women may, depending on the cultural setting, be better prepared to play.

of dedication. She worked hard; she wasn't afraid of failure; she read prolifically.* What's also notable about her is that she took her place in an area dominated by men. Lomb's case supported Krashen's theory of second-language acquisition, especially the central part of it, the "comprehensible input hypothesis," which he first proposed in the mid-1970s. Krashen argued that people can both subconsciously acquire and consciously learn language, but that the former is more important. Acquisition happens, he said, when we understand what we read or hear—not when we speak or write it, memorize vocabulary, or study grammar. This is how children get their first language—they "acquire" it. So do massive multilinguals like Lomb.

In 1941, Lomb and her husband moved into a room whose previous Russian tenants had left behind trashy romance novels. Using her beginner's Russian (pried from two ratty dictionary volumes), she began deciphering them, improving her Russian to the point that she could read literature like Gogol's *Dead Souls,* a book she had to sew into a Hungarian encyclopedia in order to disguise it from disapproving eyes. Later, she started Spanish by reading a translation of *Gentlemen Prefer Blondes*—she didn't read solely classics, in other words.

Krashen liked Lomb because she didn't claim to have a talent for doing what she did. "Her last words to me changed my life," he once said in an interview. "'Stephen, you are so young. So many years left, so many languages to acquire!' (I was fifty-four at the time.)" Afterward he "plunged" into languages—reading novels in French, German, and Spanish. His admiration aside, more would later come to light both about Lomb's methods and about the extent of her abilities.

In 2008, when Lomb's *How I Learn Languages* became available in English, non-Hungarians could finally read about the famous Hungar-

---

*Like Gunnemark, she also believed that children were not necessarily better language learners than adults. She concedes that "after 10 or 11 [years old]," one cannot pronounce like a native speaker, but she's proud of her accent: "After learning 16 languages and after more than a half a century of living in Budapest, sharp-eared people can still discover in my speech the vowels typical of natives of [southern Hungary]." The main problem of age, she said, is memory loss, but there are tricks to prevent or forestall this.

ian for themselves. Lomb's prose is spry, often sardonic. "One of my goals in writing the book was to remove the mystical fog surrounding the idea of an 'innate ability' for language learning," she says in an early eye-catching passage. "I want to demystify language learning, and to remove the heroic status associated with learning another language." What makes one successful, she says, is interest driven by motivation, perseverance, and diligence. One important point seems to be to pump yourself up: "Be firmly convinced that you are a linguistic genius."

Lomb doled out advice to the readers she encouraged to be geniuses. "The language learning method that is good is the one that enables you to learn the most reliable patterns relatively quickly," she wrote. Then you must internalize the forms to make them automatic; to do this, you must encounter them as often as you can. One way, she said, is to practice monologues or invent private language games, such as "how many synonyms for a certain word can you find?" On long train rides, she played against herself.

Though Krashen's early portrait is of someone who mainly reads ("Dr. Lomb is clearly a reading enthusiast," he wrote), Lomb in her memoir also stresses speaking practice, even if it was mainly with herself. "If I talk with myself, I am relieved that my partner will not be indignant at long hesitations, grammatical agreements difficult to manage, and vocabulary gaps completed in the mother tongue," she wrote, adding that "all I suggest is that monologues be silent." She also urged people to seek correction of errors.

(Krashen noted to me that the comprehensible input hypothesis predicts that monologues and similar kinds of practice don't do much good. Others disagree, saying that output is crucial because it builds automaticity by reinforcing neural connections. It also forces people to pay attention to grammatical structures, especially in the real-time bustle of conversing. As one researcher puts it, it's the difference between finding entertainment from watching an elite tennis player take a swing and visually dissecting the parts of the swing in order to emulate it later.)

Don't bother with grammar rules, Lomb also said. "I will sooner see a UFO than a dative case or subjective complement." Her message is clear: the fancy terminology gets in the way, so don't bother with it. "One learns grammar from language, not language from grammar," she

writes. One can almost hear the thousands of language teachers gnash-
ing their teeth in Hungary's direction.

Krashen's theory doesn't predict how many additional languages one
can acquire. The implication is that, as long as you can keep getting comprehensible input, it's potentially infinite. Yet Lomb, who had no deficit
of linguistic gumption, felt close to only five of her languages. Clearly,
there *are* limits. Russian, English, French, and German "live inside me
simultaneously with Hungarian," she wrote. This "living inside" she
defined as the ability to "switch between any of these languages with
great ease, from one word to the next." And here, age was at work:
Hungarian, German, and French were the earliest ones she'd learned.
The others came later; she embarked on English at the age of twenty-
four, Russian at thirty-two. By contrast, to translate in Italian, Spanish,
Japanese, Chinese, and Polish, her five "surge" languages, required her
to brush up for half a day. Her other six languages (Bulgarian, Danish,
Latin, Romanian, Czech, and Ukrainian) she knew only through translation work.

When I mention this aspect of Lomb's profile, some are impressed:
"She needed only half a day to reactivate her languages!" Others appreciate that an adult could be so confident and active, especially so late
in life. What struck me when I got my hands on her memoir was her
admission of a language limit. She didn't say it was because she lacks
time to practice. She didn't say it's because she couldn't travel. In fact,
she gave no sense of why. The limit was unavoidably there.

She was often asked, "Is it possible to know sixteen languages?"

"No, it is not possible," she replied, "at least not at the same level of
ability."

Again, no explanation. No matter how much time the learner has,
no matter how strong her ambition, there are unavoidable limits, as final
as gravity. Yet I expected a language repertoire closer in size to Mezzofanti's or Burritt's or Burton's. Lomb, though a fascinating character,
wasn't the linguistic summit I sought.

At this point, what I knew for sure was this: You can learn numerous
languages over a lifetime, at a variety of proficiencies. Yet no matter

how large the repertoire gets, there appears to be a limit to how many languages you can keep active at a very high level at once. You may also have a number of languages that are kept less active. It also appears that you can reactivate many more of your latent languages, at least for brief periods of time. But you could deploy even constrained vocabularies in real settings if you needed to.

Later I read a letter from Gunnemark explaining how you should be skeptical of anyone claiming to be able to speak twenty or more languages. Was he policing who gets to call him- or herself a hyperpolyglot? Why? Maybe he distrusted Mezzofanti, I thought. After all, he distrusted the grandiose claims of others, as he too insisted that speaking so many languages all at once wasn't possible.

I checked on the remaining names on Gunnemark's list of language superlearners: Czerniawski, Fazah, Juutilainen, Kenrick, Krebs, Nurmekund. Maybe one of them would claim limitless powers. But Krebs, Lomb, and Nurmekund were dead. Contact info for Juutilainen and Czerniawski eluded me. Dan Gunnemark, Erik's son, gave me an email address for Kenrick, who provided a phone number in England, but never picked up the phone when I called, so after a while I gave up.

Which left Ziad Fazah.

Chapter 8

y earliest research into Ziad Fazah turned up only a 1996 news report from Reuters with rudimentary details about his life: born in 1953 in Liberia, he was taken to Beirut as an infant. After graduating with a degree in philology from the American University in Beirut, he moved with his parents to Brazil, then married. He carried a business card stating that he "reads, writes and speaks fifty-four languages fluently." Up until 1998, he was listed in *The Guinness Book of World Records* as speaking fifty-six languages—again, it was said, "fluently." How this was determined was fuzzy—something about television, Greece, and a hyperpolyglot freak show. The footage has never been released.

Unfortunately, the poor Reuters journalist didn't sift the truth from Fazah's self-mythologizing. "Aside from his mother tongue of Arabic, and French and English, which he learned at school, Fazah taught himself all the languages. He began with German and moved on to such Far Eastern tongues as Mandarin Chinese, Cantonese, and Japanese," goes the article. At forty, Fazah was apparently still picking up languages; most recently, he'd learned Papiamentu, a creole language that combines Dutch, Portuguese, and Spanish and is spoken in certain Caribbean islands. "Fazah, who can learn three thousand words in two to three months," the Reuters writer dutifully recorded, "said Mandarin was the hardest language to learn because of the vast number of ideo-grams. Fazah claimed that in seven years he can learn the rest of the world's estimated three thousand dialects."

You could poke out an eye reading such boasts. They seemed akin to medieval beliefs that diseases could be caused by the position of the planets. Learning three thousand dialects in seven years? That was clearly intended for a naïve journalist. There are more than three thou-sand languages on the planet—by one reckoning, the actual number is closer to seven thousand. And how was Fazah going learn the two-thirds of those languages that have no dictionaries or textbooks since they're not written down?

I resolved to treat Gunnemark's skepticisms and his list of polyglots, as well as the journalist's excited account, as folklore. I didn't have to believe all of either to find something useful in them. I simply needed to press on with my own investigation.

The Internet has been a gift to those with the will to plasticity. In the last five years or so, the online world has helped language learners escape the terrible gravity of the classroom by making available podcasts, classes, tutoring sessions, blogs, games, and forums of varying degrees of quality for different prices. One website that sprang up, www.how-to-learn-any-language.com—founded in 2005 by a multilingual Swiss busi-nessman and quickly populated by thousands of language learners from all over the globe—was a hotbed of debate over self-teaching methods. It also turned out to be a gathering place for hyperpolyglots themselves. For me, it was a treasure trove.

The moderator of one thread on the site went by the moniker Arda-schir.* In an autobiographical sketch, he said he grew up speaking English but that his first foreign language was French, which he started in middle school, got to speak while traveling alone in France at thir-teen, but almost flunked as a subject in high school. As a teenager, he fruitlessly attempted German on his own, was a good Latin student in high school, and by the time he graduated from Columbia University in

---

*Ardaschir was the name of a Persian king who conquered northern India.

New York, he had a "very solid foundation" in French, German, Spanish, Latin, Greek, and Sanskrit. As a doctoral student at the University of Chicago, he added Old French, Old English, Middle English, and Old High German. For his dissertation, he analyzed Old Norse dream sagas, and after graduating he spent two years in Germany, where he "consciously banned English from my brain" and set out "to master German, paying attention to everything I heard, writing down all new words and making a point of using them actively myself until I knew them."

In the early 1990s, he moved to Handong, Korea, for a university teaching job, and at thirty-two, far from home and probably lonely, turned the full force of his mind to learning as many languages as he could. For the next five years, he spent twelve hours a day trying to learn at least one language of each representative type or from each language family, in order to read the world's great books in their original languages. He worked on thirty different languages each day in fifteen- to twenty-minute chunks. Eventually he married a Korean woman and had a son. After ten years, he moved his family to Lebanon, to take a new job at a university, because he wanted exposure to Arabic. There, another son was born. In 2006, when Israel bombed and invaded Lebanon, the family fled via a harrowing taxi ride into Syria, then evacuated to the United States. Despite these hardships, he'd become a guru on the forum for aspiring polyglots and hyperpolyglots, speaking with austere authority about learning matters and gathering biographical information about people like Fazah.

After Ardaschir posed the question "Ziad Fazah—does he exist?" a few new facts about the Brazilian trickled in: He learns languages by getting up in the morning, closing the window blinds of the bedroom, and talking to himself in whatever he's trying to learn. Or, he's bored with languages. Or even, he had quit for a while during the 1990s.

Skeptics asked how a middle-class Brazilian could afford materials for exotic languages, especially before the advent of the Internet. And if he's so talented, why isn't he richer?

Some disputed that Fazah could be fluent in so many languages.

"I've STUDIED an average of one language a year for the last thirty years so have some vague inkling of the amount of work involved to learn them and, more important, to keep each of them alive. For example I've only read books in ten languages, and although I try to listen to radio broadcasts I can only do this for a few languages each week," wrote one poster. "I would not say I can 'speak a language' until I can understand at least 85–90 percent of what is being said on satellite television and movies and can readily engage in conversation with native speakers about a variety of topics with little or no difficulties or gaps in communication or knowledge," wrote another. Doubts about Fazah were building.

Then an American, Dave Maswary, joined the discussion. He had moved to Brazil to train as a no-holds fighter and learn Japanese, in preparation for a move to Japan. His Japanese teacher? Ziad Fazah. If you don't believe what I'm telling you, and if you doubt his abilities, then call him yourself, Maswary said. An email address and a phone number appeared in his post.

One by one, forum members reported that they'd spoken with Fazah in Russian, or Cantonese, or Mandarin, or Spanish, claiming that he speaks with an accent in those languages, but he's a nice guy and clearly passionate about languages. Someone said they were going to hire him to teach via Skype.

I watched all this unfold with bemusement—Fazah hadn't shied from public performances in the past. Why wasn't he defending himself now? In this vacuum, his reputation took its final, fatal dive. In 1997, he'd appeared on a Chilean TV show, *Viva el lunes*. As with the tournament that Pope Gregory XVI had arranged for Mezzofanti, so much depended upon a single spectacle. This is even more true now, because with YouTube, where the Chilean video was eventually posted, everyone could see Fazah's spectacular failure.

A middle-aged bald man with a heavyset face sits in a TV studio, wearing a tan jacket and tie, in front of a studio audience. One by one, people stand up and ask him questions; they're native speakers of Finnish, Russian, Farsi, Chinese, and Greek. He's to translate each question for the audience and then answer it in the language. The Finnish speaker, a woman, says something about how many people speak Finnish (5 million), and that Finnish, Swedish, and Saami are the official languages of Finland. Fazah looks blank, then says something. He's not right. After he responds to the Farsi speaker, she says that Fazah hasn't actually answered his question, either; a boo rises from the audience. First blood.

"What day is it today?" the Russian asks him, in Russian.

"What?" Fazah asks.

Then a Mandarin speaker asks what the only man-made structure visible from the moon is. Fazah should have said, "Nothing." Or, to humor the speaker, "The Great Wall of China." Instead, Fazah makes an odd gesture with his left hand on his head, running it from his temple over his ear to the back of his head, and says, in Spanish, "Where did you learn Chinese? And how did you learn it so easily?" The Chinese speaker shakes his head, no. More boos. Fazah looks sweaty, and runs his finger across his head again, as if he means to dig into his skull for the answers. He's speechless.

A blogger, Magnus Lewan, on his blog, http://ardentagnostic .blogspot.com, would later express a sensible conclusion shared by many, that "it is very likely that Ziad Fazah is one of billions of people who are unable to speak fifty-nine languages." On the forum, the response was speedy and scathing. Posters judged the Brazilian a fake; skeptics paraded their vindication.

Once the video came to light, Ardaschir shut down the thread immediately, writing, "It is very clear that the only person who can shed any light upon what Ziad Fazah really knows is Ziad Fazah. And as he is aware of this forum and this discussion but does not care to elucidate, I think we should all just pass over him in respectful silence for the time being. The man exists, but the legend does not."

Like everyone else on the forum, I now had Fazah's email address and phone number. Calling him would be easy. As far as I knew, he might be a modern Mezzofanti within reach, but if I spooked him with the wrong questions, he might slip away forever. I needed to test his proficiencies—how fluent was he in those fifty-nine languages?

I needed a guide to the hyperpolyglot mind. I contacted Ardaschir, who said sure, I could come to California to meet him.

Chapter 9

 ummer in Berkeley, California. The $1 scoop ice cream store is open on Shattuck Avenue, the college girls are swinging down the hills, the San Francisco Giants are hitting home runs against the Oakland A's. For Ardaschir, whose actual name is Alexander Arguelles, a typical day begins at 2:00 or 3:00 in the morning with him at a desk in the spare bedroom, writing in a bound book with lined pages. He writes a few pages in English to help him collect his thoughts. In his first language, he says, he's the most expressive. Then he continues with his "scriptorium" exercise, writing two pages apiece in Arabic, Sanskrit, and Chinese, the languages he calls the "etymological source rivers."

"If I begin the day by writing the three of those," he said, "I know it's going to be a good day."

A page of Turkish is followed by a page of Persian or Greek, then one of Hindi, Gaelic, or other languages. He works in fifteen-minute chunks, switching to a new language at the end of each period. In languages he knows less well, he writes out grammar exercises. His goal: to write twenty-four pages a day. How many books has he filled? He pointed to three tiers of them, black-spined, atop a bookshelf. "I'm on volume forty-five now." If he's tired or distracted, the writing can drag on all day, but with focus, he can do it in four hours. When I first met him, he averaged nine hours a day of study, noting with a bit of longing that before he had children, he could average fourteen.

"There's absolutely no financial gain to knowing languages," he told me once. "It's a waste of time and energy. If I took all the time and energy that I've put into expanding my mind, my linguistics horizons, and my literary horizons, if instead of that I had turned it to practical interests, like 'I want to make money, I want a big house, I want some sort of success,' there's no question I could have done that." There was no dearth of opportunities. Doing temp jobs in the summer as a college student, he was often noticed (he said) by a boss who offered him a job. But tracking whether or not gynecologists in Utah and Nevada were accepting a certain type of credit card—one job he was offered—didn't square with his intellectual self-image.

So he's made his way here, an escape or a voyage, to a spare bedroom with bookcases filled with dictionaries, grammars, novels, workbooks, and textbooks that tower over him on three sides. They are arranged by language family, 130 languages in all. "I honestly believe, where you are right now," he said, gesturing to the shelves, "has a very good shot at being the—how shall I put this?—the world's most condensed and most complete language laboratory." The room was like a monk's cell or a space capsule: the stillness of Alexander at work could be deafening. His shelves were so full that he discovered things as we talked, like a Mandinka grammar he didn't know he owned.

Tall and thin with brown hair, gentle eyes, and a voice like a priest, forty-four years old but so young-looking you'd wonder what seminary he attends. *So this is a hyperpolyglot,* I thought. I had expected someone boisterous and charismatic, who could talk about the Giants' season so far and, oh yeah, don't you love Sino-Tibetan languages? I eat 'em like cashews. Someone debonair, not dweeby, whose life was thick with political and sexual intrigues that played out in a dozen languages— someone who could, at a moment's notice, be one with all the world, on the world's multivariate terms. A man of linguistic action. Someone fully *plugged in.*

Instead, the figure at the door was draped with loneliness. His spirit seemed at times relaxed. At other times, subdued. You'd call him lost in the past if it wasn't clear that he might be happier there. Lost in the present would be better. "I definitely could have been a very good flagellant or Jesuit," Alexander said. "I have a knack for studying with monastic discipline, as a form of trying to attain self-edification," he said. I'm not mocking him—here's someone who's living his dream, who bears its burdens, revels in its joys. On the first day I visited him, his wife was out of the house, and while we talked, his two boys, three and five years old, played quietly in the living room. When they popped in to watch, he smothered them with kisses and peppered them with questions in French, which they know alongside English and Korean. They're already writing Chinese characters in workbooks, which he— puffed with pride—showed me. That much, I thought, sounds like what a hyperpolyglot should do.

"I try to grab them and say, Let's do some Latin together. They crawl all over me. I want them to share this. I don't want to say, Get out, I'm working. I want them to be a part of it. I want to share it with them as much as they can.

"I recommend that you have two boys, spaced two years apart. It's ideal. I'm four years older than my brother, and we didn't get along when I was younger. Whereas these two, they squabble occasionally but they're really alike, they love each other, and you can see that. I just have one brother, Max, and you'll meet him. He's completely handicapped now. He was totally normal until he was ten years old and he had a devastating brain disease and has been utterly physically and mentally handicapped ever since. My parents refused to put him in a home, so they just take care of him, and he's a lot of work."

I took a chance on the next question. "Is there any way in which your learning languages is some sort of response to that?"

He inhaled and sighed before taking a long pause. "I'm not sure. I don't think so. But I think that perhaps doing it so compulsively as I do might be kind of a feeling that my brother, you know, basically lost his life, so maybe I have to do twice in this life to live my life and his."

Such an intimate story I hadn't intended to uncover, and certainly not so quickly; I felt as if I'd stumbled into a place I shouldn't be. I used to wonder why the figure of linguistic power, like a Mezzofanti, is so often compared to the native speaker of one language, when the more telling comparison is to the man abandoned by all words, reduced to meaningless sounds. As I would discover, people who have lost their language to trauma or disease have made more contributions to the scientific understanding of language in the brain than Mezzofanti and his brethren ever did. Here was that symbolic pair, the polyglot and the wordless man, in the brotherly flesh.

On many mornings, once Alexander has greeted the sun in his scriptorium, he goes for a long run in the arid hills of the park above his neighborhood, while listening to a German audiobook tape on his Walkman. (So far, he eschews the MP3.) Marathon lengths are easy for him—once, he says, he got lost in the woods and ended up running more than thirty miles, though he felt faint. Later someone told him that long-distance runners have to eat every two hours, which came as a revelation; he finds the carbohydrate goo disgusting. He eschews that, too.

One morning, he discovered the campus of a theological seminary that he now covets for a polyglot academy he dreams of starting. I asked him to show me, and on our way up the hill I learned that he doesn't know how to drive—a point that will take on significance later.

The school was made up of low, Mission Revival–style buildings surrounded by redwoods and eucalyptus trees stirred by the wind. Alexander pointed to a fire trail cutting down the hill, saying that it would be good for shadowing. Shadowing is how he gets to know a language's sounds: put a tape in the Walkman and, while briskly walking and arms swinging, you shout the sounds as you hear them. Though you won't know what the words mean, later you read the dialogues and translate them, then you shadow the same material again. For him, parsing the sounds first, then adding meaning later makes it stick. Shouting now is also an inoculation against embarrassment later.

At first, I assumed that his ambition was to speak all of his languages—otherwise, what's the point of shadowing? This turned out to be wrong. I also assumed that he might like to talk to people. That, too, wasn't right. His goal is to read literature from all over the world, classic and contemporary, in the original languages. He had shown me a recent novel by a Dutch author. "Reading this puts me in tune with the living spirit, the resonance of the language," he'd said, waving the book, "not being able to go to Amsterdam and go into a café and get a hash brownie and have them think that I'm one of them, not an American tourist." He wants to explore his consciousness, to encounter a language as a living entity, and to collect the esoteric knowledge of these encounters. "Most of the languages I've studied I've never spoken, and I probably never will," he told me. "And that's okay with me. That's nice if you can do that, but it's rare that you have an interesting conversation in English. Why do I think it would be any better in another language?"

As we walked around the seminary grounds, he pointed out a cloister, also a good space for shadowing. He cut the air with his finger, imagining himself the school principal: here he'd put Korean, here Chinese, over there Japanese, letting students drift from area to area. He'd do this, he said, because he encounters languages not as finite, divisible things, but as fuzzy clouds. Labeling something "French" or "Italian" is a convenience, not a reflection of the reality he perceives. His students should have that experience, too. What the rest of us call a "language" is, to Alexander, a minor variation on a broader linguistic theme. "For me to learn any Romance or Germanic dialect, just put me in the environment, and it would come alive," he said. "It would be building upon thousands and thousands of hours of active conscious study of other languages." Even if he were to set out today to learn a language unrelated to one he already knows, he said, "I would have to put in fewer hours than compared to, say, you."

A sunlit courtyard with a dry, cracked fountain at its center beckoned us to stop. "The way I see it," he said, "there are three types of polyglots. There are the ultimate geniuses, the ones who are so rare, the ones who excel at anything they do, and one of those happens to be languages.

"There are people who are only good at languages, like Mezzofanti, for whom it comes very easily. Then there are people like me: we're willing to work very, very hard, and everything we know, it's because we've worked to get it. I would think those would be the people you'd be most interested in: what sort of strategies do they have that they can teach everybody else?"

Walking around next to Alexander, I began to feel stupid, soft, and modern. I asked him what he thought of people who have only one language. I feel sorry for them, he replied. He maintains that every educated

Alexander Arguelles at Angkor Wat, 2011.
(*Courtesy of Alexander Arguelles*)

person should know six of them. Informality makes him uncomfortable. He gets a lot of emails that don't have formal salutations, which bugs him. The forum posts he doesn't like because they're not "scholarly." He admires figures of the Enlightenment who invented things, wrote poetry, made scientific discoveries, and learned lots of languages. That contemporary society lacks comparable polymaths he takes as a sign of civilization's decay. Understandably, he has a hard time fitting in to modern institutions. As a graduate student, a professor told him that an ambition to learn more languages would mark him as a dilettante, not a scholar. Decades later, that comment still stings Alexander so badly that he longs to prove that professor wrong.

As we got back in the car, I asked if he reads newspapers to practice his languages—I had imagined the hyperpolyglot to be someone conversant in the current events of a dozen cities.

"You know what the Greek word for 'newspaper' is? *Ephimerida*," he replied. His prickliness surprised me.

"So, no," I said.

"No." He eschews them, too.

Alexander sees himself as a rebel. Over there is the world, which drives people to specialize in ever-narrowing areas of knowledge. Over here is Alexander, who wants to embrace all literatures, all peoples. Yet he's an exemplar of the very trend he decries. Though he knows many languages, studying them is nearly all he does. For proof, look at how closely he's documented every minute of every deliberate encounter with a foreign language.

He pulled out a laptop on the neatened kitchen table and showed me how it works. Years ago, when he first started on his polyglot path, he wrote on paper in runes or Chinese characters; now he uses Excel spreadsheets and Arabic numerals. In one column go the scriptorium pages he's completed; figuring fifteen minutes a page, he calculates a total number of hours per language and language family, broken down by minutes per day—ask him how much German writing he's done, and he can tell you in the blink of an eye (fifty-seven hours). He also accounts for reading narratives, listening to recorded books while running, doing grammar drills, reviewing, and shadowing. I noticed that he never talks about parts of language or the things that delight him, and when I asked him if he has favorite vowels or verb structures or consonants, he seemed to be baffled. He talks purely in units of time, of labor. He's like someone who loves food but discusses it mostly in terms of its calories rather than its flavors.

How much time are we talking about here? Over the last 456 days, according to Alexander's spreadsheet, he's spent 4,454 hours (about 40 percent of the 10,944 hours of those 456 days) on languages, arranged in descending order by the total number of hours of study:

English—456 hours	Greek—107 hours
Arabic—456 hours	Hindi—107 hours
French—357 hours	Gaelic—107 hours
German—354 hours	Polish—102 hours
Latin—288 hours	Icelandic—83 hours
Chinese—243 hours	Czech—57.50 hours
Spanish—217 hours	Serbo-Croatian—57.50 hours
Russian—213 hours	Swedish—51 hours
Korean—202 hours	Catalan—44 hours
Sanskrit—159.5 hours	Old Norse—40 hours
Persian—153 hours	Italian—39.50 hours

Portuguese—37.50 hours	Bulgarian—8 hours
Turkish—34.75 hours	Old Church Slavonic—8 hours
Japanese—30 hours	Hebrew—8 hours
Romanian—26.25 hours	Middle English—7 hours
Ancient Greek—22 hours	Frisian—7 hours
Middle High-German—17 hours	Old High German—6 hours
Danish—17 hours	Old Swedish—5 hours
Anglo-Saxon—14 hours	Scottish Gaelic—4 hours
Old French—14 hours	Manx Gaelic—4 hours
Afrikaans—12 hours	Welsh—4 hours
Norwegian—12 hours	Breton—4 hours
Occitan Provençal—12 hours	Cornish—4 hours
Swahili—12 hours	Thai—4 hours
Ukrainian—10 hours	Indonesian—4 hours
New Norse—8 hours	Vietnamese—4 hours

He's spent from half an hour to three hours studying another sixty-seven languages. "I'll probably never know Kazakh," he said, "but I want to know what Kazakh sounds like. If I hear people speaking Kazakh on the street, I want to know, 'That's Kazakh.'"

I decided to meet Alexander's father, Ivan, who might give me another perspective on Alexander's youth. I expected someone gruff and distant, but when he drove by to pick me up, I met a shaggy grandfather in his early seventies, his white hair cut with a dramatic set of bangs hanging over his round glasses; the overall effect was of a nearsighted sheep-dog crammed into the front seat of a '90s-era Toyota sedan. Alexander's sweetness was recognizable in Ivan, who could also talk for hours about the ardent pursuit of languages if given the chance.

When Ivan and his twin, Joseph, moved to Minnesota from Mexico in the late 1940s, the other school kids mocked them: you're not Americans, you're Indians. To blend in, he stopped speaking Spanish. In the ninth grade, he fell in love with Latin—mainly because it so resembled Spanish, his Mexican father's language. He and his brother were small-town wild boys who cut romantic figures as jean jacket–wearing toughs with sensitive, artistic sides. With each other, they were so brutally competitive that as teenagers, they had divided up the world, as if it were spoils of war: Ivan got poetry and languages, Joseph took the world of art, eventually getting a PhD in art history.* Ivan inhaled the Romance languages, finding French, Italian, and Portuguese material in the library, scouring stores for books in Catalan and Provençal, finding *Colloquial Romanian* in a used-book store in Chicago. "I drove my mother crazy talking Romanian to her," he said. A Latin major in college, he also took Ancient Greek, which led to Sanskrit, his jumping-off place for Hindi, Bengali, Sinhala, and Nepali, with a detour through Persian.†️ All, except for Latin, French, and Italian, were learned outside of classrooms. He also knows German, some Old Scandinavian, Old Icelandic, Russian, Arabic, and some Chinese. "Alexander probably remembers me studying Sanskrit after my morning shower, a towel on my head," Ivan said. It was easy to imagine him like that, a young Alexander hovering, invisible, at his elbow. Then I imagined Ivan in line at the supermarket, leaning on the cart and reading some foreign tome—when he's able to read in a language that way, he says, he really knows it.

He agreed, Max's illness *had* triggered something in fourteen-year-old Alexander. The boys hadn't gotten along, and the elder boy felt guilty, his father said, horrified that maybe he'd caused it. To seek better care for Max, the family moved to California from New York, which compounded Alexander's trauma. Ivan said he watched as Alexander

---

*Eccentricity runs in his family. Joseph later changed his name to José and added an umlaut to Arguelles, becoming José Argüelles. "I don't know how much you know about New Age culture," Ivan added, "but José has become a huge figure in the New Age movement." In the 1970s, José promoted the "harmonic convergence" and later preached humankind's doom because the twelve-month Gregorian calendar was out of synch with natural rhythms. "The entire planet is operating with the wrong calendar and living in the wrong, artificial timing frequency," he wrote. For years he went by the name Valum Votan and promoted the year 2012 as the end of the world, because it coincides with the closing of a historical cycle of a calendar he adapted from the Mayan cycle. After a brief illness, he died in March 2011.

†Modern novels in Hindi and Bengali, he said, he can read with ease; it astounds him how little learning material exists for them, given that Bengali is the sixth most popular language on the planet, with 181 million native speakers.

sank into himself and "virtually disappeared as a person." Ivan eventually became a librarian at the University of California at Berkeley, cataloging materials in foreign languages, including Modern Greek and some South Asian materials, and became a well-published poet.

"We also apparently paid more attention to Max," Ivan said; "naturally we're paying more attention, but we were aware of Alexander, and we tried to be as good to him as we could, but I don't think Alexander perceived it that way. I think he felt rejected." The adolescent Alexander had few friends, and no girlfriend, which worried his father. When Alexander came home one day with records by Twisted Sister and Elvis Costello, Ivan was relieved. The boy would be okay.

In Ivan's telling, he hadn't raised Alexander to be a hyperpolyglot, in the way a football fan might bring his offspring into the yard to toss the ball and run patterns, yearning to make a star. Ivan didn't even know Alexander was learning languages until his son confessed it years later. He was flabbergasted when Alexander confessed, as an adult, to learning languages. I asked Ivan if it bothered him that Alexander knew more languages than he did.

"Oh, I have no problem at all," he said. "I used to joke, you can keep your Germanic languages, but I want the Romance languages."

Ivan was about forty years old when he decided to focus on Hindi, which meant giving up Chinese. He had realized that acquiring the skills he wanted in Hindi, such as reading the literature, would require a lot of time. "I knew that in my finite existence, I'm never going to get to the Chinese. I'm just concentrating on what I can do."

He became pensive. "I'm going to be seventy in January. I've realized, as each year passes, how much more finite my term of life on the planet is, so that if it took me this long to get where I am, how little time I have before I'm senile. So this is an awareness I've gotten in the last two years, the real awareness of one's limitations." Like his son, he is a juggler of the minutes of the day's minutes. Yet he enjoys himself more. No longer a feverish acolyte, he has passed to some other state of enlightenment in which languages don't need winning or wooing, because they're truly his friends. He told me that he'll be able to finish Persian but not Arabic, though next he'd like to embark on Tamil, the grammatical delights of which he extolled as time stole the warmth from our coffee.

———

I was surprised to learn that no one knows how many languages Alexander can speak or use to read and write, not even his father. Unlike other self-proclaimed hyperpolyglots and even some of the people who follow his instructional YouTube videos, Alexander, at the time I met him, refused to put a number on them. "If someone tells you how many languages they speak, then you shouldn't trust them," he insisted.

Come on, I said, tell me how many you know—I'll still trust you.

He begged off. Others have pressed him. "The fingers start going up, they start counting on their fingers," he said. "They don't get very far, because there aren't very many people who can name many languages."

Later I read an interview in which he says he's studied close to sixty languages and might be able to develop "real reading knowledge" in twenty.

Though he's admitted a number (for practical reasons, he'd say), he hasn't changed his position that a raw count of languages is unreliable; it's a shortcut, a way for talking to people who don't comprehend, which creates more confusion. He likened his own knowledge to a spiderweb, where newly learned items tie to other things. "How do you remember all the vocabulary?" I asked him once.

"Why should I forget it?" he retorted.

"It's just a lot of stuff," I said.

"If you study something deliberately and respectfully, it becomes part of you and it has a relationship to other things, so why should it slip away?" And he's right—we remember things better when they are tied to other things, especially strong personal emotions, but also to basic drives (like sex). Yet Alexander said he uses no mnemonics to remember words or grammatical patterns except for the etymological connections that he already possesses.

Sitting in his library one afternoon, I saw a poignant exchange between Alexander and his eldest son, who had wandered in to watch us. Alexander had tried to coax him to stay before, sometimes by saying things about languages that struck me as uncomfortably earnest.

Alexander: You're going to a Spanish school next year.

Son: No, and no, and no!

Alexander: How come you don't want to speak Spanish?

Son: Because they're hard . . . it's hard.

Alexander: What about French and English?

Son: Not . . . as hard as that, but French is a little bit more harder than English.

Alexander: Why?

Son: Because when you're starting to learn French you make mistakes, but English you don't, but only a few. But you make a lot with French and other languages.

Alexander: So English is the natural language?

Son: Yeah.

The boy giggled, squirmed away, and ran out of the room; I laughed with his father. But the exchange had a sadness, pointing to a gulf between father and son that seemed destined to widen. Or maybe it was that he was pushing them to become devout followers of his religion when they still too young. We attribute great linguistic abilities to children, but the pursuit of the mystery of languages, like the pursuit of God, is for adults alone.

Alexander doesn't get strident about it, but he doesn't want me to talk about the brain, his or anybody else's. You won't find any answers there, he says. The few times I posed questions about talent, aptitude, or anything cognitive that he might have been born with, Alexander let me know that he doesn't possess those things. I get the sense that he wants his discipline, his scholarly mien, and his incisive (if fusty) appreciations—his personality, in other words—to get the credit for his accomplishments. As far as the will to plasticity goes, focus on the will, he was saying, not on the plasticity.

Yet plasticity is what it looks like. Here he was in his early forties, still learning new things. He had adjusted his tasks to stretch his cognitive skills without overtaxing them. By reading and writing and depending on dictionaries when he needs to, he can make his use of languages the easier receptive, not productive, feat. Also, he can worry less about how his knowledge of English will interfere with the word order and other syntactic variations in other languages, because he's not generating new sentences in real time. His shadowing exercises make him familiar with pronunciations, but they can't prepare him for the etiquette of a culture. He's not bothered by this gap in knowledge, though. He can do what's expected in English, Korean, German, and French. If he spent enough time in a country, he said, he could compile what he knows and talk to people. He also reduces the challenges he faces by not striving for a native accent. Once, he snapped at "a coterie of critics who always surface to harp on the lack of a native accent (as if such a thing were desirable, let alone attainable)."

Alexander's languages have made him more efficient at learning more languages. It's commonly accepted that learning a second language within the same family is simpler, and this is true (it saves time with vocabulary, for instance). But Alexander and others with his capacities can take advantage of experience across families. People like him have honed the learning strategies that work for them and use them more often. Presented with a new language, he has an easier time grasping its sounds and its patterns, but he needed five or six languages before his hard work began paying off.

One person I met later claimed to have "cracked the code" of Arabic verbs, which are usually taught in the past tense first, because those are the shortest. Then people learn the present tenses, and with a lot of difficulty learn the exceptions. This person figured out that it's easier to learn the present tense first, and then to derive the past. "I found very beautiful rules, almost without exceptions," he exclaimed, "so that means the system had been upside down for centuries!" Another person had a system for learning the tones of Mandarin, Hmong, and Thai that involved practicing all of the possible two-tone combinations. He did this mainly to help in accurately perceiving and producing the tones; along with knowing each tone in isolation, you eventually have to know the transitions to and from every adjacent tone.

Just as they can become peculiarly invested in certain language structures, hyperpolyglots report emotional reactions to languages that drive or repel them. Alexander said he doesn't like the way Mandarin sounds, so it was easy for him to stop working on it. From a woman who'd majored in four languages in college and went on to serve as a military interpreter in Russian, I heard that she had been unable to learn Arabic during her deployment in Iraq because it was the enemy's language. A man reported that in middle school he'd chosen German over French, which he perceived as a "sissy" language, a perception that stayed with him for decades.

Neither are all parts of the grammar of a language equally friendly. Christopher, the "polyglot savant," got stumped as readily as normal speakers by the meaning of a word in a language invented by researchers (the word meant something different depending on where it was placed and whether it was attached to the third word of a sentence or appeared in a sentence's third clause). The hyperpolyglot who "cracked" Arabic said that Russian verbs had stumped him. As in many languages, these verbs have two forms, one for finished action (the perfective), one for unfinished action (the imperfective). In Russian the rules for perfective and imperfective are complex, with many exceptions. He felt you'd have to be brought up in a Russian family to get the verbs right. The great Mezzofanti himself suffered a nervous breakdown after struggling with Mandarin Chinese in Naples and lost every language he knew except his mother tongue, Bolognese.

Does Alexander have superior analytical abilities? He won't even speculate. On such questions, he seemed bizarrely preoccupied with what it would tell about language learning more broadly. Once I tried telling him about research on a small group of accomplished adult learners of Dutch and the factors that contributed to their success. At first he listened respectfully, then he stopped me. "It's just this teeny tiny group of people. How is this going to help the other people who are studying Dutch?" I enumerated some of what exceptional language learning could provide, but he didn't want to change his mind, for fear he'd have to admit some biological gift not of his making.

I regarded him for a moment, then took up a thought and speared him with it: *Speak, brain,* I wanted to lean close and whisper, *tell me the secret thing that's in you, tell me what drives you. You've traced the human languages, each one a richly layered symphony, to the place where they become the simplest of hummable tunes. And you've looked in the eye of the Ur-language that lies buried in our heads and radiates its timeless mystery. And yet, when asked why you can do what you do, you cannot say one syllable! Speak, brain!*

If Alexander didn't entertain my interest in his cranium's contents, he was downright discouraging when it came to my interest in Ziad Fazah. Clearly he disapproved of the way Fazah had sullied polyglottery with spectacle. Or so he perceived it. A couple of days into my visit, he revealed that when he lived in Beirut, he found out things about Fazah that he'd never revealed to the polyglot forum. Fazah had said he'd learned his many languages from sailors, but "there just aren't that many sailors," Alexander said. "Are there Azerbaijani sailors walking down the street in Beirut? You just don't find them."

Fazah also claimed to have gained notoriety among local diplomats. Thirty years later, no one in Beirut had ever heard of Fazah, Alexander said. You'd think that someone who had made that sort of splash would have been better known. "I had some acquaintances who were journalists, and I asked them to look in archives there over the past couple of decades and see if there had been any reports," he said. "They couldn't find anything."

"Whatever else is going on, there is one patent lie," he added, "that he got the materials that he needed to do this from the public library in Beirut. *There was no public library in Beirut when he would have been living there.* The resources were not available. I think the whole thing is a Borgesian fiction," he concluded. I thought, to be honest, all of you could have been imagined by Jorge Luis Borges, who wrote about people with perfectly accurate memories who are crippled by remembering, and about an infinite library of Babel that contains translations into all languages of every book that had ever been and would be written. A man who knew every language ever spoken and invented yet could say nothing to anyone? Seems like a quintessential Borges character. So was the case of one polyglot judging another polyglot, not by going head-to-head with languages, but by circumstantial evidence.

He told me about a blogger named Ryan Boothe, who had actually gone to Brazil and met Fazah. "He believes in Fazah," Alexander said.

That's interesting, I thought. Was hyperpolyglottery a matter of belief and not fact, in the same way that one can continue to believe in Bigfoot or UFOs? Later, Boothe told me that he didn't believe that Fazah speaks fifty-nine languages fluently, but, as he said, that's not the point: "It's not that he speaks fifty-nine languages fluently or that he doesn't speak any languages at all."

He added, "To be frank, those who claim to speak dozens of languages are being misleading unless they qualify their abilities with phrases like, 'I'm fluent in three, conversational in twenty, and can read another thirty quite comfortably.' Conversely, it would be nice if people were a little better informed and understood that speaking a foreign language is a skill much like playing the piano. Once you've acquired the skill it's actually not too hard to reacquire it after years of neglect."

Boothe had offered to test Fazah, to which Fazah at first agreed, as long as he could make some money at it, but then they fell out of touch, and Fazah again disappeared.

From afar, the hyperpolyglot is a glowing example of the sort of human being who, in myth, all humans once were and whom we should all aspire to be again: someone who builds towers in hopes of encountering the divine.

Then see this figure up close, as I did. See him sitting in his sunlit study. See his spreadsheets, his tapes, his books double-stacked on the shelves, and his living room empty, his refrigerator bare. Alexander may be a language god, a kind of archi-polyglot, but the truth about his life is far from the divine. His family was traumatized by their narrow escape from Lebanon. Alexander taught for a few semesters at a small college shut down by the financial crisis of 2008, and he'd cashed in some long-term investments to pay daily expenses. When I met him, he was living on unemployment checks and Korean translation work.

As for me, I felt abandoned by him in the labyrinth of this topic, since he wouldn't help me with Fazah and wouldn't agree to a test of his language aptitude. Then, after visiting him twice and transcribing hours of our interviews, we developed a jokey relationship, and I came to consider him a holy man. Others do yoga; Alexander does grammatical exercises. He tracks his linguistic progress through the hours as saints once cataloged their physical self-sacrifices. And like a linguistic whirling dervish, he inspires by the excess of his ecstasy, a man who doesn't need schools or corporations but will make a place, a home, for hyperpolyglots. No wonder his YouTube channel has thousands of subscribers, and his online friends, many of them hyperpolyglot hopefuls, respect him and seek his pronouncements: they want to touch him, and thereby gain a piece for themselves of what he represents. I was not immune.

Alexander, the hyperpolyglot guru, asked me, "What language do you want to work on? We could work on something while you're here." He radiated optimism that I could, in fact, do this.

"I've done Spanish and Mandarin before," I said. "Hindi's caught my eye, for some reason."

"You can definitely do all of that," he said.

I hadn't told him about Russian yet.

A couple years back, I felt that my brain needed a certain type of exercise I knew I could get from studying a language, which had to be a language I could read. Russian fit the bill, and I signed up for a class at the community college, excited to be there and to work hard. The teacher, a part-timer, wasn't a native speaker. He was a short man in his sixties, probably someone who'd dropped out of a doctoral program and been hired for his Muscovite accent. I nicknamed him Mr. Bombastic.

I'd floated into the class on a cloud of good feelings; I was doing my duty as a global citizen, broadening my mind, becoming more sensitive to foreign cultures. Quickly the experience soured; instead of Russian, I learned speechlessness. There we were in the early twenty-first century, reciting unlikely sentences from a book and pointing at pictures. *Is it an elephant? Yes, it is an elephant.* Sixty years have gone into researching foreign-language pedagogy and second-language acquisition, and none of it had touched Mr. Bombastic, who taught Russian grammatical rules like this: write a rule on the board, give a few examples, make students recite. *Voilà.* Then he'd move on to the next rule. He taught like a jaded stripper. In violation of other precepts, he piled reading *and* writing in Cyrillic print *and* cursive on top of grammar and vocabulary work, as if this were a premed weed-out class. Even the girl who had lived in Moscow was crushed into silence. Good feelings evaporated.

Later, I would meet with Andrew Cohen, an applied linguist at the University of Minnesota, who also happens to be a hyperpolyglot—he's studied thirteen languages as an adult and learned four of them to a very high degree—and he sympathized. "We're force-fed a lot of rules that are useless. Rules for certain kinds of articles we use in English. I know that Asian students have long lists with fifty-seven rules, and they memorize whether to use 'the' or 'a.' Native English speakers just know what it is. But why waste your time and energy on that?

"When I was studying Japanese, we had a lesson on buying a tie in an elegant department store in Tokyo, and we had to memorize for the test the words for 'subdued,' 'gaudy,' 'plaid,' 'polka dot,' and 'striped.' In my mind I'm going, Why? When I buy a tie I never talk to anybody—I just go to the rack and take it. Why are they making me learn this stuff? There was another lesson on talking to my doctor about what kind of diarrhea I had. I said, if I'm that sick, I'm going to an American doctor, or at least someone who speaks English. When I'm sick, it's not time for a language lesson." Talking to Cohen and other hyperpolyglots, I realized that, unlike me, they can learn no matter what the teacher's method.

I lasted as long as I did being tortured by Mr. Bombastic because I adapted the class to my own needs—I stopped writing homework in cursive, for instance, because I'm too old for penmanship. What would he do, fail me? I didn't need a grade. It also helped that I sat in the back row with a sprite of a high school language nerd named Elizabeth who was taking the class for fun. When Bombastic insisted that we speak in complete sentences, "in good Russian," as if Russians only speak in complete sentences, Elizabeth muttered, "The rain in Spain falls mainly on the plain."

I should have quit but didn't. I wanted to be studying Russian. So I invented some games to make the best of it—which, I realize now, is what a prisoner does. It's common sense that when you teach the words for family members, you ask students to bring in photos of their real families, to tap into one's emotions as a pedagogical aid; I've taught it myself that way, when I taught English in Taiwan. Because Bombastic did not exert such effort, we sat pointing to imaginary photos. *This is my mother, she is a doctor. This is my father, he is an architect.*

The best solution: outdo the absurdity. *"This is my mother,"* I said to Elizabeth, pointing at an imaginary photo, reciting aloud to the class. *"She is a woman who works on asphalt."*

"So is mine!" Elizabeth said.

"This is my father," I said. *"He is a veterinarian of elephants."*

"So is mine!" Elizabeth said.

Some classmates chuckled. Most were astonished. Bombastic let fly a smirk. "In the old Soviet Union, people had to meet certain production quotas. These two," he said, "are like the guy who goes over the quota."

Bombastic wasn't happy with my customizations. One evening, he gave us a practice exam that didn't test what we'd been studying, and for me this was the final straw. Furious, I told him the exam wasn't fair, and he accused me, incorrectly, of slacking off, as if I were a freshman punk. We almost came to blows in the front of the classroom. He scurried away, and I never went back. What I am left with is the confidence that if I should find myself in Moscow, I will be able to correctly identify an elephant.

"What do you want to work on?" Alexander asked.

"Hindi," I said.

Hindi it was.

At a nearby park, we met up with a lanky Berkeley undergrad named Justin, who had recently been exasperating Alexander, his tutor, by not shadowing as prescribed. So the polyglot sent him on a looped bit of path running down into the shade, then back up into the sun, past young women sunning in the grass. Part of the advantage of shadowing in a park is that people are going to stare, so you get used to it. The problem is, Alexander joked, that in Northern California, to get people to stare, you have to be *really* strange.

After several circuits, Alexander ambled next to Justin, encouraging him to shout more "Italianly." As the two men orbited by, shouting and gesturing dramatically, as if they were declaiming opinions in the midst of some vehement argument, I spoke to one sunbather, who had wandered down the hill.

"Does this look weird to you?" I asked.

"Kind of," she said. "What's going on? Is he learning Italian?"

"The guy on the right, he's the teacher," I explained.

"He's good."

"Do you speak Italian?"

"No, I speak Spanish, but I've been to Italy. Where is he from in Italy?"

"He's not Italian, he's American," I said. Her eyebrows went up. "Actually, he knows a lot of languages, he says, and he wants to start a school to make more people like him."

"Oh, like a language cult," she said, as if this were a commonly recognized phenomenon.

When Justin finished, Alexander offered the tape recorder to me. I'd chosen an Assimil Hindi tape. *Le Hindi sans Peine,* the label read.

"You've just promised me Hindi without pain," I said.

"I've promised you nothing like that," he said.

I started walking, gesticulating, the stiff foam earpieces flapping on my ears and leaking warbly Hindi sounds into the afternoon air. I felt a few of the sounds going into my ears and come out my mouth. Then I felt a few more. Progress. No one else in the park seemed to notice me, because half an hour of Justin and Alexander's declamations had bored them. Stand up straight and talk louder, I told myself. This was hard. I couldn't make out the long words in a phrase and had to stop speaking to listen. *Garam garam hai.* Oh. What does that mean? "Hai," sounds like "hay," over and over. *Garam garam. Mera naam.* Suddenly it sounds to me very Sanskrit. I have a yoga teacher who opens class with a Sanskrit chant whose parts sound like *garam garam cai hai. Ji ha. Mera naam.* Is there some grammatical ending for asking questions, the *hai?**

At a certain point Alexander came to my side; in the valley of Hindi syntax, the polyglot saint walketh beside me, and I had no fear. Amazingly, he was speaking Hindi too. How? He said he has it "internalized." After three lessons on the tape, I stopped and apparently had done

---

*Good guess, but it's not: Hindi keeps the copula, the "to be" verb, at the end of the sentence, so the sentence "The tea is hot" appears as "Tea hot is" in Hindi.

so poorly that Justin critiqued me: stand up straighter, talk louder, he says. Shout! Alexander nodded approvingly. You looked worried, he said. Well, yes, because I couldn't make out the words on the tape and I wanted to say, Forget it. We sat on picnic benches and went over the pages of dialogue in the textbook. Do you want to do it again? Sure. This time, you have to be louder, faster, straighter. Yeah, yeah.

After shadowing three dialogues again, it happened: Hindi opened up. I'd never sought out methods or secrets; all I knew was what I knew about studying: you plug away, you memorize, you write out sentences, you practice endlessly. Flash cards. At first shadowing had seemed absurd. Yet the gates to Hindi were—I could feel it—parting before me.

"You have promise, you definitely have promise," Alexander says. "You know more than I thought you did. You surprised me."

Sunshine, sunshine. Now give me someone from whom I can elicit words. Let me play board games with a little kid. Give me a hyperpolyglot, who will baptize me in his confident shadow, who has no inhibitions, even though he's not a native speaker.

In the next year, Alexander's life will change again, for the better this time, though only after, on the advice of a friend, he stopped describing himself on his résumé as a polyglot. He's now a language specialist for the Southeast Asian Ministers of Education Organization in Singapore, a multilingual city that could be a polyglot's playground, but he hasn't had time to explore Malay or Tamil, two of the official languages there; because he can't get Beirut out of his head, his most active language pursuit is Arabic. He maintains his aspirations to open a polyglot school and is proud of his sons' achievements in languages. When his eldest son wins a prize for his poetry, however, it's in English, not Chinese or French.

I'll always remember how, after the Hindi lesson in the park, we went to a used-book store, where Alexander mooned over dusty tomes of German philology that he couldn't afford. After we browsed the foreign-language section together, I headed to the natural history shelves, alone. Alexander popped up to ask, "You're not telling me you have a well-rounded mind, are you?" Somehow, my performance in Hindi had lightened him to teasing. I shared his buoyancy; I'd been complimented by a hyperpolyglot.

One sweltering afternoon in August, I went to World Bank headquarters in Washington, D.C., to meet another kind of hyperpolyglot, even more rare: a woman. At the front desk, the guard said there was someone frantically looking for me. As I stood there, the phone rang, and the guard, holding the receiver away from her ear, raised her eyebrows at the person shouting on the other end. *That's her,* she mouthed. A couple of moments later, Helen Abadzi, a tallish woman in a short skirt and a state of brisk disarray, swept into view.

Back in her office, quietly tucked behind her desk, she described how she flies all over the world evaluating the progress of educational programs, particularly in literacy, that have received World Bank funding. Born in a small town in Greece in the 1950s, she said that one thing she wanted to be was weird, and that "one way to be weird in a town that once teemed with Sephardic Jews was to learn Hebrew." So she took Hebrew classes at fifteen and was fluent at twenty-one—this linguistic knowledge she later applied to Arabic.

Helen Abadzi talking to school principal. Gambia, 2010.
(*Courtesy of Helen Abadzi*)

Overall, Helen says, she's studied nineteen languages to at least an intermediate level, and she says she gets her analytic skills from her father, who learned Turkish, Bulgarian, and German, all without books.

She uses Greek, English, Spanish, French, and Portuguese (the last four official World Bank languages) every day. Others she keeps on ice until she goes on overseas missions. Some she learns anew, building an extensive linguistic patchwork all her own. For an upcoming mission to Tanzania, she's learning Swahili for the first time. But a trip to Cambodia will intervene; she has to put down Swahili to pick up Khmer. Speaking local languages isn't a job requirement, but she finds that it makes her more effective, because she can talk to teachers and students and follow along when they demonstrate their reading abilities. It also allows her to circumvent local bureaucrats who might try to sanitize the reality by presenting it in English. Two things stymie her. One is not having enough time to practice. The other is her age. She's fifty-nine, and finds that retaining material for the long term isn't as easy as it once was.

One of her age-defying tricks involves a machine called a digital language repeater. Made in China, it's a square silver box with a tape player. Instead of playing the tape directly, it stores the sounds in a digital buffer that can play snippets over and over at different speeds. She looks for language materials with audio recordings or pays local people to record texts, then listens to them at least fifteen times, until she knows all the vocabulary and grammatical expressions. She also uses other technologies: an old Sony PDA and an iPod.

Even with the language repeater, Swahili has been a challenge for her. Other languages she's learned all have suffixes, so words are easy to look up in dictionaries when she doesn't know the grammar. But the Bantu logic of Swahili means there are prefixes that are affixed with changing meanings, so one has to know the grammar to translate them. She rails a bit against this. On the other hand, "At my age, as I like to say, it's good to do the things you *don't* usually do. These have become anti-aging exercises! I have three centenarian relatives, so maybe I have good genes, maybe I don't"—she laughed—"and so we have to keep the mind sharp. And the way to do this is to keep learning challenging things."

"If you knew it would be so hard when you were younger, what would you have done differently?"

"I would have learned fifteen more languages," she quickly replied.

Another strategy she uses is called "timed review"—going back to review previously learned material at regular intervals. (She likes to ride her bike while listening to audio files.) One such "memory schedule" was developed by Paul Pimsleur, of the Pimsleur method for learning languages. He recommended reviewing any learned material (words, grammatical rules, and the like) at intervals of five seconds, twenty-five seconds, two minutes, ten minutes, one hour, five hours, one day, five days, twenty-five days, four months, and two years. These intervals were based on the natural rate of memory decay; with successive reviews, the time span extends between reviews, because each subsequent review slows the overall rate of decay.

The mind retains a certain amount of material without timed review. Psychologist Harry Bahrick once tested native English speakers who had studied Spanish as long as fifty years before. Not surprisingly, the better grades someone had earned back then, the more Spanish they could access now. What is surprising is that what one remembers doesn't decline steadily over a lifetime. Rather, what you remembered after three to six years would stay with you for decades.

Hyperpolyglots seem to have superior recall. One unusual feature of Christopher's memory abilities is that his recall improves after a delay; for most people, delaying without rehearsing means that recall fades.* One woman said that half a day of exposure to written material is all she needs to revive some of her languages. Someone else told me, "The enemy of the language learner is forgetting. You can only prevent this by regularly studying. It's not revolutionary."

Another key asset for the hyperpolyglot, from Mezzofanti to Abadzi, is an ability to monitor what they say before it comes out of their mouths. This is the thing that Robert DeKeyser, the linguist I consulted before going to Bologna, had predicted would be the case. Hyperpolyglots can also keep bits of a sentence in mind as they are heard, a related ability.

Doing both requires what scientists call "working memory." A frequently used metaphor for working memory is the carpenter's work-

---

*Christopher's performances on a variety of memory tasks are so unexpected, he may be a better candidate for studies of anomalous memorizers than of language.

bench, the space for holding information required for solving problems. The size of the workbench determines how much information goes into the solution and the time taken by the process. We use working memory in all aspects of our daily lives. You have to be able to hold in mind the beginning of a sentence to make sense of its end, just as you have to hold in mind what you intend to cook for dinner as you're shopping for its ingredients in the market. As defined by the British psychologists who first explained it, working memory is "the capacity to maintain temporarily a limited amount of information in mind, which can then be used to support various abilities, including learning, reasoning, and preparation for action." Working memory ability has emerged as the best predictor of intelligence; it could also be a major component of what's traditionally called "foreign-language aptitude."

Helen, who lectures to audiences around the world about literacy and learning, talks a lot about working memory. It often comes up in her work on overcoming illiteracy among impoverished people. *Aha*, I thought. *Finally, someone who can let her brain do the talking.*

"Imagine that you have the biggest bottle in the world," she said. On her computer monitor was a sketch of this bottle, which represents long-term memory. *Her* long-term memory. "There's no bottom to this, and you can put connected knowledge in here to no end. This bottle has a very narrow neck—and it will only open for twelve seconds at a time and hold seven verbal items.

"Let's say you enter a store, locate a box of cereal, read the price, and take out money to pay. If you read haltingly, by the time you finish a sentence on the box you may forget the beginning. If you count slowly, by the time you count all the coins you may have forgotten the price." These are limitations of working memory, which can hold things only for a certain amount of time—and only a specific number of them.

It works this way with language, too. When someone asks you a question, she said, "You have to structure a reply. You're doing a conscious search of what you know that you can use to respond. Those conscious searches had better bring stuff quickly."

When you write or read, that window is less relevant than when you're listening and conversing, activities that occur in real time. When you talk, you're finding four to five words every second. Let's say someone asks Helen, "How many students come to this school, and did they have breakfast before they went to school?" To reply, she has to be able to conjugate a bunch of verbs and do it quickly.

She boosts her working memory by making language patterns as automatic as possible: repeating grammatical patterns and lists until she can access them with the smallest amount of conscious cognitive effort. *"I have bananas. We have bananas. You have bananas.* It drives you crazy. It's boring, but it sticks," she told me, with a passionate snarl that made me think, *She doesn't find it so boring, actually.*

Unlike Alexander, she admitted to using what she called "pointers," or memory schemes. She said that her mnemonics can be etymologies or visualizations of the actions in the words. She also memorizes songs in her various languages, which give cues to grammar or vocabulary. Once, in the Delhi airport, she was changing money and speaking Hindi with the teller. Do you come to India often? he asked her. *Kabhi kabhi,* she said. "Sometimes." This happens to be the first line of a popular song, which the teller begins to sing. *Kabhi kabhi,* he crooned. And she crooned back: *Mere dil mein khayaal aata hai.*

"So all of a sudden there is a teller in the New Delhi airport and me starting to sing this song!" she exclaimed. Bollywood is real! In the airport! "This is the stuff that really makes my life!" She laughed.

In 1990, her husband, Theodore, heard about a contest being held in Europe to find the most multilingual person. She doesn't promote her own abilities enough, he thought. I'll enter her name. A few days later, the contest organizers surprised Helen with a phone call in which she talked to nine native speakers of nine languages, one after the other, to see if she qualified. She protested; she doesn't keep all her languages active to the same level, she said, and likes to use later-learned languages one at a time. Otherwise, she says, they interfere with each other. Even so, she received an invitation to the contest, where she was one of only three women out of twenty contestants. She was flown to Brussels, and in a large conference room she went from table to table, speaking to native speakers from embassies or universities.

This must have been the contest that Robert DeKeyser described! I thought, I have to find out more about it. All those hyperpolyglots tested in one place. *Tested.* Had a modern-day Mezzofanti been among them?

"The winner," she said, "his name I've forgotten. He had twenty-six languages." I longed to meet the man whom I knew only as the Polyglot of Europe.

Alexander and Helen kept most of their languages in reserve. Helen is prepared to use around five on a daily basis; Alexander uses English, Korean, and French in daily life, in addition to the language he's focused on at a given time. From talking to both of them, I could see that their lives were structured just as Erik Gunnemark had said a devoted language learner's should be. Their daily exercises were aimed at three tasks: improving their familiarity with the sounds of the language and their ability to reproduce them, drilling themselves on grammatical patterns, and working hard to stem memory decay. Mezzofanti had apparently done the same, but still, he possessed one ability that they didn't: he could switch between languages with ease, which doesn't appear to be an ability that improves much with practice.

Someone who heard Mezzofanti speak in seven or eight languages in half an hour asked how he never confused them.

"Have you ever tried on a pair of green spectacles?" Mezzofanti asked him.

"Yes," replied his companion.

"Well," replied Mezzofanti, "while you wore those spectacles everything was green to your eyes. It is precisely so with me. While I am speaking any language, for instance, Russian, I put on my Russian spectacles, and for the time, they color everything Russian. I see all my ideas in that language alone. If I pass to another language, I have only to change the spectacles, and it is the same for that language also!"

In his biography of Mezzofanti, Charles Russell described several instances of Mezzofanti's flitting among languages. The Bolognese hyperpolyglot had been ordered to Rome by the new pope, Gregory XVI, to join the Propaganda Fide, an official Church body designed to bring Catholic men from all over the world in order to learn the evangelizing arts. Every January 6, the school would hold its *Accademia Poliglotta,* a spectacle in which all the students would recite poems in their native languages. It was a fitting date. In the Catholic calendar, January 6 marks the visit of the three kings to the infant Jesus in Bethlehem. Because the kings represented the outside world of Gentiles (or non-Jews) drawn to the divine babe, the Feast of the Epiphany was also known as the Feast of the Languages. As a symbol of missionary work, the celebration was appropriate, and Mezzofanti's skill made the ceremony resound with a claim of global power.

When Russell attended this ceremony, the head scholar gave an introductory speech, in Latin, to open the proceedings. Then the students each took a turn. They'd been assigned to write a poem with a holiday theme, the Illumination of the Gentiles. Students presented in forty-two languages that day. (Some years there were fifty or sixty.) Then the real extravaganza occurred.

Mezzofanti, whose presence was accompanied by restless excitement, was mobbed by students, and he spoke with them this language, then that one, "hardly ever hesitating, or ever confounding a word or interchanging a construction," in a "linguistic fusilade," Russell wrote. If it seemed like a circus, it had no ringmaster. A group of young Chinese men crowded Mezzofanti; then a Burmese youth who spoke Peguan had his turn. From the flank came a gentleman with a joking complaint that he'd heard no Russian poems—which provoked a long conversation in Russian with the cardinal. By the end, Russell had heard Mezzofanti speak no fewer than ten or twelve languages without hesitating, and he was dazzled.

For a sense of what Mezzofanti was doing, one can look at what ordinary multilinguals do when they switch between languages. One theory says that they don't switch languages on and off; rather, they have them all mentally activated at the same time, but put a lid on the unwanted ones. It's the equivalent of turning on all the lights in the house, but covering up the bulbs you don't want to shine. A speaker has to do two things: stop the response in one language, then initiate a response in the other one. A friend of mine who grew up with English, French, and Spanish said that even if only one language is coming out of his mouth, he feels as if he's speaking them all at the same time. The trick of the polyglot has a contradiction at its heart: to say something, many things must also go unsaid. This might explain why someone like Lomb Kató could have only five languages simultaneously. It's not that she couldn't keep more than those activated; it's that she couldn't keep more than those *deactivated*.

This switching mechanism is what enables interpreters to move between languages so rapidly. It also helps bilinguals insert words or phrases from one language into utterances of another, or code-switch. Fluent speakers can switch within sentences, flipping between languages without violating the grammar of either one, a process that requires some powerful neural hardware.

Switching between tasks—or languages—is the central job of something called *executive function*. This is a group of cognitive skills that give a person the ability to manage and focus on a task. Think of executive function as how you control your mental airspace—how many planes you have in the air, how many are landing, how much room you have in your airport. Working memory, as Helen described it, is an important component of executive function.

Scientists know that mental airspace control is located in the prefrontal cortex, but they know very little about where language switching takes place. An area called the posterior parietal cortex was once nominated to be a "language talent" area of the brain, and it was believed that this area had something to do with switching. Someone with damage to this area would sound like a patient known as HB, an eighty-year-old man observed by the neurologist Ellen Perecman. After a car accident caused bleeding in his brain, the recovering HB rattled on, fluently, about nothing. Most strikingly, he mixed up German (his mother tongue), French (a second language), and English (which he learned as an immigrant to the United States). The doctor asked him why he was in the hospital, to which he replied, *"Eine sprache* to *andern* [to change a language], you speak a language that comes to you." Many of his utterances were polyglot salads, such as *"Vorständig* thickheaded" and "Standing that means *ständig ständig führen stein."*

The idea of a "language talent" area didn't work out. So whether switching is controlled in some other specific place or more broadly, a healthy multilingual person can switch between languages voluntarily. Doing so for the purposes of translation, as in a courtroom, is a skill to be learned and honed. But if someone could have a superior facility for switching, would that person behave like a Mezzofanti? Could they, for instance, switch among more languages, which would mean having more of them active at once?

A bilingual person is, in essence, a linguistic multitasker. As a result, he has more powerful executive function skills. Children who speak two languages test higher on executive function skills than do their peers with one language. Presumably, it's because their brains are constantly juggling languages, selecting one and inhibiting the other. On simple tests, bilingual and monolingual adults perform at the same level, yet lifelong bilinguals always do better when their executive function is truly challenged. Scientists also speculate that a lifetime of living with two languages may protect people from the effects of cognitive aging— the constant exercise working memory, focus, and inhibition builds up a "reserve" that people carry into older age. One doesn't have to be a Mezzofanti to see such benefits, either.

In Bologna I'd ruminated on the case of Mezzofanti, a man who had escaped some elemental linguistic curse by taking advantage of his unique circumstances and, most likely, drawing on something hard-wired in his brain which wasn't just memory. Mezzofanti was a myth, Erik Gunnemark hissed. I didn't agree—sure, the size of his repertoire may have been inflated, but who really knew? Science had relegated him to a dusty cabinet of curiosities; no one had looked as seriously at him as I confidently thought I could, bring proficiency tests, institutional scales, and other metrics for judging language proficiency. The tests, I found, didn't suit the evidence. And the cobwebby evidence was incomplete. The only solution was to interrogate a live person.

Thinking I would meet a pop culture polyglot, I found instead Alexander, a man who practices the polyglottish lifestyle that he preaches. Alexander doesn't pursue oral communication, though he could say a lot of things in his languages. Once, to humor me, he logged on to Skype with a fellow language aficionado and had a conversation that switched from English to Russian to Korean to Arabic. Mostly, he reads. He criticizes the modern language-learning paradigm of shopping, migration, and tourism that artist Rainer Ganahl identifies as characteristic of our era. Instead, he longs to learn languages for the reasons that drove monks and philologists centuries ago, a semimystical desire to touch the origins of literary texts. It dates, he said, from adolescence. He read many authors in translation, but "felt even then that I was not doing them justice," he told me. "For I seem to have an ingrained dictum that if something is worth reading, then it is worth reading as the author wrote it."

I, too, desired an encounter with some harder proof of his proficiency than a library of books, but he declined to have his proficiency or his aptitude tested. No scientific test can capture his experiences, he said. I brought it up a few times, then dropped it. I figured I could find someone else to test.

Alexander and Helen are both very good at managing the filters their native language makes them hurdle when they are learning new sounds and words; it was harder for me to tell how well they could deal with the word orders of new languages, which had also stumped Christopher. Believing that language learning isn't easy and takes work, they commit themselves to using their time efficiently. With a balance of motivation and aptitude, they know how they learn and how languages tend to work. That demonstration of expertise—something they'd undoubtedly achieved after lots of hard work—might, in some people's thinking, make some organic advantage unnecessary. After all, there were tragic turns in their lives that languages assuaged. In addition to Alexander and Helen, Ken Hale had suffered the extended illness of a sibling and the turning away of parental attention. Even Elihu Burritt, the Yankee polyglot, appeared to take up languages partly to compete with his deeply loved older brother, partly to grieve when his brother succumbed to fever in Texas.

Yet I couldn't escape the sense that Alexander and Helen and all the others were somehow beyond expertise. Experts who hadn't sought expertise. They *loved* languages, not as a writer or poet loves a turn of phrase, a way of making meter or rhyme; they loved them as objects— or, rather, they loved the encounters, both occasional and sustained, with those objects. Does the expert surgeon love the scalpel and the tissues it parts? Does the expert programmer love the code?

There was also the way they persisted, despite social isolation and economic hardship (more so in Alexander's case). True, they seemed sustained by pride. What else? It wasn't money or achievement they were after. Burritt had described his achievements to an admirer as the result of a "plodding, patient, persevering process of accretion which builds the ant-heap—particle by particle, thought by thought, fact by fact." Why would Burritt have submitted to anthood if he didn't find some pleasure in it? By "pleasure," I mean the thrill their neurological systems get when they put sentences together, parse sounds, choose words. I mentioned this to someone, who laughed and asked, isn't all pleasure neurological? Sure, I replied. Anyone who learns another language or two has to appreciate this at some level. And the hyperpolyglots, they *really* seek it out. I think the usual way to make sense of this is to say, of course they enjoy it, they're good at it. But this seemed backward to me. Why not acknowledge an inherent pleasure that initiates the journey to success?

I found one answer in the work of Ellen Winner, a psychologist at Boston College, who works with exceptionally artistic children. She identified one of their attributes as a "rage to master." This is, she says, the drive to immerse one's self in a particular area because one enjoys both the cognitive problems it poses and the experience of solving them. In Winner's formulation, one doesn't develop expertise because one works hard; one works hard at tasks that one finds rewarding, causing expertise to emerge, over time.

As Winner argues, precocity and talent have an innate, biological component. Even if you can't locate them precisely in the brain—after all, only a few of the really complex cognitive processes can be located this way—that doesn't mean these differences don't exist. Artistically talented children learn more rapidly than others; they make their own discoveries, without much help from adults; and they do things that ordinary artists their own age don't do. For example, their drawings are more realistic and reproduce volume and relative size more accurately than those of their normal peers, even if all of them have had the same amount of explicit instruction. Most important, as Winner puts it, is that "they are intrinsically motivated to acquire skill in the domain (because of the ease with which learning occurs)."

Does the structure of the hyperpolyglot brain give its owner a boost?

Do these people use neural circuits more efficiently, or create more of these circuits than other people? Maybe their sleep consolidates their long-term memories more effectively. Maybe their bodies produce more neurotransmitters, or are more sensitive to them. Contemporary knowledge about the brain offered any number of possibilities. Alexander and Helen had hyperpolyglot brains worth looking at, but they were still using them. Perhaps a brain preserved in a jar would provide suitable answers.

And the good news was, I had just found one.

Part 3

REVELATION:

The Brain Whispers

Chapter 10

I n May of 1917, Emil Krebs, a German diplomat and hyperpolyglot, arrived in San Francisco with his wife, Amande, and her two daughters. Known to be a cranky, unpleasant person, he ranted about the storm clouds of war that greeted them. For the last two months, they'd been on a Dutch steamer escaping from China, where he'd been posted. Eastbound on the steamer, they heard via radio that the United States had declared war on Germany. He might have feared that when they landed, they would become prisoners of war, but a diplomatic deal was arranged: the family could journey to the East Coast to catch a ship to Europe, but they would have to travel in a sealed train car across the United States. No visitors, no exits, not even windows, for an entire week. Which was fine—bookish Krebs had his whole library with him and probably would have paid little attention to the rugged landscape unrolling before his eyes.

He was a man with many languages traveling across a country that was on its own journey to having only English. The United States was in the middle of a transformation from a proud, mostly tolerant polyglot land to a xenophobic, English-speaking one—a change that found its final hastening in the very conflict between the United States and the government of Kaiser William II that Krebs represented.

Had Krebs toured San Francisco, where several generations of Chinese speakers lived, he could have conversed in the many languages from China, his specialty. Krebs didn't know any indigenous American languages, which once numbered in the many dozens in California, making it for a time one of the most linguistically diverse places in the world. Linguists now figure that as late as 1800, more than 100 languages were spoken in the area that would become the state. In fact, when Europeans arrived in the Americas, the northern and southern continents contained half of the entire world's linguistic diversity, an estimated 1,800 languages in all.

As the train crossed the Midwest, it went through towns and cities full of Germans, Swedes, Norwegians, Pennsylvania Dutch, Polish, Italians, Greeks, living their lives in their native tongues, publishing newspapers, educating their children, going to church—and eventually learning English. In 1910, there were 13 million white immigrants over the age of ten in the United States. Most spoke English, German, Italian, Yiddish, Polish, or Swedish as a mother tongue; and 23 percent of the population reported that they couldn't speak English at all. (The number wouldn't be this high again until 1990, when 26 percent reported not speaking English well or at all.) Native Americans had been forcibly educated in English since the 1870s and even earlier, but the sounds of proud immigrant cultures were just now being silenced.

In the throes of anti-German mania after the declaration of war, American patriots outlawed the teaching of the German language, regulated German newspapers, and burned German books. In South Dakota and Iowa, the governors proclaimed that it was illegal to speak any language but English over the telephone or in public places. Children took oaths of loyalty to English. In 1910, 433 German-language newspapers were published every week; by 1960, the number had fallen to 29.

Had Krebs known about disappearing languages in the country he was crossing, as a language lover, he might have mourned their loss. Like Mezzofanti, he was a carpenter's child, and similarly, his passion for languages launched itself. Somewhere he found an old French newspaper, and two weeks after a teacher gave him a French dictionary, he showed up at the teacher's desk speaking French. No parent as a model. No multilingual community. He simply bent toward foreign languages as a sunflower leans to find the sun.

By the end of high school, he is said to have spoken twelve of them. After law school, he went to the Foreign Office school for interpreters in Berlin and was asked which language he wanted to study. By then, he had studied Latin, Greek, French, and Hebrew in school, and Modern Greek, English, Italian, Spanish, Russian, Polish, Arabic, and Turkish on his own. I want to learn all of them, he replied.

You can't learn them all, he was told.

"Okay," Krebs reportedly said. "I want to learn the hardest one."

That was Mandarin Chinese. He began Chinese courses in 1887 and took (and passed) his first exam in 1890. In 1893, he became a diplomatic translator for the growing German presence in the Chinese cities of Tsingtao and Beijing, and took two further exams in 1894 and 1895, receiving the rating of "good." By 1901, he'd risen to the rank of chief interpreter. There his language abilities brought him literally to the seat of Chinese imperial power.

One day, an exacting Chinese imperial official inquired who in the German legation was writing such elegant Chinese documents. It was Krebs. From then on, the Empress Dowager Cixi often invited him for tea, which they drank out of translucent porcelain cups. She "preferred to converse with him as the most careful and best Chinese speaker among the foreigners." Chinese authorities asked him questions about the languages in their realm (Chinese, Mongolian, Manchurian, Tibetan)—because they had no tradition of polyglottery, they wouldn't have known these languages themselves. One story told about Krebs is that Chinese officials, unable to read a letter sent from a rebel Mongolian tribe, asked Krebs to translate it.

"Throughout Chinese history," said Victor Mair, a Sinologist at the University of Pennsylvania, "practically the only Chinese who learned Sanskrit were a few monks who actually traveled to India and stayed there for an extended period of time. Merchants and others (e.g., some officials who traveled widely within China) learned several Sinitic languages (so-called 'dialects') in the various places where they went. There was no interest in learning other languages out of sheer intellectual or linguistic curiosity." Steven Owen, a Harvard professor of Chinese literature, added that some of the Chinese population learned Manchu when the Qing ruled China (from 1644 to 1911), but that they were specialists working for the emperor.

"As an intellectual endeavor," Owen said, "meaning learning languages that are not proximate or needed, with an attendant interest in the culture—I don't know of any cases among the educated [Chinese] elite before modern times."

One reason was most certainly cultural. In the West, polyglottery had its earliest roots in Christianity, which was, from the start, an evangelical religion with no single language (Jesus himself spoke Aramaic and Hebrew, and maybe Greek) and whose central text was propagated in many languages. Polyglottery also stemmed from European exploration, colonization, and empire building. By contrast, in China, the main pursuit of the intellectual class for thousands of years had been trying to either join or rise up in the civil service. This required such extensive literacy—being able to read and write upward of one hundred thousand characters—little time was left for much else. Moreover, the one writing system itself linked intellectual cultures across time and space in a way that, in the West, required fluency in many languages. Perhaps most significantly, the Chinese perceived themselves to be the center of the world, so they could hardly be expected to learn barbarian languages. The barbarians should first learn some Chinese.

One shouldn't think that the hyperpolyglot is uniquely Western, however. I was connected with a historical document from sixteenth-century Java which outlined the responsibilities of someone called "the Polyglot," who was a real or imagined figure in the royal court's intelligentsia. The Polyglot held linguistic knowledge of all the communities in the Indian Ocean world that Sundanese traders might contact, as well as "all other kinds of foreign lands." Exactly what sort of abilities this Polyglot had in all those languages (and there were nearly five dozen of them) isn't known. But as linguist Benjamin Zimmer noted in his fascinating analysis of this document, it provides "a striking example of the linguistic outward-lookingness that has pervaded the Indian Ocean world" for centuries before the Europeans arrived. Exactly the time and place where a hyperpolyglot would have flourished, in other words.

———

In 1913, at the age of forty-five, Krebs married Amande, a German divorcee. On a honeymoon tour, at a stop at the tomb of Confucius, he read the inscriptions in Mandarin, Manchurian, Mongolian, Kalmuck, and Turkish. Frail and perpetually underpaid, Krebs (or "Krebsy," as his wife called him) sat down the following year and wrote a list of what languages he could use—he could, for instance, translate into and out of German in thirty-two languages.* Later he would be said to "know" sixty or sixty-five languages. His stepdaughter appended her own note to the list: "It is a great difference between whether one can speak, write, and master a language, or whether one is able to finish correct translations as a proven interpreter." Be that as it may, during his lifetime he passed government tests in Chinese, Turkish, Japanese, and Finnish, and possibly more.

Similar to other hyperpolyglots I had met or read about, one of Krebs's most stunning traits lay in how quickly he could learn. Werner Otto von Hentig, a young German attaché in China, described how Krebs had jumped up in the middle of breakfast to find out from two strangers what language, "foreign to him, had been battering his ear." Armenian, he found. After ordering books, he spent two weeks on the grammar, three on old Armenian, and four on the spoken language. "Then he was a master of them too," Hentig wrote.

If the anecdotes about Krebs's language genius—and his obsessive passion—are as rich as those of Mezzofanti, they differ in one respect: they tell of a character who was rude and impatient. Hentig related that Krebs once refused to speak to his wife for three months because she had told him to wear an overcoat in December; in one year, he fired

---

*He listed them as "Arabic, Armenian, Bohemian, Bulgarian, Chinese, Danish, Dutch, Norwegian, English, Finnish, French, Georgian, Greek, Hindi, Hungarian, Italian, Japanese, Javanese, Croatian, Lithuanian, Malay, Manchu, Mongolian, Persian, Polish, Romanian, Russian, Swedish, Thai, Serbian, Spanish, Turkish, Urdu." By his death in 1930 he also had Egyptian, Afghan, Albanian, Altarmenisch, Basque, Burmese, Estonian, Gaelic, Gujarati, Icelandic, Irish, Catalan, Keilschriftsprachen (Sumerian, Assyrian, Babylonian), Coptic, Korean, Latvian, New Arabic, New Greek, New Hebrew, New Persian, Portuguese, Sanskrit, Serbo-Croatian, Slovak, Slovenian, Swahili, Syriac, Tatar, Tibetan, and Ukrainian.

a succession of eighteen Chinese cooks, none of whom pleased him. Once, in order to satisfy a bureaucratic requirement, Krebs had to take a test in both Finnish and Japanese. He intimidated the examiner with his knowledge, scaring the man from the room. In China, Krebs made it perfectly clear that he wanted to study languages rather than do his job (especially since he was often sleeping during the day, having stayed up all night studying).

In another revealing anecdote, Hentig described having to fetch Krebs for a meeting.

"His Excellence wants to see you!" Hentig shouted over the walls of Krebs's compound. There was no answer. "Herr Krebs, the legate needs you!" No answer. "The Herr Minister is asking for you!" Finally Hentig heard a grumble.

"The legate knows me, leave me in peace," Krebs grumbled.

"May I help you get dressed?"

"Go to hell!"

"They really need you."

"They always say that," Krebs muttered.

One contemporary said that Krebs had never learned the "technique of life." He was someone who could tell you off in dozens of languages. He had translated the phrase "kiss my ass" (known as the Swabian salute) into forty languages. Something of a joker, he gave a German journalist the Chinese name Bu Zhidao, "doesn't know." In daily life he was so disagreeable that no one wanted to work with him, which became a liability later in his career, when no one was willing to promote him or accept his work in languages other than Chinese.

Like Alexander Arguelles, Krebs reviewed his languages on rotation: a strict schedule that assigned Turkish to Monday, Chinese to Tuesday, Greek to Wednesday, and so on. With a book in hand, he walked around and around the dining room table from midnight to four in the morning, naked, smoking a cigar, drunk on German beer. His library was organized by language and language group. For each book he wrote a summary, which he regularly reviewed. At his desk, he stood. He refused to eat anything but meat, and sought out social interaction only if he could use one of his languages. "He knew 32 languages, not in the way we often see with polyglots, but elegantly and well spoken in Arabic as well as Russian or Italian," Hentig wrote. His Tuscan dialect was so good, the Italian ambassador in Beijing offered to cut Krebs's hair, just to be able to hear Tuscan.

Unavoidably, writers of the time compared him to Mezzofanti, but in the eyes of German writers, Krebs was superior. "Against whatever kind of displeasing experiences are told of the Mezzofantis, who know all languages, but none fundamentally," wrote Ferdinand Lessing, a German translator in Tsingtao and later a professor and polyglot himself, "this wonderful talent bites its thumb."

If they could have roamed freely once they reached New York, the Krebs family would have found a city filled with immigrants from Europe—in fact, there were more daily newspapers published in other languages (Italian, German, Hungarian, French, Croatian, Spanish, etc.) than in English at the time. In addition to twenty-two English newspapers, there were ten Italian, seven German, seven Yiddish or Hebrew, three Greek, three Hungarian, two French, two Bohemian, two Croatian, and one apiece in Spanish, Serbian, and Syrian. Perhaps the Krebs family was detained at Ellis Island, the main through-point for immigrants arriving on the East Coast. There he could have met professional language learners who, like himself, had been employed to deal with the polyglot huddled masses. One of these was an Italian immigrant named Anthony Frabasilis, a renowned scholar of Greek philology at the University of Athens, who was hired at Ellis Island as a Greek interpreter in 1909 and also worked in Italian, Spanish, French, German, Polish, Russian, Turkish, and Armenian. He's said to have known fifteen languages, and to have spoken them all well.

Starting in 1909, a civil service exam tested interpreters' writing, reading, and speaking abilities in some (or all) of the languages in which they worked, which provides hard evidence for a cluster of real hyperpolyglots at Ellis Island. Another interpreter employed there was Reuben Volovick, a native of Russia, who knew Yiddish, Russian, Ruthenian, and many other Slavic languages. Another was Peter Mikolainis, a Lithuanian native, who knew seven languages. They would meet with passengers, sorting and directing them through medical exams and legal interrogations. Except in rare medical cases, the interviews were simple enough: What's your occupation? Your race? Your ethnicity? Have you ever been an anarchist? A polygamist?

Finally, the Krebs family boarded a ship for Europe, leaving behind Emil's extensive library, which eventually was sold to the US Library of Congress. Back in Germany, Krebs turned to languages with full force, "surrendering to his great ambition for language study," as his great nephew, Eckhard Hoffmann, wrote. The Foreign Office was offering 90 deutschmarks for every language that someone could speak. "You'll be a millionaire!" family friends told him. But officials informed Krebs that he would be restricted to testing in two languages. He made nothing for being able to read the cuneiform writings of Assyrian, Babylonian, and Sumerian.

One afternoon in March 1930, while he was translating something (what isn't known), Krebs collapsed, and he died soon afterward. The news spread quickly, and later that day, his wife received a chilling call: Would the family donate his brain to science? The request came from Oskar Vogt (1870–1959), a pugnacious specialist in brain anatomy and the director of the Kaiser-Wilhelm Institute for Brain Research. The brain would be a fine addition to Vogt's collection of elite brains, and the only brain of a *Sprachgenie*.

Vogt, devoted to the study of elite brains, had a trail of scrapes and narrow escapes behind him. In 1924, he'd been invited to Moscow to study the brain of Vladimir Lenin. At the time, political maneuvering in the young Soviet Union, particularly by Joseph Stalin, saw the importance of creating and sustaining a cult of Lenin as a revolutionary supergenius. "It also appeared a brilliant idea to obtain, if possible, a confirmation of Lenin's 'genius' from some respectable source, preferably from abroad," wrote Igor Klatzo, a biographer of Vogt and his wife, Cécile. By 1927 Vogt had soaked Lenin's brain in formalin, embedded it in paraffin, and sliced it into 31,000 sections. From there, he faced a huge challenge: how to remain scientifically principled yet not offend his Soviet sponsors? How to explain certain features of Lenin's brain without referencing the fact that he might have had syphilis? (He didn't— Lenin apparently had a family history of atherosclerosis.) And what if Lenin's brain didn't match other elite brains?

Vogt solved the problem by describing the rich array of pyramidal neurons in Lenin's cortex and explaining that they must have been involved in rich imaginative, rational thinking. To great Soviet acclaim, his paper was published in 1929, and Vogt turned to other projects.

Little did he know he would be collecting a hyperpolyglot brain the next year. He met Krebs's sister-in-law and his stepdaughter in the church where the funeral was to be held; by law, brain extraction required family members to be present. Toni and Charlotte-Luise, who had stepped away because they couldn't bear to watch, could hear Vogt's hammering and sawing. The mood must have been one of Frankensteinian gloom: the dark church; the flickering gaslight; and Vogt walking away with Krebs's brain, jiggling in a glass jar.

It was this brain, I hoped, that would have something to say for itself.

Chapter 11

T he brains that have added the most to our understanding of language abilities belong not to the Mezzofantis or Krebses of the world but to people who have lost those abilities. One of the more famous of these was a man named Leborgne, an epileptic laborer in Paris who had barely spoken for years when he was brought to the hospital in 1861 for an inflammation of the legs. He could only say "tan" (though he could say it with different intonations) and gesture with his left hand. The hospital staff, and later the medical literature, knew him as Tan Tan.

When, several days later, Leborgne died, his doctor, Paul Broca, performed an autopsy and found, on the left front side of Leborgne's brain, an area of tissue damaged by syphilis. Later, Broca collected the brains of others who had the same broken speech as Leborgne (we now call it aphasia) and damage to the same part of the brain. This led Broca to propose, against prevailing scientific opinion, that he had found the brain's locus for speech functions. Also contrary to ideas of the day was his proposal that speech control was located only on one side of the brain (in most people, on the left). More confirmation was needed, but the outlines of Broca's notion soon passed into fact. Now scientists recognize that this area is responsible for more functions than previously thought—and also that languages are controlled in other places besides "Broca's area." But it was an important discovery nonetheless.

To get a sense of where exactly Broca's area is, imagine a globe, perhaps one of the glass or plastic globes you'd find in a classroom or library, mounted on a metal bracket, the sherbety chunks of nations spread across it. My globe happens to be a vinyl inflatable one, which I'm going to use as a rough model for the geography of the brain. To start, turn the globe so that Europe faces you, and the imaginary north–south line, the prime meridian, which runs through Greenwich, England, lines up with your nose. This puts the prefrontal cortex, the seat of human consciousness and cognitive control, in an area that ranges from the equator northward to the north pole, east to the Middle East, and west across the Atlantic Ocean in line with the northern coast of Brazil.

This means that when I place my hands at the equator on opposite sides of the globe and hold it front of me (the prime meridian in line with my nose)—my left hand on the brain's right hemisphere, my right hand on the left—the edge of my right thumb will be right next to the Arabian Peninsula and the Arabian Sea. This is the area of the brain that Broca associated with speech control. (There's an analogous area on the right hemisphere right off the coast of Brazil, though for most people it plays a less important role in language. Not for Emil Krebs, as we'll see.) About thirteen years after Paul Broca made his observations, a German scientist named Carl Wernicke announced that people with damage to another area of the left hemisphere also had communication problems. If you return to the globe, this area is in far eastern Mongolia, or where the end of my right index finger lands.

Broca's area usually gets the attention when people talk about language. But recent scientific work has revealed a broader story, thanks mainly to imaging technologies like functional magnetic resonance imaging (fMRI), positron emission tomography (PET), and diffusion tensor imaging (DTI). In that broader story about language in the brain, language doesn't reside in any single place. Instead, it is spread over parts of the brain in networks that are more widely distributed than had been thought. There are two main networks, which have also been called "streams." One stream maps speech sounds onto strings of motor commands, so that a person can turn sounds they hear into sounds they say. On the brain-as-globe, this stream goes north, from north India to eastern Mongolia. In most people, this stream is located on the left hemisphere of the brain. The other stream maps strings of speech sounds onto stored concepts in the brain, which is how you're able to comprehend what someone is saying to you. This network seems to spread in both hemispheres, on the left hemisphere from north India to northern Taiwan, on the right from south Texas to Hawaii. Greg Hickok (at the University of California at Irvine) and David Poeppel (at New York University), the two neuroscientists who put together this "dual stream" model in 2000, call the first one the "how" stream (since it tells the system how to produce meaning in speech) and the second the "what" stream (since it metabolizes a stream of speech sound and translates it into meanings).

The "how" and "what" model has been backed up by neuroanatomical studies that have traced the bundles of nerves that connect these areas to each other. As a complete picture of everything linguistic in the brain, it has shortcomings—it's mainly a model of words, even though human language obviously involves grammar. But it illustrates that languages aren't filed away like library books in the brain; there's no "French" neural pathway living next to, or occasionally overlapping, a neural pathway that's dedicated to "English." Instead, what you have are meanings with different sets of strings of sounds attached to them, some of which the outside world identifies as French or English. It also helps to illustrate some of what's going on when languages are learned. Learning how to speak a new language will involve the "how" stream, engaged mainly on the left side of the brain (under my right hand); learning how to comprehend a new language will involve the "what" stream, which is likely working on both sides of the brain (under my left and right hands). Getting those two streams up and running makes up a lot of the work of foreign-language learning.

If this seems very distant from everyday life, I find it extraordinarily useful for understanding why my seventeen-month-old son can understand me better than he can speak, and why he can understand words that he can't say. It's because the "what" stream doesn't involve anything mechanical, whereas the "how" stream uses lots of moving parts. And knowing that his brain is plastic also helps explain why his pronunciation of the same word varies so much from day to day—the motor commands haven't become concrete yet.

The fact that early languages, no matter how many there are, utilize the same streams implies that the brain doesn't have a native language. The brain can only reflect the fact that a set of neural circuits was built and activated for a certain period of time. Nor does the brain care if those neural circuits map onto things that the rest of the world calls languages or dialects. It really cares only about what activates those circuits. Thus, the brain patterns that typify language use across skill levels can be mapped.

Brain imaging technology monitors the intensity of oxygen use around the brain—higher oxygen use represents higher energy use by cells burning glucose. The deeply engrained language circuits will create dim MRI images, because they are working efficiently, requiring less glucose overall. More recently acquired languages, as well as those used less frequently, would make neural circuits shine more brightly, because they require more brain cells, thus more glucose.

Using imaging technology to study these circuits, you'd also see the location of oxygen use change, depending on skill level. More recently learned languages engage areas all the way on the other side of my plastic globe, somewhere under my left hand. This is the signature of a brain that's recruiting higher-level cognitive processes, not automatic ones, to perform language tasks in relatively new languages. Given enough time and practice, however, those tasks would consolidate into the streams under my right hand. By making expected, predictable tasks automatic, expert brains save up cognitive resources to deal with unexpected, novel tasks.

Building the "how" and "what" streams in adult brains doesn't happen without conscious practice. But, as Dick Hudson noted, people who practice the same amount vary in their ultimate performance. It makes sense that there must be some sort of underlying capacity that enables those streams to be faster, stronger, or more durable. Because the functional anatomy of the brain is still largely a mystery, mapping that kind of capacity is a challenge—or, to put it another way, just because no structural or anatomical difference has yet been pinpointed doesn't mean that it can't exist.

"Neuroscientists will tell you that brains are as different as faces, perhaps as different as bodies," John Schumann, an applied linguist at

UCLA and an expert in the neurobiology of language learning, told me. Partly this is because of gene shuffling at fertilization—you get 50 percent of your parents' genes but not the same 50 percent as your siblings. The other reason is that the genes don't determine the exact placement of neurons in the brain. "During embryonic formation, as neurons are formed and migrate to what will be the brain," Schumann said, "their trajectories are stochastic, and they depend on the chemical and mechanical milieu of the brain."

One result is that brains are similar in gross anatomy, while at a microscopic level, they are markedly different. Some of those "microramifications" could point someone toward high performance.

Schumann speculated that hyperpolyglots might have different brains than normal language learners. "During embryonic development," he said, "there's some neural migration, perhaps to the area between Wernicke's area and Broca's area." This would correspond on the globe to the swath of Central Asia between Saudi Arabia and Mongolia. As a result, Schumann said, there would be more robust formation of brain matter, the neurons and neuropils, dendrites and neuroglia, and support cells. All these I would be learning more about later.

One example of such a brain is Einstein's. Though its overall mass (at 1,230 grams) was average, its inferior parietal lobe was slightly larger than others' brains, and it was also more symmetrical from side to side. This "exuberant expansion" would have "allowed him to think and reason and imagine in areas of mathematics and imagery," Schumann said. Fortunately, he pointed out, Einstein was born at a time when his theories were understandable—you can't separate the genius from his context.

So, as a fetus, the person who would become a hyperpolyglot could land extra neural equipment in parts of the brain that are responsible for learning words, for being sensitive to grammatical structures, or for parsing and mimicking speech sounds. Maybe they would get more equipment in one of the three areas. Or maybe they would get more equipment in all three.

That's what the brain of Emil Krebs looked like.

Chapter 12

Sitting in a chic hotel in Düsseldorf, Germany, I heard a knock on my door. My guide had arrived: a woman in her late fifties with round cheeks, silver spiked hair, and fashionably chunky glasses. Loraine Obler is an American neurolinguist at the City University of New York who was spending part of a summer teaching in Potsdam. She had told me about a team of German neuroscientists in Düsseldorf who had used new methods to analyze Krebs's brain. What they found sparked outpourings of linguistic pride in Germans. If you wanted to know more about the brains of exceptional language learners, as Loraine and I did, it was galvanizing work that promised many answers. We were off to meet the neuroscientists and hear more about their work.

Loraine's journey toward talented language learners began in college, when she was in Israel studying Hebrew. Good at French in high school but not at Latin, she found Hebrew a breeze—she "inhaled" it—all the while watching a classmate, a smart Mormon kid, who just couldn't get Hebrew to stick. This disparity stayed with her. In graduate school, she studied Arabic and went into linguistics. She wrote a dissertation on Arabic, mainly in Israel, where she also began to study people with more than one language who had lost the ability to find words or produce coherent sentences. Damaged brains, especially those with more than one language, became her focus. She cowrote an influential book, *The Bilingual Brain: Neuropsychological and Neurolinguistic Aspects of Bilingualism* (1978), one of the earliest attempts to explain how it all works, and coedited *The Exceptional Brain: Neuropsychology of Talent and Special Abilities* (1988), a collection exploring the "neurological substrate" of talent and unusual abilities—what talented brains are like, where they come from, the personalities of people who achieve, and the social context in which they develop.

In her introduction to *The Exceptional Brain,* she explained that exceptional outcomes come from a storm of tiny, interlocked interactions between a neurological bent, a cultural frame, nurturing relationships, and pure happenstance. Some of the loops we understand. Some we haven't found yet but might be able to understand when we do. Many more are untraceable, especially by currently available methods and modes of thinking. This was one reason why I wanted her as my guide in Düsseldorf.

The other reason was that she'd done important early work on language talent. She'd begun by studying hyperlexia, a cognitive disorder in which children who are otherwise intellectually impaired are able to read fluidly at a very early age. Though they don't comprehend what they read, they have powerful word recognition capabilities. (It had been suggested that Christopher was hyperlexic.) This phenomenon got her thinking: Why are some people better readers or language learners than others? Recalling her Mormon classmate, she got a colleague to post flyers around town: DO YOU OR DOES SOMEONE YOU KNOW LEARN LANGUAGES VERY EASILY?

That's how they found C.J. He was a Harvard graduate student, white, twenty-nine years old, raised in a monolingual English-speaking family in the States. In high school he encountered French first. Success there led him to German. He studied Latin and Spanish for a semester apiece. A college French major, he went into the Peace Corps in Morocco, where he learned Moroccan Arabic more easily than his peers, then spent time in Spain and Italy and picked up their languages. He reported that native speakers of his five languages had found him easy to understand, even native-like. (The researchers took him at his word and didn't assess his language proficiencies.)

Crucially, Loraine and her colleagues also looked at how C.J. scored on a battery of IQ and cognitive tests. Hyperpolyglots aren't necessarily exceptionally smart; C.J. turned out to have a fairly average IQ of only 105. (In this he resembled Christopher, whose performance IQ was lower than his verbal IQ, which itself wasn't stellar.) So high verbal IQ also isn't a prerequisite for language talent. As a child, C.J. had been slow to read, and his grades indicated mediocre high school and college performance. However, on most parts of the Modern Language Aptitude Test, a test developed in the 1950s to help the US Army find people who can learn foreign languages, C.J. scored extremely high.* He also excelled on any test that required him to spot complex patterns in strings of numbers, letters, or words. His verbal memory was very good: like Christopher, he had a sponge-like memory for prose and lists of words.

Anecdotally, musical ability and foreign-language ability are often tied together: languages and music both are formal systems involving sequences of discrete units, and an individual must be disciplined to perform well. It's true that speech sounds and music share areas of the brain, and that there's also a basic similarity in visual and auditory pattern recognition. But when C.J. took the Seashore Tests of Musical Ability (developed by Carl Seashore in 1919), his scores on a memory test for melody and for sequences of rhythm and pitch were average. In his case, at least, the anecdotal connection didn't hold.

Possible explanations for talented language learning fall into two general areas. One view says: What matters is a person's sense of mission and dedication to language learning. You don't need to describe high performers as biologically exceptional, because what they do is the product of practice. Anyone can become a foreign-language expert—even an adult. In fact (the story goes), language learners run the gamut, and the successful ones represent the very, very successful end of this spectrum. Their native languages may be as jealous as anyone else's, but somehow these people aren't held back from hearing and producing new sounds, words, and grammatical patterns. Believing that language learning isn't easy and takes work, they commit themselves to using their time efficiently.

---

*According to Madeline Ehrman, the MLAT's grammatical sensitivity subscale predicts later outcomes best, but C.J. scored in the 50th percentile on this.

The other view says: Something neurological is going on. We may not know exactly what the mechanisms are, but we can't explain exceptional outcomes fully through training or motivation. C.J. came to play an important role in this view, because Loraine had measured in him the cognitive features that support quick, easy foreign-language learning by adults. Presumably these features are more genetically determined than others; though trainable, they seem to be improvable only within certain margins. In time, C.J. would appear as a case study in other people's work, including linguist Peter Skehan's at the Chinese University of Hong Kong. Skehan suggested that what's so special about C.J. "seems to be the capacity to deal with large quantities of material to be memorized quickly and easily."

Both Christopher and C.J. have talents that aren't centrally about language at all, Skehan argued. Rather, they possess cognitive abilities that happen to be very well suited for learning languages. That is, they can recognize patterns and remember learned material. These skills are suited for languages, which are "relatively simple codes which can be learned and operated quickly, and which then can be the basis for the retention of material." When Skehan wondered "whether there can be an exceptional talent for learning languages, qualitatively different from high [linguistic] aptitude," his answer was a resolute yes.

Both types of language learners would share a couple of traits. They "would have a high range of lexicalized exemplars, considerable redundancy in their memory systems, and multiple representations of lexical elements. . . . It is assumed that such learners would not value form highly," he wrote. To translate: they know a lot of words, have many different words for the same meanings, and do not care too much about avoiding errors. People like this have to be biologically different, Skehan suggested. "Exceptionally successful foreign language learners consistently seem to be characterized by the possession of unusual memories, particularly for the retention of verbal material," he wrote. "Such exceptional learners do not seem to have unusual abilities with respect to input or central processing." In other words, they learn languages in virtually the same way everyone else does; they just have better memory retention and retrieval.

What does better retention mean? The average person, over a lifetime, will find it easier to learn new facts than to learn new motor or cognitive skills. In the same way, the average adult language learner will have an easier time picking up new words than picking up grammatical rules. And we know, at least in the early stages of foreign language learning, average adults lean quite heavily on "declarative memory." This is the part of the memory system that remembers facts and words. It remains fairly robust as one ages, though the plasticity of procedural memory, where motor and cognitive skills as well as grammatical rules are stored, becomes less assured. So "better retention" may mean that hyperpolyglots can cement declarative memories in their brains more quickly. Or that their procedural memories remain plastic longer than most. Or maybe they just have declarative memories with a lot of capacity. The degree to which Christopher, the polyglot savant, has superior memory retention suggests that he's less like an average adult language learner than he might at first seem.

For her part, Loraine thought something more might be going on.

C.J. forgot images and numbers as fast as anyone else did. Why should someone have a good memory for sounds and words but not for other things? In music, he was average; tests of visuospatial ability stumped him; he said he couldn't read maps or figure out new routes. This intrigued her, since it's often thought that exceptional verbal abilities are associated with limited visuospatial abilities, or vice versa.

To give these overlaps some order, she looked to a complex theory known as the Geschwind-Galaburda hypothesis, which links co-occurrences among dyslexia, gender, handedness, and other traits. As examples, there's a predominance of left-handers among talented visual artists, and males are overwhelmingly more often dyslexic and autistic. In the 1980s, neurologists Norman Geschwind and Albert Galaburda looked to brain development for an answer. They observed that the left hemispheres of the brains of fetal rats developed more slowly if testosterone spiked at certain developmental moments. The cells destined for the left hemisphere migrated to the right hemisphere, which acquired more of the raw materials for building dense brain connections.

If the same thing happened in humans, Geschwind and Galaburda suggested, that asymmetry could create clusters of talents and deficits. Their theory might explain why children with left-hemisphere-related disabilities (such as dyslexia or stuttering) tended to have higher-than-normal abilities in right-hemisphere abilities, such as putting together puzzles. And it may explain why left-handedness (or ambidexterity), homosexuality, autoimmune disorders (such as asthma or allergies), learning disorders, and talents in music, art, and mathematics all seem to happen together, if not in the same individuals, then in families.

C.J. fit the profile. He was an identical twin, though his brother had no apparent special abilities; neither was strongly right-handed (C.J. was left-handed and his brother was ambidextrous); C.J. had hives and allergies; he was homosexual; and he got lost easily.

Doesn't it disprove the theory that C.J.'s brother had no language abilities and wasn't gay? No, said Loraine. "Just because you have a lot of left-handers with no talents, that doesn't hurt the explanation, because these cluster in families," she said.

You're not looking for a specific gene for deficits or talents; you're looking for genes that affect how hormones work. According to Geschwind and Galaburda's theory, fetal genes drive the production of testosterone and determine vulnerability to hormonal spikes. Neither genes nor hormones determine each other or any particular outcome. Rather, they take a zigzag course: the right inputs at the right moment under the right conditions might produce a certain brain asymmetry that would lead to behaviors that, culturally speaking, would be interpreted as talents or deficits. Whether the hyperpolyglot learned languages very quickly, could use a lot of them, or both, his or her talent was the result of intersecting lines of circumstances.

As any good expedition begins with a meal, Loraine and I considered hyperpolyglots over sushi. Tomorrow we'd be visiting the brain institute, and we had much to discuss.

Even if one doesn't agree that hormonal disarray creates a cluster of traits, the clustering is still of interest. Loraine wanted to know if any of the people I'd met manifest attributes of the Geschwind-Galaburda cluster. I told her that most of the hyperpolyglots seemed to be men, and a number were gay and left-handed. Alexander couldn't drive. He'd taught himself to write with his left hand, and his father was an identical twin. I also told her about a translator I'd met at the European Commission in Brussels, forty-three-year-old Graham Cansdale, British by birth, who came from a "resolutely monolingual family" (as he put it), yet had studied, or dabbled with, a total of twenty-two languages (including Guarani, the indigenous language of Paraguay, and Vietnamese, which stumped him); he uses fourteen of them professionally (French, Spanish, Italian, Swedish, Russian, Portuguese, Hungarian, Danish, Greek, Czech, Slovak, Arabic, Turkish, Finnish). When I met him he was studying Arabic, Chinese, and Turkish in his spare time.

"People think it must be lots of hard work," he told me. "In my case I couldn't agree. I don't spend a vast amount of time doing this. It comes so easily. If it is hard work, it doesn't feel like hard work. Actually, I just remember it because I do. It just goes in. I'm not forcing things in my head."

Graham was unable to learn how to drive and had an excellent memory for language-related things but not for, say, history facts. And he was gay, married to a Slovakian man. He wasn't a word accumulator but a system builder; he was content with the geekish thrill of being able to decipher the verbs on the small print of a menu or to read the street signs that he encountered on his extensive global travels.

This was an anecdotal sample, but the Geschwind-Galaburda hypothesis helps make sense of it. As a theory of both biology and society, one that accounts for individuals as well as families, Geschwind-Galaburda explains a lot, and has the virtue of not claiming that people with traits A and B are bound to become a Y. It doesn't indulge a crude determinism but instead tries to map a set of possible influences. Another virtue is that it treats handedness, immune disease, talent, and even sexuality as falling along a spectrum.

Yet its assets—and, indeed, its power—also make it difficult to establish. To dig into it, you'd have to know genetics, cognitive science, epidemiology, and endocrinology, all in great detail. You'd also have to gather a big sample, many families, and ask them the right questions. Attempts to confirm some of the correlations have had mixed success. One study, for instance, found no connection between left-handedness and higher spatial or mathematical abilities, though researchers did find that left-handers often reported having speech problems. Various studies have shown that people with autism have higher rates of non-right-handedness. Yet another study found, as the Geschwind-Galaburda hypothesis would predict, that there are more males than females who perform both very high and very low on mental rotation tasks, though, outside of Loraine's work with C.J., no one had ever linked verbal abilities in a foreign language with any of the Geschwind-Galaburda traits.

We discussed how I might capture similar information about clusters of traits from as many people as possible, and I eventually designed an online survey that collected information from nearly four hundred people from around the world from January 2009 to January 2010. People who claimed to know six or more languages were directed to the survey via English-language linguistics blogs and language learning websites like http://how-to-learn-any-language.com. There they gave their consent to answering questions about their background, their language learning, and their cognitive styles.*

The results, which were analyzed by an academic statistician familiar with this type of data, give support to some parts of the Geschwind-Galaburda hypothesis. For instance, people who reported knowing six or more languages and who said that learning foreign languages was easier for them were more likely to report homosexual behaviors, preferences, and/or orientations than would be predicted. This finding was statistically significant.

This same group also was more likely either to have immune diseases themselves or to have family members who did. However, neither of the other traits (handedness and twinning) had any meaningful relationship with either number of languages or ease of learning.† Despite an anecdotal connection between homosexuality and verbal abilities, no connection between language talent and homosexuality had ever been shown in research before. Again, this isn't saying that people who speak a lot of languages or learn them easily are necessarily gay; it's that there are more gays—and people with immune diseases, for that matter—

---

*Just a note about this survey: I chose six languages as the limit because of advice from Dick Hudson that five languages were the most spoken in a community, so people who speak six are outside the norm.

†One major caveat is that the survey draws from people who are online, so the overall make-up of the online population can skew the results.

among talented language learners than you'd otherwise predict. Testing this with numbers allows us to move beyond anecdotes and to suggest why these patterns exist.

This survey's groundbreaking results were many months away; Loraine and I were still sitting in the sushi restaurant, preparing for our visit with Krebs's brain. She said, "There's one difference between C.J. and people like Mezzofanti, Krebs, and the other people you're interested in. C.J. hadn't started to accumulate languages when we met him, and we don't know how well he switched among them. Rather, he was notable for how fast and easily he learned his languages to a very high level. I'm interested specifically in those people," she said. They may or may not overlap with those who *accumulate* languages. The question was, are they the same? Or are there two separate groups?

I repeated a phrase that had been coined by someone named Loren Coleman, who writes and comments prolifically about the search for hidden or unknown animals, from Bigfoot to newly discovered frog species. Coleman once summed up such uncategorized creatures, also known as cryptids, as "out of time, out of place, out of scale." In the case of the coelacanth, they're living fossils, thought to be extinct, so they're out of time; they're out of place, like a monkey escaped from the zoo who is sighted rooting in suburban trash cans; or they're out of scale—like giant Amazonian snakes or mastodons. The term fits hyperpolyglots perfectly—they do things with language that are out of scale with what normal people do with language. They don't usually live with other hyperpolyglots, so they're also out of place. Some of them bear the distinct whiff of the past or are perfumed with the future. That takes them out of time. C.J. and Mezzofanti, Alexander and Helen, Ken Hale and Christopher—all of them out of time, out of place, out of scale. I felt lucky to have found them in their place, and to have seen the scale you'd need to measure them.

Tomorrow we'd see Krebs's brain in a glass jar, trailing bits of tissue in some murky formaldehyde juice. I looked forward to peering at it, hoping it would simplify matters. To our delight and surprise, the next day had something else in store.

Chapter 13

"I'm really good at finding four-leaf clovers," Loraine said from the backseat of the taxi, as we drove to the Cécile and Oskar Vogt Brain Research Institute. "It's my only gift." Anywhere she goes, she finds them, and after being in Germany for a few weeks, she had found quite a few. There are two possibilities, she says. Either Germany really has more four-leaf clovers, or she's relaxed and noticing them more. Maybe it's genetic, I said. Well, my grandmother also could find a lot of them, she said.

At the institute, we sat at a conference table and drank coffee with the archivist, Peter Sillmann, who had brought out some articles about Krebs, a brief memoir, and the black-and-white photo you see here.

I thought of Geschwind-Galaburda; Krebs was right-handed. Sillmann, who was

Emil Krebs. (*Courtesy of the Cécile and Oskar Vogt Brain Research Institute*)

speaking to Loraine in German, kept saying "crepes." Crepes? Loraine explained: in German, they devoice the final consonant. Ah. *Krebs.* I hadn't tackled any German for this trip. Sillmann had other photos: Krebs sitting at a desk in his office in China, his legs crossed, looking out the window, a potted palm by the wall; a photo of his headstone in Potsdam, near Berlin. There was also a photo of Krebs's postmortem brain. The stroke that killed him had blown a dark hole in his brain's right temporal lobe (on the brain-as-globe model, northern Mexico). The dark withered edges of the hemorrhage resembled a mushroom cap's moist underside.*

Our hosts arrived. The director of the institute, Karl Zilles, tall and thin, looked like a dashing financier, in a tan jacket and light blue shirt; Katrin Amunts, a professor of neurology at RWTH Aachen University in Germany, was petite, with dark curly hair and rimless glasses. Why were you looking at Krebs's brain in the first place? I asked her when we settled down again with cups of coffee. She said she had wanted to try out some brain-mapping techniques and chose to look at language functions because it's more or less well known where they occur in the brain.

Does the brain collection have any linguistic geniuses?† she had asked Sillmann.

It did. Sillmann had brought Amunts the box of glass slides containing Krebs's brain. After collecting the brain, Oskar Vogt had photographed it, then removed the brain stem and the cerebellum. The four remaining lobes were cut into blocks, and these were soaked in a series of baths—formaldehyde, alcohol, chloroform—then hardened in paraffin. The waxy blocks of tissue were sliced with a microtome, which uses a spinning knife to carve off microscopically thin slices of tissue. These slices were mounted on glass slides and stained, then stored. Which meant that the brain wasn't stored in a jar.

Naturally, I was disappointed that about this, but the sliced brain might have been a bigger gift to Amunts, because she could locate slices

---

*Because the stroke had killed him instantly and because the hemorrhage was on the right, not the left, side of the brain, the damage didn't affect the results of the analysis.

†Musical abilities are also very localized; the library also contains the brain of Belgian violinist Eugène Ysaÿe (1858–1931).

from the Broca's area on the left and on the right. Others before her had looked at Krebs's Broca's area, notably Vogt himself; looking for cell densities to explain genius, as he had with Lenin's brain, Vogt had shown that Krebs had an unusual density of neurons in this area.

In even older exams, other scientists had associated a large number of accumulated languages with a visibly larger left Broca's area. In the 1860s, British doctor Robert Scoresby-Jackson proposed that only the lower portion of Broca's area was crucial for the mother tongue; the upper area could hold others. Eventually this was disproven by Ludwig Stieda, a German anatomist, who performed an autopsy on the brain of German hyperpolyglot Georg Sauerwein (1831–1904). How Stieda got the brain and where it is now isn't known, but he reported that Sauerwein's brain had a normal-size Broca's area. He examined other polyglot brains (without saying how many languages they spoke), which also contradicted Scoresby-Jackson, and with that the pursuit of a large Broca's area, at the level of gross anatomy, anyway, was abandoned.

Unlike his predecessors, Oskar Vogt and his wife and collaborator, Cécile (1875–1962), looked at brains in microscopic detail, particularly at the arrangement of cells and other brain tissues. They were still dividing the brain into its various territories, each lobe and nodule given its own name and jobs. But they searched for the real differences under the microscope.

For decades, neuroscientists had bickered about the significance of comparing the density of neuronal cells to the amount of surrounding tissue, called "neuropil" (the interwoven nerve tissue that makes up the greatest amount of the brain's gray matter). Vogt and others eyeballed the tissue landscape, each coming to different conclusions about what they saw.

In the 1980s, Karl Zilles, with a colleague, frustrated by findings he found unscientific, developed a microscopic scanner for areas 20 by 20 microns square (about as much surface area as the thickness of a human hair). The scanner mapped the cells and the surrounding fluid. Then it turned their ratio into a curve. With a glance, one could see the density of cells at each of the six layers of the brain's surface. This was the tool that Amunts used on Krebs's brain slices.

Not only did Amunts take slices from Krebs's Broca's area on the left and right sides, she also took slices from an area related to vision. These areas were known by the labels given to them by Korbinian Brodmann, one of Vogt's chief assistants, who subdivided Broca's area into what are now called Brodmann's areas 44 and 45. Like the map of the American West, the territory of the brain is named by its explorers, who had a penchant for honoring each other with slices of cerebral territory. The vision sample came from Brodmann's area 18. (On the brain-as-globe, this would be in the Pacific Ocean, at the back of the brain.)

Amunts found that in Krebs's brain, the neural cells in Brodmann's areas 44 and 45 were layered in more heterogeneous patterns than in eleven other brains she'd sliced and stained for the purposes of comparison. This arrangement suggested that the cells had unusual ways of interacting with each other. What did this mean for the way his brain actually worked? It's unclear. You'd need to scan a similar hyperpolyglot brain. But at that microscopic scale, even modern scanning technologies may not pick up anything significant.

Another surprise was the pattern of development of Brodmann's areas 44 and 45 in Krebs's brain. An overdeveloped Broca's area on the left wasn't a huge surprise—since Krebs used it a lot, it had responded by building more connections between neurons. Rather, the biggest difference between Krebs's brain and the eleven comparison brains wasn't in areas 44 and 45 on the left; it was in area 45 *on the right*. Such symmetry in 44 and asymmetry of 45 across the hemispheres was unusual. How did it happen?

One answer is that both adults and children who are just starting out with another tongue engage more of their right hemisphere in verbal communication. Certain tasks (such as making sense of words) need help from nonlinguistic cognitive processes whose networks run through the right side of the brain. Another answer is that the Geschwind-Galaburda hypothesis predicts that in talented language learners, language will be represented in both the left- and right-brain hemispheres. It's known that the right hemisphere can even take over some responsibility for language when the left Broca's area has been damaged by stroke. Also, in the dual stream model of language, the "what" stream (which is involved in the perception of speech sounds) spreads in both hemispheres of the brain (but doesn't reach into Broca's area).

Early on, it was thought that only the left hemisphere was responsible for language. Since then, the right hemisphere's responsibility—even among healthy, right-handed people—has been acknowledged for fixing incoherent sentences, storing pragmatic knowledge, and cogitating about language itself. "In this context," Amunts wrote in her analysis, "E.K.'s language performance may be related to special meta-linguistic abilities far beyond automatic speech." That is, the thinking about language that he did, he did with his right brain.

The overdevelopment of the right Broca's area may also have something to do with Krebs's Chinese. In 2009, a team of British neuroscientists found that speakers of Chinese had denser gray and white matter in the right anterior temporal lobe (located on the east coast of China) and the left insula (a part of the brain folded within the cortex that lies somewhere deep under the Arabian Sea) than those who didn't speak Chinese. This effect was found even among non-Chinese people who learned Chinese. This makes sense: tonal languages such as Chinese seem to require the right hemisphere to assign pitch to the meanings of words. But it's unlikely that a single language would have been solely responsible for the right brain's overdevelopment.

All this means that Krebs probably did possess the talents attributed to him: he could process language structure differently from others; he was more sensitive to intonation and prosody (which would have been crucial for Chinese); and he was generally more sensitive to speech sounds.

I'd like to know something else about Krebs's brain. We know that you can match neural signatures of language proficiency with language biographies, as an Italian research team revealed in 2009. People who'd been multilingual for a long time, including children, had most language-related brain activity consolidated more or less in one spot. But people with languages they'd learned later had more diffuse activity, including activity on the right side. Was it possible for a brain to be an ultraconsolidator, to put all of its languages on an efficient central circuit, even if they'd been learned later? To answer a question like that, you'd need a living hyperpolyglot brain. Ideally, you'd need more than one.

The Vogt archive contains a transcript of an interview with Amande Heyne, Krebs's wife, from the year of his death. How many languages did he speak? Sixty-eight, she said. How many could he read but not speak? He had knowledge of more than one hundred languages—when he learned languages, he wanted to read, write, and speak them. Did he have a good memory? Yes, an extremely good one. For names? Yes. For numbers. Yes. For everyday things? As long as they interested him, she replied. Did he read? He read all the time, and he read everything. His favorite author was a cartoonist.

"He was a very strange personality," Zilles said.

"He wasn't talkative," Amunts said.

"He learned all these languages, but he wasn't talkative," Loraine marveled. (Amanda Heyne had said that he could be socially engaged, "if the people interested him.")

When Zilles told me that he thought Krebs might have had a mild case of Asperger's syndrome, I groaned inwardly. I didn't want to think about a link between Asperger's and hyperpolyglottism. I hoped language talent was its own thing, not something you'd only find in savants like Christopher. I couldn't very well go back to Alexander or Helen and inform them that they were autistic.

Outside, rain pounded on the windows—a typical German summer day, the secretary joked. But I was intent upon this question, and unprepared for what happened next.

Chapter 14

Before meeting Loraine Obler in Düsseldorf, I had interviewed the Greatest Living Linguist, according to *The Guinness Book of World Records,* an American named Gregg Cox, who lived about 170 miles away in the city of Bremen. Though Cox was credited with speaking sixty-four languages, fourteen of them fluently, it is not clear to me what Cox, now in his late forties, had ever been able to do in the various languages he claimed. I did, however, learn that he was the product of a broken home in Los Angeles, and that his teenage fascination with languages brought him, in the 1980s, to the Russian school at the Defense Language Institute, where the US military provides most of its recruits with language training.

While serving in the US Air Force, based in Europe, Cox accumulated certificates and test results from dozens of language courses. He sent sheaves of paper to *The Guinness Book of World Records,* which was impressed enough in 1999 to crown him the "Greatest Living Linguist," ousting Ziad Fazah from the title. I figured that the *Guinness* title didn't deserve that much credence (they'd once crowned Fazah, after all), but I wanted to meet Cox all the same. When I had sent out a note looking for highly talented language learners in a DLI alumni newsletter, Cox had called me within minutes of its online release. I expected to find him struggling to make a living, as Alexander had been. Contrary to type, he'd built a cozy bourgeois life, working as an executive at a dental implant company, a job he'd gotten because the company's founder was impressed by his polyglottery. His certificates were packed away in his house, and he pled that he was too busy to retrieve them for my visit.

When I was setting up my visit with Katrin Amunts, I told her I was visiting Cox. She responded with an excited, almost gustatory email: We can scan his brain!

This was exciting. As far as I could tell, the most languages seen at work in a scan of a single brain was four, in a group of Swiss men and women. Different languages activated overlapping areas of the brain, and the more fluent languages activated a more central area. Studying someone with more than four languages would put us at the brink of a true frontier.

The next day, Amunts wrote back: Forget about scanning Cox.

At the time, I'd been puzzled. Now, sitting across from her, I could ask, "When you wrote back saying no, was that because it would produce another case study?"

Amunts smiled. At first, she said, she felt the same excitement about Cox as with Krebs's brain. "*Of course* I'm interested, and of course we could do all these fancy tests on language, cognitive abilities, general intelligence." Ultimately, though, she decided not to pursue it, because "we would arrive at the same point, that it is a case. *A case.*"

The ugly history of the study of elite brains had surfaced. Many scientists have been motivated by ideological arguments about the superior intelligence and culture of this country or that race, Zilles explained, which the natural historian Stephen Jay Gould had taken up in his 1981 book *The Mismeasure of Man*. Too many bad studies on elite brains have made journals cautious, Amunts said. No one wanted to publish a study on just one genius, especially one on a German genius by German authors.

I saw the opportunity immediately, but Loraine spoke first. "Suppose you had *three* people," she said.

The atmosphere in the room visibly shifted. I quickly added, "I'm in contact with five people who claim at least two dozen languages." I knew I'd meet more. (And I did.)

"Two dozen languages," Amunts whispered, then turned to Zilles and muttered in German.

We'd want to look at functional connectivity, glucose, and oxygen use, Zilles said. We'd want to know how parts of the brain communicated with each other. It might be, he suggested, that a language-gifted person has more or faster connections in certain areas than a normal person. We'd have to test their language proficiency, of course. It would be good to have a range of ages and native languages, too. As we talked, it all seemed possible. The world's first neuroimaging study of a sizable group of hyperpolyglots dawned in front of us. A door into the future had opened, and if we seized the opportunity, we would do something that science had never attempted before.

"Let's do it," Zilles said.

Silence in the room. Maybe the rain was coming down, but I'd stopped hearing it. We were finally going to get the brains of hyperpolyglots to speak for themselves.

When the meeting was over, Zilles took Loraine and me upstairs to the brain library, a quiet, grayish room where rows and rows of small wooden boxes sat on metal shelves. Here, human brains, Zilles said; there, brains of the great primates who'd lived in zoos. He seemed proudest of the major collection of insect eaters and bats. "A very rare collection," he said. He took down a box from the human section, opened it, pulled out one of the glass plates, about five by seven inches, and put it under a microscope. Loraine and I took turns peering at the gray, grainy amalgam of the cortical slice.

But focusing on what was in front of me was difficult—I was thinking about the living, breathing brains we'd finally get to see in action. And which, someday, when the Oskar Vogts of the future came asking for them, might settle into collections of their own.

Even though Krebs's brain had a very different cell structure from normal brains, it wasn't clear whether those differences might have existed before he encountered his first foreign language. I asked our German hosts about this. "How long would it take for Krebs's brain to develop like that? Could it happen in a year? Or is that the lifetime of change?"

"That's an interesting question," Loraine said. "Or was he born like that?"

Zilles said he didn't know. Such changes can come from training, he said. They can also emerge quickly—cellular-level changes in the brains of pianists, for instance, can occur in a matter of weeks. And intensive use gives musicians different brains from nonmusicians' brains. Studies of rats have shown that training increases the number of synapses and glial cells and makes the capillaries supplying oxygen denser. Jugglers and taxi drivers have markedly different brains from nonjuggling, non-taxi-drivers. Persistent overuse could be a simple reason for the cells' peculiar arrangement as well as his brain's remarkable symmetries.

"When you look at a histological section, you see the cell bodies that are stained, and in the cell bodies there is unstained tissue," he said. "But there is something there, in those unstained areas. There are dendrites. There are synapses, and the glial cells, and the blood vessels. But most of this volume is for dendrites, synapses. For contacts. These contacts are very fast-moving structures, so such a synapse can change within hours. When you do training, then you will get an effect on the synapses, and so the space between the cell bodies changes its size."

Amunts disagreed with her colleague. To her, Krebs's cytoarchitecture could have caused or enabled his linguistic predisposition, instead of resulting from it. His parents were neither educated nor rich; other people paid for his schooling. If the story of Krebs and the French newspaper was to be believed, he brought a distinct cognitive foundation to learning foreign languages very early on.

"I'm convinced that there's something in his genes," she said. "You cannot say this is only the environment. That is rather simplistic."

Here the story of Krebs's abilities might have stalled in another endless round of arguments about the primacy of nature or nurture. In the popular mind, only one of these can drive outcomes, not both. Meanwhile, scientists are trying to describe how biological resources and experiences in the environment interact, on what schedule, and with what impact. It turns out that genetic mechanisms not only make you; they also determine the range by which you can be made by your environment.

One such genetic trait that Krebs might have possessed was the way his brain regulated its plasticity—how sculptable and moldable his brain was in response to things in his environment. Overall, his tendency toward more or less malleability would be driven by genetic factors. No matter how someone without that plasticity practices, they won't be able to speed it up or make it stick more. It's widely known that babies and other young animals have an "exuberant plasticity" that allows them to learn about their world very quickly. Yet neuroscientists now also think that the brain's essence—at any age—is to be changeable. What happens in adulthood is that the plasticity has been "braked" for one very good reason: in order to survive and succeed, adults have to have a certain amount of reliable neural structure that is usable over months and years. One of the ways that Krebs's brain might have been unusual was that it preserved more of its childhood plasticity.

Even among normal learners, there's a lot of variation between individuals when the malleability of childhood hardens. Bilingual kids also enjoy an advantage in remaining open to new language input. And, in some rare cases, language learners appear to enjoy a plasticity past the point where it's shut off for others. Unfortunately, because linguists have been most fascinated with the acquisition of native-like skills, more is known about people who are able to learn one or two more languages very deeply rather than about those who can acquire a good working knowledge in a larger set. Again, it was the bias for the "all or nothing" view over the "something and something" view of language abilities.

Young humans use their exuberant plasticity for learning many things; one of the most important is for language. The notion of a critical period for language learning was first formulated in the 1960s by linguist Eric Lenneberg. "Automatic acquisition from mere exposure to a given language seems to disappear after [puberty], and foreign languages have to be taught and learned through a conscious and labored effort," Lenneberg wrote. The exact nature of this critical period for language has long been debated, even though its biological mechanism isn't known. One limit is puberty, which means hormones are likely involved. But is puberty the end of plasticity or simply the beginning of the end? No one knows for sure.

Ever since Lenneberg, researchers in second-language acquisition have taken the adult's decline in plasticity—the closing of the critical period window—to refer almost exclusively to the impossibility of learning a language like a native speaker. Even though the brain has no native languages, only focused activity in certain neural circuits, *linguists have looked only at how "linguistic insiders" are produced.* Some researchers have even fiercely defended the claim that no one who begins learning a language outside the critical period will ever have native-like abilities. In one recent study of Swedish learners, none of the adult learners passed a nativeness test, and only 3 of the 107 child learners did. If a child learning Swedish can't become a native speaker, then who can?

Opponents of the critical period hypothesis have taken on these claims directly—by trying to find adults who have, in fact, achieved nativeness in languages they didn't grow up with. Some have figured that only 5 percent of adult learners can do this. Some put the number even lower, at fewer than 1 percent. Even so, these opponents are bound by "nativeness" as the sole criterion of success at learning a language— they've let the proponents of the hypothesis set the terms by which the debate is waged.

In one recent dissertation, forty-three non-native speakers of Dutch, a language they'd started learning after the age of twelve, were asked to do some tasks with a type of sentence that's hard for people to learn.* If you knew languages close to Dutch, as some participants did, you could borrow and apply what you know. If your native language was one like Turkish, you'd have nothing to fall back on. Your language lacks this sentence structure completely. Of the forty-three, nineteen were able to produce this kind of sentence like native speakers did. Most were

---

*These are sentences called "dummy subject" sentences, in which the subject of the sentence, the doer of some action, is not in the place where the grammatical subject is usually found in the sentence. In English: "It is the man who threw the ball." In Dutch: *"In de krant wordt beweerd dat hij dronken achter het stuur gezeten heeft."* ("It is claimed in the newspaper that he was drunk while he was driving.") Dummy subjects are so hard that native speakers can't describe all the patterns, which aren't things you learn in school or from books, but only from hearing and using them.

women; most were also more likely to speak German and French than Turkish, and had spoken Dutch for a long time. Interestingly, all had either studied a third language as well, or had worked as teachers, translators, or some other language-related job. This was significant, because the answer didn't lie in their fondness for languages—every single one of the forty-three subjects had said that they liked to learn languages.

In another project, an exhaustive battery of proficiency tests was given to nine non-native English speakers who'd been mentioned or referred to the researcher as having excellent English. All nine had learned English after age sixteen and had lived in the United States for at least five years. Only three of them performed like native English speakers on tests of grammar, pronunciation, vocabulary size, politeness, and storytelling. All three were women. They were all from Eastern Europe, had studied English for at least five years before coming to the United States, and lived with native English speakers (two of the three were married). They also used their first languages infrequently.

For these cases, what predicted good English was using a lot of English. No other biological factor—gender or age of arrival—predicted good English or vocabulary size. You just had to live longer in the States, preferably with a native speaker. On the surface, it appeared to be a victory for the power of practice and immersive experience to trigger changes in the brain. But other individuals might share those same biographical facts and still not speak English well enough to be referred for a study. The studies didn't provide a cognitive profile of the high performers, either. They couldn't speak to the cognitive skills that those individuals brought to their tasks, nor could they account for how one person's brain might be more plastic than another. Could a measurement of brain plasticity be a better way to predict language learning outcomes?

One day, after my trip to Germany, I was at home in the apartment, dealing with a clogged bathroom sink. The landlord came over with his son-in-law to fix it. In the course of chatting, the landlord asked what I was working on, and I told him, a book about people who speak a lot of languages. Really? my landlord said. He speaks a lot of languages, he said, pointing to his son-in-law, who was half sticking out of the cabinet. He's from Iran, and he's lived all over. He speaks six or seven languages. He's a genius.

Is that true? I asked the son-in-law.

Yeah, it's true, he said, from under the sink.

How many languages can someone learn? So far, I'd pursued an answer among massive accumulators and high-intensity learners, many of whom came from monolingual communities. I knew little about places where normal people, inheritors of a normal biological endowment, regularly learn to speak many languages. I knew I had to venture out for a closer look to see what else I could learn about the brains of Babel.

Part 4

ELABORATION:

The Brains of Babel

Chapter 15

ver the palm trees, the sun was barely squinting, and already the traffic lashed the dusty intersection in front of the Hotel Diamond Point. Streams of small trucks; battered motorcycles; shiny compact cars; yellow, three-wheeled auto-rickshaws; scooters; bicycles; pedestrians; and the occasional oxcart converged from five directions onto the same point, creating a chaotic whirlpool in the middle of the intersection. No signs channeled the crush, no lights controlled it; there were no lanes, hardly even curbs.

I was watching this on the street in Secunderabad, a south Indian city whose entire population seemed to be trying to pass in front of the hotel in one unstoppable throng, at that very moment. When you're in a vehicle, the traffic feels crushing; then you realize that you're not being crushed; then that you're making slow progress toward your goal. After a couple days of crossing Secunderabad and neighboring Hyderabad (with a population of four million) on roads like this, you realize that the visible chaos has predictable patterns. Maybe that's what kept drivers so eerily calm as they headed into the whirlpool—keep your speed, make no sudden movements, and you might stay safe. Maybe the policeman, a lone man in a white hat, shaped these flows. No, I realized, he's just a witness to the gridlock's wonder. On a giant poster high on a building, the face of a beatific swami gazed upon the waves of disorder.

A couple of streets over, my hosts Sri and Kala,* a retired couple in their sixties, have returned from yoga class for breakfast. They live in a big house with a rooftop garden, ceiling fans, televisions, and a kitchen shrine that befits their Brahmin roots. Sri used to be a manager at a manufacturing company. A short, round man with a sharp jut to his lower lip, he laughs easily, loves a joke, and loves to eat. At breakfast he pulls out a jar of chutney and adds a creamy glop to my plate; every lunch ends with a rich, cardamom-infused ghee dessert or ice cream that he's forbidden to eat for health reasons. Slender Kala, trained as a botany professor, spent time every morning threading white jasmine blossoms into a garland for her kitchen shrine while watching Hindi soap operas.

Enthusiastic to begin, I asked our hosts about their language repertoires on the first morning. The glimpse left me hungry for what else we'd find. Though their mother tongue is Tamil, they speak to each other in Hindi. When they were first married, this surprised Kala. Hindi was the language they would have likely spoken outside the family. "I thought, why is he talking to me as if I'm a friend?" she says. They also speak English—it takes a day to adjust to their accents, but they seem to have no problem understanding me or my wife, who had joined me for this leg of the journey.

The whirl of languages gets more complicated. Sri also uses Hindi with his two grown sons. With one of his daughters-in-law, he uses Tamil and English; he speaks in Kannada with the other. With his sisters he uses Tamil, though with one of his nieces, he speaks in Telugu. He speaks in Kannada with Kala's sisters. Though he speaks Hindi, Kannada, Tamil, Telugu, and English, he reads and writes only in Hindi and English.

Kala's language life was a bit more easily mapped. She talks to her sons and one daughter-in-law in Tamil; with the other, in Kannada. With her own sister, she uses Kannada. She also knows Telugu, Hindi, and English. She watches Hindi soap operas and reads the newspapers

---

*Out of deference to their hospitality, I'm going to use only their first names and those of their family throughout this portrait.

in Hindi and English; out in the markets she uses Telugu, the language of the state.

The morning we mapped this out, my head swam; it seemed so much like the intersection at the Hotel Diamond Point. How do they know what language to use with whom? How do they know who they are in each language? Is that even relevant? What order underlies this apparent chaos?

On that first morning, I explained to Sri and Kala why I had come. I'm writing a book about people who can speak a lot of languages, I said— like, dozens of languages. I knew there are places where it's common for everyone to speak a lot of languages, but I didn't know anything about them.

Many of the same myths about multilinguals applied to hyperpolyglots. Maybe, by looking at one, you might get closer to the other. One myth about multilinguals was that they can use all their languages equally well. Another was that they have one cultural background per language. Yet another was that they know languages somehow imperfectly, and that imperfect knowledge couldn't count. I surmised that hyperpolyglots were more different from multilinguals, though, who were numerous and also lived in communities that develop a shared standard for what it means to speak those languages. Rooted in such a sensibility, they beget more multilinguals. And, while polyglots fade in and out of the historical record, multilingual communities have been around forever, direct descendants of the time before civilizations tamed our tongues.

India isn't the only place where one finds multilingualism. One of the best-known multilingual hot spots exists, or used to exist, in the northwestern Amazon basin. The American anthropologist Arthur Sorensen made the tribes who live there famous in the late 1960s. "In the central part of the Northwest Amazon, there is a large multilingual area encompassing many tribes, each possessing its own language, where almost every individual is polylingual—he knows three, four, or more languages well," Sorensen wrote in an article about the place. At the time, about ten thousand people lived along the Vaupés River, in an area the size of New England. There, each one of twenty-five tribes has its own language, which (among other things) determines whom an individual can marry, because individuals have to marry outside of their language groups. As a result, children grow up at least bilingual, and perhaps learn other languages from people who live around them. This outmarriage system powers the quadrilingualism that Sorensen observed, though some individuals speak more. Linguist Alexandra Aikhenvald reported meeting someone in the Vaupés who spoke ten languages well.

Yet the timeless multilingualism of Amazonian hunter-gatherers is, well, neither. (Hunting-and-gathering is also on the decline.) To prepare to go there myself, I interviewed Jean Jackson, an MIT anthropologist who did fieldwork in the Vaupés in the 1970s. She told me that the marriage system isn't millennia old, but is a more recent adaptation to migration pressures and population declines, which emerged about a hundred years ago. That system itself is on its way out, broken by outside pressures; very few people speak four languages fluently anymore. Bilingualism is still prevalent, but increasing numbers of people rely on Tukano, the language of the most populous tribe, as a lingua franca. Even if I could have gotten around the problem of not knowing any of the local languages, I would have found very little there that I hoped to see.

Another of the world's linguistic hot spots is the Mandara Mountains in northern Cameroon, where the average mountain tribesperson speaks three languages; many speak five or six. What this means in reality, reports Ohio State University anthropologist Leslie Moore, is that a typical person will "speak only two or three of them well and have stronger receptive than productive skills in the other languages." Like a hyperpolyglot, it didn't seem unusual, at least for multilinguals in this part of the world, to know lots of bits of lots of languages.

Another expert on the same area, anthropologist Scott MacEachern, has described the multilingualism as very old; people have spent centuries trading, warring, intermarrying, jockeying for political advantage. Connections to the outside world have encouraged some people to learn more languages. Take as an example a man in his mid-twenties, Michel Kourdapaye, who worked as a translator for MacEachern. He "speaks *pelasla, wuzlam,* and French fluently," MacEachern wrote. "He also speaks *mada, wandala,* and Fulbe with varying levels of efficiency; as is usual, he can understand the latter languages rather better than he can speak them. He can also understand some *muyan.* He insists that his linguistic facility is not very unusual in the region." (The italics are MacEachern's.) Such an expansive repertoire is more common among younger men, who learn more languages in order to take advantage of opportunities beyond the mountains, the anthropologist added. Before European contact, he supposed, speaking three or four languages was the norm.

While pondering whether or not to go to Nairobi, another very multilingual city, I came across a prickly quote by D. P. Pattanayak, an Indian linguist and a champion of India's multilingual society (some 428 languages are spoken there), about how multilingualism was always explored from the perspective that a viable society could maintain only a finite number of languages and finite amount of cultural diversity. He proposed a question that turned the assumption over: "Given ethnic and linguistic diversity," he asked, "what does the viable political order look like?"

If India was the place to catch a glimpse of a more expansive way to live with many languages, that's where I wanted to go. I decided to go south to Hyderabad, a former Muslim stronghold with a large Urdu-speaking population, in the state of Andhra Pradesh, where Telugu was spoken. Which language would I learn a bit of before going? I had a little Hindi in my head from shadowing with Alexander, *garam garam hai.* But Hindi isn't a good choice in south India, where the Dravidian languages are proudly spoken and Hindi has in the past been openly resisted.* South India has four main Dravidian languages, two of which, Kannada and Telugu, were spoken in two of the Indian states I was going to visit. Don't worry about it, my friend said. Everybody speaks English. Which wasn't exactly true. But there was a lot of English, which benefited me tremendously.

---

*In 1965, riots in the southern state of Madras (later called Tamil Nadu) were sparked when Hindi nearly became the country's only official language. But there haven't been language riots in the so-called Dravidian states since the 1980s, and language nationalism is waning.

On that first morning in Secunderabad, once I finished sketching my book project for my hosts, Sri told me that I had to meet his cousin's brother, a former ambassador of India, who speaks lots of languages, including non-Indian ones such as Chinese. Soon he was on his cell phone, setting up our visit in another city. I was amazed. In a family where many languages are spoken; in a city where, depending on where you are, the signs are printed in Urdu and English, or Hindi and English, or Hindi and Telugu; in a country with uncountable hundreds of millions of people speaking two, three, or more languages, the polyglot was still powerful—it wasn't just in my own monoglot country. Over and over I would present the case of Mezzofanti, and people would shake their heads. *Incredible.*

One of the first things to understand was how people knew what language to speak to whom. Where I've lived in the American Southwest, choosing to speak in English or Spanish based on how someone looks is risky. If you try English and they don't speak it, you can switch to Spanish if you know it. But if you start with Spanish, you might offend: *You don't think I speak English?* This can be the case if you're Anglo, even if you speak Spanish very well and had just heard the other person speaking Spanish. When I described such a scenario to Indians, they couldn't relate—to them, choosing the wrong language wasn't embarrassing or politically charged. Or so they said.

"Doesn't anyone get offended?" I asked a doctor whom Sri had brought us to meet.

"No, why should we be offended?" She seemed baffled by the question.

Sri, who had heard me ask this question several times, cut in, a little exasperated. "No, you just say, I'm sorry, I cannot speak your language, please speak in English."

One day we took a bus tour of Hyderabad's popular sites: a white marble temple to Vishnu, a gaudy, fluorescent-lit museum filled with the vast collections of a rich official, a palace of a Muslim ruler, and the zoo. Aside from one other foreign couple on the bus, everyone was

Indian. As we drove from place to place, the tour guide, a young man, hung on to the luggage racks as the bus jolted, rattling off descriptions and instructions in English. I was intrigued that by the end of the day he'd added Hindi to his narrations. When the tour ended at a pearl jewelry store (Hyderabad is famous for its pearl trade), I pulled him aside to ask why he had switched.

He gestured to the women, older, dressed in saris, who were looking at pearl necklaces at a counter. He knew from the start of the tour that they'd want Hindi at some point.

"How did you know?" I asked him.

Based on how someone walks, from their clothes, and from their appearance, he can tell what their mother tongue is. He himself also spoke Kannada, Telugu, and some Marathi. Others told me they judged (or guessed) based on skin color: people from the south tend to be darker than those from the north. (These are problematic stereotypes, though; it may well be that talking about skin color is code for other attitudes.) You might also choose a language if you can hear the influence of their mother tongue in their Hindi. If one person can hear Kannada in another's Hindi, they say, Let's speak in Kannada. As their mother tongue, it's what people want to speak anyway. In this vast country riven with differences, you grasp any connection you can.

One afternoon Kala and Sri took us to a Hyderabad fairground where textile merchants had set up booths: Kashmiris with wool shawls, Rajasthanis displaying skirts sewn with tiny mirrors, fine chikan embroidery from Lucknow. Throngs of women (about half of them covered by black chadors, the other half dressed in vivid *salwar kameez* and scarves) circulated, checking out the cotton prints, silk saris, and lustrous brocades. We stopped in one booth so my wife could look at a blouse, where the clerk, a young man, let slip to Sri that he's from Bangalore. Sri perked up, then spoke Kannada. After some back-and-forth, the salesman said to us in English, "Since you can speak Kannada, I'll give you a discount." Everyone laughed: a safe harbor.

"See how that works?" Sri said to me as we walked away. "Language builds closeness. We started speaking Kannada, and we felt some closeness."

In the days that followed, we met many members of this family, each of whom spoke multiple languages—even the four-year-old grand-niece knew Hindi, English, and Telugu. Some languages were reserved for certain settings and people, and new languages seemed to follow jobs, not the other way around. The four-year-old's mother, in her early thirties, said she speaks Telugu, Hindi, Marathi, Sanskrit, Tamil, Punjabi, Bengali, and English. *How well?* One presumes she could use them as she needed them. I was tempted to say that it's hardly an environment where saying you have more languages means higher status, as it might in the West. Here, too, mentioning foreign languages is a power play; so is including Sanskrit as a language you speak, because *Sanskrit is no longer a spoken language*. Even her recital of a list of languages was an expression of identity of class and caste. The four-year-old's uncle, Ramu, also in his thirties, is a salesman for a company that builds textile looms—he grew up with Tamil at home and in elementary school, lived for a while in Bombay, where he learned Marathi, and knows Hindi, English, and Sanskrit. In college he studied German and later picked up Japanese to communicate with visiting Japanese engineers. Fortunately, his teacher was a native Japanese speaker who also knew Hindi, a convenience since he not only taught in Hindi but could highlight its grammatical similarities with Japanese.

As an aside, Ramu remembered, he can understand Telugu. "There are so many languages," he said, laughing, "you forget." He picked it up for business because local CEOs want to speak it. "It doesn't matter if it's perfect," Ramu said. "If you're an outsider, they're happy that you're trying." Most of his office is run in Hindi, though official email is always in English. Yet, once in a while in business meetings, when all the attendees realize they know Telugu, they switch.

In Mysore, we met Sri's cousin's brother, a slim, bald ninety-two-year-old man with great fronds of eyebrows who'd been born and educated largely abroad. I'll call him Siddhartha. "I don't speak English." He sniffed grandly. "I speak Shakespeare and Milton and George Shaw. I'm a plagiarist. I'm a pariah dog who speaks whatever he can pick up and carry off." It was much like meeting George Bernard Shaw must have been, if Shaw had worn a dhoti and ran a preschool on the second floor of his house. It was hard to pin down exactly how many languages he'd known over his lifetime or how well; he dismissed other language accumulators as fantasists, including a civil servant he knew who claimed sixteen languages yet knew only a few words in most of them. It didn't matter, though. I hadn't really come to find another hyperpolyglot. I appreciated him more for his seasoned dismissal of a unified thing called "English." That sensibility about language would prove valuable.

One morning we drove with Siddhartha about ten kilometers outside Mysore, to an elementary school he founded. As we walked toward the assembly grounds, we could hear children's voices singing prayers from the Vedas, a beautiful sound that grew louder as we approached. After the prayers, he addressed the orderly rows of uniformed students about developments in Israel and Pakistan, and the recent financial news. Global in his outlook, he also promotes Sanskrit in the school, which is controversial because it's a classical language more associated with the elite; in the West, the equivalent would be teaching Ancient Greek to schoolchildren. "They connect me with being an ambassador of India," he told me later, "so they think it's not their cup of tea."

After the assembly, he had to meet with some teachers, so my wife and I waited in the school library—stocked with his personal English literature collection—where we met a female student, Ananya, who said that her father knew ten languages, all Indian ones. She herself knew three and was learning Sanskrit, too.

As our ability to access foreign languages with a mouse click has exploded, our sense of the world as a place where many languages are spoken—and that we might speak, too—has expanded. Is India the way we're all headed?

Taking a trick from Siddhartha, I'll leave aside the idea of a unified India to focus on south India. There, multilingualism in at least some of its forms arose out of circumstances that evolved over millennia, after migrations, the rise and fall of empires, and invasions. All this turmoil helped to create a unique language phenomenon called a *Sprachbund*, in which people speaking many languages are all learning what every-one else speaks.* Existing side by side for centuries, the languages have melded and merged—not just in the words people use but in the gram-mars that structure them.

If you live in a place where the people who speak languages A and B never confuse A with B, it may be hard to appreciate the fluidity of this situation. So it's helpful to review three of the events that were so important for India's linguistic history—and that couldn't have been duplicated anywhere else.

One was an extended southward migration by Indo-European peo-ples, which began around 1500 BCE. They brought with them Indo-Aryan languages such as Sanskrit, which they imposed on speakers of Dravidian languages in the south. Embedded in Dravidian languages (the largest groups now are Tamil, Kannada, Telugu, and Malayalam speakers) is the story of how these people learned, though imperfectly, the Indo-Aryan languages of the arriving conquerors, and changed those languages, too. Over the next three thousand years, the languages of the two families gradually fused. Trading and borrowing between them became more complex, going as it did in all directions, and far beyond nouns to the deeply patterned stuff that's invisible to a language's speaker. The languages borrowed each other's sound patterns: most of the Indian languages, whether Dravidian or Indo-Aryan, have conso-nants a speaker makes with the tongue against the teeth that contrast with consonants a speaker makes with the tongue curled back. Word forms, word types, and grammatical patterns—all of which take a long time to migrate among languages—were borrowed, too. For instance, Sanskrit, though it's an Indo-European language, eventually acquired very un-Indo-European grammatical features that clearly come from the Dravidian group.

What you see and hear is a situation in which languages are less like apples—neat and discrete—and more like oatmeal. It's always been oat-meal in India, and all the varieties of oatmeal continue to merge, despite

---

*Instances of *Sprachbund* (which in German literally means a "language union") exist all over the world; famous ones are located in the Balkans, in southern Mexico, and southeast Asia, among others.

political pressures to name them as if they were marbles. The languages that people speak to each other do have sharply etched borders within regional varieties of the same language (such as Hindi), the dialects of different castes, and the pidgin languages born where speakers of different languages come in contact.

The evolution of the *Sprachbund* is so glacially slow and massive that it's basically invisible; because it moves so slowly, people can still give a separate name to each of the linguistic varieties they use. This produces an odd situation: people speak five languages, but they're not really five languages. To put it another way, the cultural reality has five languages, but the cognitive reality doesn't. As with the hyperpolyglot, the number of languages can't be the relevant unit of measure here. The relevant unit is the whole of the linguistic "something and something" that someone knows. As Vivian Cook suggested, "It's their multicompetence."

South India's second significant invasion was its slow conquest by Persian-speaking Muslims, starting around 700 CE. Crossed with the military jargon of the invaders, Sanskrit birthed a language called Hindustani. For complicated political reasons in the mid-twentieth-century, Hindustani split into Hindi and Urdu.

Added to this mix was the third invasion, the arrival of the English. First introduced in 1583, when Queen Elizabeth sent the first exploratory mission to India, English became institutionalized with the rise of British political influence in 1757. In the ensuing 250 years, English became something other than merely a foreign language, though how many Indians speak English is disputed—figures range from 5 to 50 percent of the population. Upper castes such as Brahmins were historically incorporated into the British imperial structure and given access to English educations; later, they inherited the power structure along with independence.

Both Muslims and the British found a cultural landscape that was already thick with languages. British official George Grierson surveyed the colony's languages in the late nineteenth century and found that "there are parts of India that recall the confusion in the Land of Shinar where the tower of old [that is, Babel] was built, in which almost each petty group of tribal villages has its own separate language." He also found "great plains," thousands and thousands of miles square, "over which one language is spoken from end to end."

Then as now, counting Indian languages completely and accurately is a task that would craze a generation of survey takers. But there are some statistics that give form to the linguistic landscape. In 2005, the language with the most speakers was Hindi, with 180 million mother-tongue speakers and 120 million second-language speakers—rivaling the number of native English speakers worldwide (328 million). The next most populous Indian languages are Bengali, with 70 million speakers, and Telugu, with 69 million. Ninety-five percent of the population speaks one of twenty-two languages; it's not exactly known how many speak more than one.

According to the 1991 census, India had 20 million bilinguals and 7 million trilinguals, a very low number that will probably increase in the next full national survey. But you don't need a survey. Just flip through the cable channels or visit the newsstand to see the modern version of what Grierson encountered: newspapers are published in at least 34 languages and radio and television broadcasts in 104.

I sat in my hotel room and watched Hindi television, where English words and whole sentences mixed with Hindi. The mixing of languages apparently has had a very long history in Indian literature, but all of it was lost to me; I longed to know enough Kannada and Telugu and Hindi to be able to identify their fusions, too.

The Hindu cultures have been pluralistic for millennia, celebrating tensions and moving fluidly among them. Plurilingualism seems to be a natural extension of this. One metaphor for Hinduism that seemed to capture this quality comes from religion scholar Wendy Doniger, who called it "one house with many mansions," which also captures the linguistic life of the south Indians I met. In the West, a person with multiple identities and affiliations seems obliged to struggle or feel confusion. Here, the more the merrier.

This expansiveness was on display in what I could piece together of Sri and Kala's family history. About three hundred years ago, Sri's ancestors left the southern kingdom of Madras (now the state of Tamil Nadu) and migrated north to Bangalore, bringing Tamil with them. Rather than dropping Tamil for Kannada, the language of Bangalore, they simply added Kannada to the mix. Around two hundred years later, in 1911, his father moved to Hyderabad, and instead of dropping Tamil and

Kannada, family members broadened their repertoire, again, by adding Telugu. Meanwhile, formal education and professional work brought together Hindi and English. By the time Sri and Kala's sons were born, in the early 1970s, the family had accumulated so many languages, they didn't have a single "mother tongue."

"We speak Hindi a lot," said one of Sri's nieces. "All of us speak Telugu, but when more of us are together, we speak Tamil. Then, when we get even more together, we speak Kannada." They are exposed to so many languages from a very young age, they don't really know how many there are, she added. By the time she was five, she had five languages (Telugu, Kannada, Tamil, Hindi, and English) and now she can understand three others (Malayalam, Gujarati, and Marathi). For her, each language presumably has its own resonances. Speaking them all is a reenactment of family history, a way to transport the accumulated past into the present.

India is no multilingual utopia, however. Neither is it a model for how to build a peaceful society with multiple languages. People's feelings about language spark conflict and violence all over the world; why should India be any different? Deep discontents about languages roil, and the history of the country is checkered with intolerance and violence.

You only need a few examples to get the flavor of the problem. In 1999, language police in the state of Karnataka objected to a sign that was written in three languages and three scripts: English, Hindi, and Kannada, in that order, with the words running from top to bottom. Then the police began to bicker: Shouldn't Kannada be on the left, a place of honor, since it would be read first? Or should Kannada be in the center, a place of respect, since it would be flanked by the other two? Just the fact that "language police" monitor signage reflects deeper tensions. Or perhaps they're just thugs, like the ones who beat up shopkeepers in Mumbai who use English, not Marathi, on their signs.

In Hyderabad, Kala said that in the 1960s, her stepmother never sanctioned Kala's sister's marriage to a man who, though he was from the same caste, spoke Kannada. Fifteen years later, when Kala's other sister married a Telugu speaker, the stepmother was forced to accept the husband. Why should people be open about language differences, when they are such a convenient index of other attitudes? (I learned

later that the language difference would be taken as a sign that the marriage wasn't a traditional arranged marriage but a more controversial
love marriage.) In the weeks we were in India, Hindu fundamentalists
attacked Indian women dressed in Western clothes (in one case, drag-
ging women out of a Mangalore bar and beating them), accusing the
women of being untraditional and of not being able to speak Kannada.
In another incident, one girl, the daughter of a member of Parliament,
was dragged from a bus and beaten for talking to a Muslim teenage boy;
one news report I read suggested she'd been unable to extricate herself
because she didn't know Kannada.

Also complicating Indian multilingualism is that the languages don't
have the same social or economic status. Those who speak a global,
brand-name language tend to have higher status than those who claim
a mother tongue with fewer speakers. (By no means is this peculiar to
India.) English and regional languages like Telugu, Kannada, and Tamil
are already locked in a slow-moving war. In this case, it's the tectonics
not of grammars but of actual politics. Given the sheer number of their
speakers, none of those languages seems endangered—Kannada has 35
million speakers, Telugu 74 million, Tamil 68 million. But as journalist Sugata Srinivasaraju wrote in *Keeping Faith with the Mother Tongue,*
the Kannada language (and presumably the other Dravidian tongues) is
endangered less by English per se than by a "very amorphous techno-
global identity" called "cosmopolitanism." To become a member of the
world society, a global citizen, you have to learn English. To the degree
that people perceive that the global stage is their only goal, they are leaving local languages behind.

"Local languages and mother tongues seemed to be slipping away
into the realms of nostalgia without a serious functional purpose in
the outer world," Srinivasaraju wrote. "They were being forced into a
clipped and compromised existence in the drawing rooms and kitch-
ens of their speakers." Himself a proud Kannada speaker, Srinivasaraju
noted how writing in English left him without the time to devote to the
Kannada literary movement, an elite that was itself dwindling. Once
it lost its public face, the language began losing its power. Columbia
University Sanskrit scholar Sheldon Pollock wrote in a 2008 editorial
in *The Hindu* that many classical texts in Indian languages were in dan-

ger of being forgotten because no scholars were being trained to read them. "Within two generations, the Indian literary past—one of the most luminous contributions ever made to human civilization—may be virtually unreadable to the people of India," Pollock wrote.

"We are not one people," Siddhartha, the ambassador, said to me, referring to Indians. "We are castes and tribes. Anything that divides us, we love."

It would be gauche for an American visitor to gawk at instances of this, but they were right there in the Sunday newspaper, with its pages of classified ads for available brides and grooms, who were categorized by profession (architect, doctor), others by previous marital status (divorced, second marriage), and even immigration status (non-resident Indian/US green card). Looking at these pages, you couldn't say that caste, language, or region didn't matter: there were sections for Tamil and Telugu brides, as well as Brahmin grooms. In the weeks I looked, the biggest sections were for Brahmins and cosmopolitans: "Wanted: Slim good looking, educated, vegetarian girl, 30–33 years, 165 cms in India or US for a Tamil US citizen." "Dubai-based parents invite compatible match for July 73 born 6'1" very fair handsome US based MS computers working reputed software company."

Raju advocates what he calls "rooted cosmopolitanism," a bilingual ideal in which humans depend upon a central identity, or at least develop one part that's more neutral. The political order needs to gather those neutral identities as the basis for political unity among its citizens. In a place with so many identities in flux, nothing's neutral—every language, religious view, cultural practice, is charged, for someone, somewhere.

English is now considered India's one neutral language, and it has become a de facto official language in the country. In 2006, a Dalit writer and activist, Chandrabhan Prasad, provoked a media firestorm by calling for Dalits (otherwise known as "untouchables") to give up Indian languages. English, he said, should be their mother tongue. His reason? Anything Indian, including Indian languages, reeks of caste discrimination. English is the key to opportunity.

This suggests that, in fact, English is not at all neutral, and the notion is obvious in the painting *Goddess English,* which Prasad unveiled after his speech, depicting the Statue of Liberty standing on a computer, holding a pink pen. Construction on a temple to this goddess has already begun in the village of Banka, where a BBC reporter said women singing *"Jai Angrezi Devi Maiyaa Ki,"* or "Long Live the Mother Goddess of English," could be heard.

"Goddess English is all about emancipation," Prasad wrote. "Goddess English is a mass movement against the Caste Order, against linguistic evils such as Hindi, Marathi, Tamil, Telugu, and Bangla for instance. Indian languages are more about prejudices, discrimination, and hatred and less about expressions and communications." Indian languages should just "wither away."

English gives you access to more education, better jobs, a cosmopolitan lifestyle, and especially the high-tech industry, where caste origins begin to be irrelevant. As one Dalit boy put it, "They just assume that anyone working with computers is a Brahmin."

"What I speak, if spoken in Hindi," Prasad said in a newspaper interview, "doesn't make an impact at all. I am dismissed but if I say the same things in English, I am heard and applauded. Also, you may have noticed that English-speaking people tend to wear suits and matching shoes. Better dressing elevates your position and makes you heard."

Many Indians also seem to have a restless linguistic appetite. They talk about learning languages as if it were a natural activity required by the body, such as breathing or eating. Were they obliging my willingness to be amazed (which I didn't try to hide)? Perhaps. Over and over I asked, How did you learn language X? The same answer would come back: Oh, I picked it up.

A Japanese teacher at the English and Foreign Language University in Hyderabad told me that her students are "shameless learners"—they're not afraid of making mistakes, and they love to brag about what they can do. "We're all conditioned to speak languages in different contexts," another person said. "You're open to new sounds. You're open to new ways of thinking." A public relations officer at the Microsoft Research lab in Bangalore, a native of the city of Kolkata, told me that he speaks Bengali and Tamil as mother tongues, learned Hindi and English in elementary and secondary school, and then learned Spanish in college. Presenting these language repertoires (as I've been doing) can seem pointlessly repetitive—until you see that he knows languages in four families.

Then he added that he speaks Kannada.

"How did you learn it?" I asked.

"Well, I live in Bangalore," he replied.

"No classes?"

"No, you just pick it up." He added, "Lots of Indians will say that." He paused. "Well, you'll find that mostly with south Indians. North Indians are a little put off by the nature of south Indian languages." The Dravidian languages are perceived to be harder; plus, people in the north tend to be monolingual Hindi speakers.

In Bangalore, I ate dinner with Zainab Bawa, an urban studies graduate student who learns languages for her research by hanging out and living with families. "The best way to learn a language is to sit with four-year-olds," she said, because they don't talk about very complicated things, and they don't have high expectations of your time together. They just want to play. She said she learned Kashmiri and Bengali this way. To learn Kannada, she went to professional meetings, built a list of words that kept appearing, and then asked friends if the words were important. "You don't pick up the language in a sequential manner," she said, adding the now familiar refrain: "You just pick it up."

In what seemed to be a society built around brain plasticity for languages, I wondered if Indians had the same facility with non-Indian languages. In Hyderabad I visited the French government–run Alliance Française, which offers French classes and cultural programs around the world. Tucked in a back office was Frédéric Dart, a short, bald Frenchman who served as the director of the Hyderabad office. He told me that Indians were remarkably enthusiastic about learning basic French but that they didn't stay with advanced classes. There may be a thousand students in the beginner classes, but only thirty in the advanced classes. "They're the fastest beginners I have ever seen," he said, "but they leave after one hundred hours, because they have enough to survive." Before coming to India, he'd been in Japan, where the reverse was true: few Japanese started French classes, but those who did stuck with the language for years.

I asked Sri's nephew, a management consultant and journalist who'd been educated in Britain, if he thought south Indians might have a genetic predisposition for learning languages.

"It's not a genetic predisposition," he said. "It's an economic predisposition. If you don't speak, you don't eat. It's as simple as that." Near his house there was a shopkeeper whom he'd heard speak eight languages in only five minutes.

What proves difficult, and this was true of the Americans and Europeans we met earlier, was changing their accents. In India, the valuable accent was a neutral one that didn't trigger the ire of English-speaking American callers. "Indians have a lot of pronunciation problems," I was told by Joshy Eapen, the owner and founder of the Bangalore School of English, who is originally from Bangalore. "A lot of Indians can't understand other Indians in English, because each region has its own accent."

One example: the English word *zoo*. Because Indian languages don't have the *z*, the word is pronounced "soo" (in the south) or "joo" (in the north). This sort of native inflection can keep people from getting jobs in the booming call-center industry in Hyderabad and Bangalore, two huge, bustling cities that are home to high-tech companies and the "business process outsourcing" industry.

Eapen's school was one of dozens teaching the "soft skills": team building, negotiation, and English pronunciation. Students were paying him 6,000 rupees (about $126 US) to help them neutralize their accents in English; he himself has a crisp British accent, which he honed working in Kuwait and Dubai. The courses last for three months, five days a week, two hours a day. "We're the only place that teaches phonetics," Eapen said. Other schools teach only grammar, which exacerbates the formality of their grammar school English so that students say "I purchased a book," not "I bought a book." Eapen said he starts from scratch, drilling them in phrasal verbs and common expressions.

As we talked, women sat clustered around computer monitors doing pronunciation drills, then students filed in for class. Most of the women were in their twenties, staff nurses in local hospitals who wanted to move to Canada, England, Australia, or South Africa. A few were housewives who wanted to enter the workforce. Most of the young men were engineers; one was a Catholic priest (the school turns out to be in a Christian part of town) being sent overseas. Only one of the students was mono-lingual; all the others claimed between two and five languages.

I tried to engage them in conversation but found it hard to under-stand their English. I didn't expect them to sound American or British, but they weren't yet intelligible to my ear, accustomed as it had grown over a few weeks to Indian pronunciations. It was obviously going to take more time.

The drive to speak English is common, but access to English train-ing is politically loaded. If you go to an Indian public school, you'll have classes in three categories of language: your mother tongue or the regional language, one of the other official languages of the country, and another modern Indian language or a foreign language.* This lin-guistic smorgasbord comes on top of a curriculum loaded with math and science courses as well as a competitive testing regime.

Rooting around in the library at the Central Institute for Indian Lan-guages in Mysore, I came across a study from the 1970s that hoped to find out if the system loaded too many languages on elementary school and high school students. Impressively, 69 percent of students said in a survey they preferred to learn four or more languages in school. Lan-guages would help their education, get them good grades and jobs, and give them a way to talk to people and enjoy mass media, they said. Only 28 percent said they wanted to study just three languages.

Though they were all enthusiastic about language learning, they also said it wasn't easy for them. Nearly half of both boys and girls said that different grammars were an obstacle, as were lack of opportunities to practice. The parents who were surveyed agreed with their children: 61 percent of them wanted their kids to study four or more languages, again for very practical reasons—to get a job, to travel, or to get more education. The economic predisposition prevailed.

Human brains don't handle languages; they handle bundles of electrical signals that are more or less distinct, that can't be allowed to interfere

---

*In one school, if their home language was Tamil, Telugu, Urdu, Marathi, or Hindi, then they had to study Kannada and either Sanskrit, Arabic, or Persian.

with each other, and that fade or strengthen over a lifetime. When I ask the question "How can brains handle so many bundles?" it sounds as if I'm marveling at south Indians (or any multilingual) through the lens of monolingualism. "If you were writing a book for a *montagnard* or a Dutch audience," anthropologist Leslie Moore (who does field-work among Cameroonian tribespeople) wrote in an email to me, "you would ask a different question: Why do so few Americans speak more than one language?"

I know why so few Americans speak more than one language: a large geography and distant borders; a culture of assimilation; an indifferent educational system; and a mother tongue that also happens to be (at least for now) a global lingua franca. To the Dutch or the Cameroo-nians, American monolingualism must make a boring story. What they might find compelling is an explanation of why they know *only* six lan-guages, not ten or twelve.

The easy answer is that individuals respond to their cultural and lin-guistic environment, speaking as many languages as are around them. But in the part of Cameroon that Leslie Moore and Scott MacEachern knew, thirty languages are spoken, and neither of them had mentioned a case of someone who knows all thirty, even to varying levels. The groups in the marriage system along the Vaupés River speak twenty-five languages. No one speaks all of them.

Why not? If a given person in these communities could learn as many languages as he or she needed, why does the motivation to acquire lan-guage stop expanding *exactly* at the drop-off of utility? It's like saying that your hunger will be sated by the amount of food on your plate. Utility does have its limits. But it's ad hoc to suggest that individual motivation drives higher linguistic proficiency and then to claim that motivation has run out where the repertoire does.

Perhaps there's an economic limit. In an "unseen hand" sort of way, individuals calculate the utility of knowing a language (including the costs of learning it) against the costs of not having it. Using game the-ory, the political scientist Josep Colomer once figured out the optimal number of languages you'd have to speak in order for most of your interactions with some random person—who may be speaking some other language—to be successful. A "successful interaction" is defined as one in which you know the language of the person you meet. (The game doesn't account for differential abilities that exist in real multilingual societies.) In this game, monolinguals have many failed interactions. So do bilinguals, especially if their society has more languages. Colomer calculated that the optimal number of languages to speak, if a given society has ten languages, is three.

Living in that environment, someone who speaks three languages will have successful interactions 89 percent of the time. The reason that three would be optimal is that the utility of learning a third language is much higher for a bilingual person in this ten-language society than the utility for a trilingual learning a fourth.

Yet a lot of people—as I saw in south India—learn *more* than three languages.

A more complete answer is possible if you ask how much of our brains we've evolved to devote to languages. What's the cognitively optimal size of the linguistic patchwork? How much can someone devote to their linguistic multicompetence? Because we have to use our brains for other things, the patchwork can't be too large. As a consequence, we balance the social benefits of knowing languages with the expense of having to keep them sorted in our minds. One can imagine the evolutionary advantages that more competent individuals would have (more mates, more economic advantage, perhaps more social power). Of course, individuals' abilities vary. Even in one or two languages, some kids talk earlier than others. Some adults talk more and faster; others talk less, use fewer words, and have smaller vocabularies. Even controlling for educational differences, they differ in their linguistic abilities. And yet they would all count as native speakers.

Oceans of ink have been spilled either scolding users of this or that language for their misuse of the grammar or defending them as legitimate users of the language. This is true in English (E. B. White and William Strunk's *The Elements of Style* and, more recently, Lynn Truss's *Eats, Shoots & Leaves,* come to mind as prominent examples), in Dutch (Jan Renkema's *Schrijfwijzer,* or "Style Guide"), and in Russian, Czech, Polish, or Hebrew. Japanese adults berate the young for not knowing polite speech for formal situations; the Mainland Chinese argue about proper pronunciations. All these and many more, including the efforts of the

Académie Française, Real Academia Española, and the Svenska Akademien, are attempts to reconcile the many ways to be a native speaker of a language. Not only is any language like a big tent, but its sides are flapping open and its visitors spilling in and out.

Then you have places like Singapore. Four official languages. Myriad ethnic histories and identities, and a lot of multilingualism. All of it different, because different cultural groups are taking up English at different rates. Varying standards exist here for how two languages can be mixed, by whom, and in what social settings. The human brain can handle all of these differences.

In south India the answer lies in social dynamics that are clearly organized along cognitive lines. One way that Indian brains are able to manage so many languages, according to the University of Chicago linguist and Tamil scholar E. Annamalai, is the *Sprachbund*. That overlap between languages is a result of generations of people trying to reduce the cognitive load of having to learn and remember so many of them. Another way to put it is that the *Sprachbund* is a cultural adaptation to two fixed constraints: a set of spoken entities whose boundaries will never blur, for cultural and political reasons, and the limits of the human brain. Something had to give. What gave was linguistic complexity itself.

Annamalai suggested to me that the adaptation included a "monogrammar" that underlay all of the languages. While they sound different and use different vocabularies, he said, the grammars are nearly the same. Thus, to learn a new Dravidian language, you substitute new words into templates that some languages share. To use a radio metaphor, it's like picking up the same broadcast at a different frequency. In that sense, the brain isn't a container, it's a receiver device that allows you to "pick up" the language.

The other way that Indians handle linguistic diversity, Annamalai contended, is by judging linguistic ability by what people can get done in a language, not by the institutional criteria that represent the "all or nothing" view of what it means to know a language. An Indian multilingual's proficiencies might be low by the standards that a school or company might devise. But if judged (and self-judged) by what they could get done and how others perceived them, they might do just fine. Such speech is often dismissed. It's "kitchen Hindi." It's "bazaar

Telugu." But this is comparing monolingual apples to multilingual oranges. In fact, "bilinguals know their languages to the level that they need them," François Grosjean, a prominent researcher on bilingualism, has written.

I don't mean to diminish the cultural richness of these societies or individual lives. But when you know these linguistic realities, it helps put claims about multilinguals into perspective, something that monolinguals wouldn't otherwise have. If it dampens the enthusiasm for counting languages, perhaps it will also sharpen the search for some other measure of a person's total linguistic competence. I don't intend to make the people I met or the situations I saw or read about representative of all multilingual communities; in other places, the dynamics of languages will certainly be different. I went to India to learn something about hyperpolyglots. And I did.

One afternoon in the library at the Central Institute for Indian Languages, in the middle of reading various Indian scholars' work on multilingualism, I jotted in my notebook that "the hyperpolyglot is the plurilingual individual in the West—the presence of language fluidity in the West." There's a truth to this, though I can't shake the notion that they're really doing something different from the Indian multilinguals whose lives I glimpsed.

One difference is that individuals living in multilingual communities seem to settle on an optimal cognitive load. The hyperpolyglot possesses a similar patchwork of linguistic proficiencies. Yet he or she exceeds this optimum with a conspicuous consumption of brainpower.

Another difference is how learning these languages ties a person to his or her community. For multilinguals, learning languages is an act of joining society. There's no motive, no separable "will to plasticity" that's distinct from what it means to be part of that society. Being a hyperpolyglot means exactly the opposite. The hyperpolyglot's pursuit of many languages may be a bridge to the rest of the world, but it walls him off from his immediate language community.

Taking my lead from Dick Hudson, I began my project by identifying hyperpolyglots as people who knew more languages than they needed to merely "belong" or get along in their local communities. I would go further, however. *Hyperpolyglots are people who have the multicompetence to belong to a real or imagined global community.* In order to learn more languages, they borrow tricks and adaptations to lighten their cognitive load from people in multilingual settings: they keep their languages at different levels of proficiency; they read and write only in some of them; they develop receptive knowledge in some languages and tend to know other languages that share vocabulary and grammatical regularities. Sometimes they count languages that they long ago studied but no longer (or rarely) used.

When I describe hyperpolyglots, some people wrinkle their noses. They have the sense that hyperpolyglots are doing something deviant. *They're not communicating,* someone said. That's what language is for, right? As much as they're admired, they're seen as socially isolated, devoid of their own culture. But the hyperpolyglots I met are no more shy or more reclusive than any other gifted, eccentric person—or any shy person, for that matter. And it's not true that they don't communicate. In fact, they do.

In one way, that's *all* hyperpolyglots do, passing meaning back and forth like someone volleying balls across a tennis net. Recall that Mezzofanti knew a sequence of conversational starters in at least one language, Algonquin, and probably others as well. Or that Christopher has difficulty with word orders that differ from that of English. Or the cautionary tale of Ziad Fazah, who couldn't take questions in languages he said he knew because he wasn't expecting those questions or those languages. Even for Ivan Arguelles reading his Tamil in the supermarket checkout line, communication is a foregone conclusion. It's like living in a script, an interaction between speakers that can only unfold seamlessly in the way it had already been composed.

Language, however, encompasses more than the communicating we sometimes do with it. If language had evolved solely for communication, we'd rarely misunderstand each other. Instead, we have a system in which words mean more than one thing, in which one can devise many sentences to capture the same idea, in which one moment of silence means more than a thousand pictures. No animal species could survive this intensity of ambiguity. Moreover, people don't appreciate how little of our meaning is in our words, even as we decipher hand gestures, facial movements, body postures automatically every day. What we mean is *implied* by us and then *inferred* by our listeners. Meaning is outside the words, beyond them. But not so for the people I met.

Also, if you're a hyperpolyglot, you live outside a language's evolution. Languages change because the new people learning them (mainly children) modify them to suit themselves. A hyperpolyglot receives the future of any language he knows. He doesn't actively make it—not in the same way that a four-year-old Indian living in Hyderabad and learning Hindi will. Being a hyperpolyglot likely also means that you're fine with this. You reserve joking and verbal intimacies for only a few languages; you don't intend to be able to enjoy them in all of your tongues. And if you're outside the communities that shape a particular language, then so be it, because that's the point: *to be a professional outsider.* You don't appear on any map.

For people like this, "nativity" is simply the wrong standard to use to make sense of what they're trying to do. They're massively non-native. In one of my surveys, people said they focused on being intelligible and clear (if they were speaking). Like the counting of languages, "native-likeness" as shorthand for measuring language acquisition was relevant in a world in which people didn't cross what were then distinct boundaries between speech communities. That's not the world we live in now. That's probably not the world we've been living in, either.

What will replace nativeness as a goal of proficiency? I suggest we need something brain-based. Something to weigh someone's competences in all their languages, as unequal yet as dynamic as this group of things would be.

I began my search for hyperpolyglots with the sense that no matter what I found, the truth about language geniuses might help temper some of the contemporary anxiety over learning languages. Indeed, I confirmed that we mortals regard such people with a mix of envy, fear, and fascination. We hunger to know what the linguistic future holds— what's the best preparation to give our children? I learned a lot about myself, too: that I grieve for the languages I might have learned when my brain was more malleable and that my fascination with unsolved linguistic mysteries might outstrip my ability to deal with them.

Eventually I met a number of hyperpolyglots—perhaps more than anyone has ever met before—and researched others. From what I now knew about the beatific Mezzofanti, the crabby Krebs, the feisty Lomb, the obsessed Alexander, the excitable Helen, the shy Hale, and all the others, I built a picture of what qualities combined to make a polyglot. In accumulating languages, they followed their own interests and needs—refusing to bend either to an evolutionary logic or to social convention. Their attitude—and their success—made them models of the will to plasticity that permeates our era.

It's still not clear what neurological story to tell about them. The powerful Geschwind-Galaburda hypothesis suggests that a certain fetal environment could produce a brain that's linguistically superior and that verbal gifts will accompany visuospatial deficits, along with other traits. People I'd met fit into this. Any real results would require a larger study.

I'd also seen proof that Emil Krebs had an unusual brain. This raised more questions, however. Had his brain been remarkable even before his encounter with French? Was it at all like other hyperpolyglot brains? A brain-imaging study of the population to confirm differences in the structure and functioning of their brains awaits a pioneer—at this writing, the project with Zilles and Amunts has yet to find its feet. Franco Pasti's taunt echoed in my head. I might be a positivist—but I'm not a determinist.

How to explain why a hyperpolyglot brain might not produce a hyperpolyglot? This led to the next question: Do people with exceptionally powerful memories, especially for verbal material, and a fascination with language amount to something more than random single cases? Is there a more widespread phenomenon worth investigating? If so, what is it?

One day as I was writing this book, I reread Loraine Obler's introduction to *The Exceptional Brain*. She suggests that talent can't simply be a product of genes, since the activities in which a person could be "talented" would be culture-determined. A proficiency for programming computers wouldn't have been recognized before computers. Surely, I thought, geek tendencies existed before computers. The skills would have been lying dormant in humans all along, waiting for cultural evolution to give them a stage on which to bloom. Who knows how many such hopeful talents the human species contains?

Language superlearning seemed to me like just such a talent, something given a purpose in a globalizing world, where language materials were widely available, travel was cheap, access to telecommunications was easy, and the borders of nations were melting away.

The history of culture is, in a sense, the process of uncovering certain talents while burying others—taking away the contexts that give certain abilities value. What if there were a neural tribe—a group of individuals who possess neural hardware that's exceptionally suited for a particular activity, who have a sense of mission about undertaking the activity, and who cultivate a personal identity as someone who does that activity? Their mental ability would predate our civilization and stand outside it, though it would manifest itself according to the social and cultural makeup of the time.

As I read, it dawned on me. Hyperpolyglots don't belong to a country; they work outside of institutions—beyond even their own communities. *Hyperpolyglots are a neural tribe.*

Chapter 16

I f you have ever taken an aptitude test—to see if you should be a doctor or a teacher or a pipefitter—then you've encountered the basis for the concept of a neural tribe. You also encounter it in psychology's long history of trying to map mental difference: IQ tests, "multiple intelligences," cognitive styles. Not only are these strengths and weaknesses varied across the human population but human neurological development takes more than one path.

You've also encountered the concept of a neural tribe if you've heard of *neurodiversity,* a term coined by Judy Singer, an Australian disability activist, and first used in print by Harvey Flume, an American writer. Early on, it referred mainly to people living with autism spectrum disorders. Later it became a rallying cry for groups of people living with autism spectrum disorders who are building identities and even community around neuroatypicality. As a concept, the scope of "neurodiversity" has expanded. In a 2010 book, *Neurodiversity,* Thomas Armstrong describes people with autism, ADHD, dyslexia, mood disorders, intellectual disabilities, and schizophrenia as "neurodiverse." Armstrong also stresses the cultural frame used to define these as disabilities or gifts. Humans with typical neurologies would flourish in nearly any culture or time; the atypical ones require specific contexts, otherwise they're marginalized or exploited. These days, the world is ripe for polyglottery.

Now surfacing, the hyperpolyglot tribe has long been lost to view—though hints of its existence pop out from time to time. Madeline Ehrman, a research scientist now retired from the Foreign Service Institute's School of Language Studies, observed accomplished language learners who scored a level 4 (out of 5 possible) on FSI proficiency tests in reading, speaking, or both. There are relatively few level 4s—it's difficult to score so high (only 1 percent of people who have taken the test have ever scored as high as natives)—and Ehrman found similarities among them. They tend to be meaning-oriented and pattern-seeking, and the majority of them were introverted intuitive thinkers. Using the labels of the Myers-Briggs personality type test, most of these were INTJs (Introverted, Intuitive, Thinking, Judging). This means they're highly analytical people, introverted and intuitive, logical and precise, and prone to thinking in terms of systems.

Ehrman also found an advantage for what she and a colleague have called "synoptic" learners, who acquire information unconsciously and "trust their guts." A pure synoptic learner can quickly reach an intermediate level because their intuitions promote flexibility and discovery. On the downside, their skills tend to plateau. They might eventually be outperformed by people who take conscious control of their learning, a group she labeled "ectenics."

Most frequent among adult learners with very high levels of language proficiency were those whom Ehrman calls "synoptic sharpeners." They blend the best of the synoptic—flexibility and openness—with an attention style, known as sharpening, where close attention is paid to minute differences among sounds, words, and meaning. It's not enough for them to call something "green"; the sharpener is precise and must identify it as "dusty olive." They *notice* (which is a key skill that both Erik Gunnemark and Lomb Kató recommended). Synoptic sharpeners benefit from strategies that let them encounter language as it's really used and, at the same time, notice linguistic details in those realms.

Whether you call these attributes "cognitive style" or "personality," there are elements of each that come with us when we're born, and that we might pass to our descendants.

———

My survey provided a thumbnail view of this neural tribe. Most hyper-polyglots will claim that learning languages is easier for them than for others. They'll also say that this is because they possess an innate talent. They don't have high IQs; they aren't savants. If they seem reclusive, it's not because they're social cripples—I found some of them to be the most talkative shy people I'd ever met. Some hyperpolyglots are women, but far more are men, even though women tend to score higher on tests of verbal abilities than men. On my survey, of those who claimed more than six languages and said that learning languages was easier for them, 75 per-cent were men. It's worth noting that the Geschwind-Galaburda hypothe-sis doesn't predict that 100 percent will be men, since the male hormones that affect brain development are present in biological females as well.

Some only read their languages; others aim to develop oral skills. Each hyperpolyglot has a variety of uses for his or her languages. Though the great majority seem to be autodidacts, others are quite happy to learn with teachers and fellow students; their methods range widely. (See the Appen-dix for a list of methods from people who reported eleven languages or more.) Their lifetime repertoire of languages can be quite large, though the upper limit of fluently spoken, simultaneously accessible languages ranges from five to nine. More numerous latent languages can be "warmed up" or "reactivated." As I've described, having a dynamic repertoire that consists of both "active" and "surge" languages is a near-universal feature of the tribe.

They are also rare, even in highly motivated populations of profes-sional language learners. Edgar Donovan, a US Air Force officer and a Defense Language Institute graduate in Persian-Farsi who has studied several other languages, sent me his scores from official tests of his lis-tening and reading proficiencies in fifteen languages. At DLI, these proficiencies are measured by the Defense Language Proficiency Test (DLPT), which ranks language abilities on a scale of 0 to 5. (Getting the highest rating, 5, means that you are "functionally equivalent" to the well-educated native reader or listener.)

Given that DLI is a high-pressure school attended by ambitious peo-ple, you'd expect that many of the graduates would have multiple lan-guages. Yet only 402 people out of the thousands who have attended have ever scored 2 or above in both listening and reading in at least three languages. And while only fifty-three people had four high-proficiency languages, Donovan was one of only twenty people who had at least five high-proficiency languages. *Only twenty out of thousands.* (True, there might have been others who hadn't bothered to be tested, but given that more proven abilities could mean higher salaries or better postings, the number of people who didn't bother is probably quite small.)

The online survey I designed captured information about two overlapping groups: those who reported that they knew six or more languages, and those who said that learning a foreign language was easier for them than it was for others. There are two groups because a talent for learning isn't always realized, and because not everyone with many languages found learning them easier. A more accurate picture emerges if potential is separated from actual achievements.

Figure 1 summarizes some of the facts about these two groups. Both are mostly men between the ages of twenty-five and forty. It is not necessarily true that only English speakers become polyglots, though most of them grew up with only one language. It's also not necessarily true that either talent or achievement is linked to IQ (the high skew probably stems from the fact that IQ was self-reported).

Figure 1 N = 390		
	Category 1: "I know >6 languages" N = 172	Category 2: "I learn languages more easily" N = 289
Gender	69.2% male	65.6% male
Age	44.8% 25 to 40	41.7% 25 to 40
Mother Tongue	43 reported >1 mother tongue; 84 had English as (one) mother tongue	53 reported >1 mother tongue; 162 had English as (one) mother tongue
IQ	45.7% reported IQs over 140; 42% reported IQs 120–140	35.3% reported IQs over 140; 50.4% reported IQs 120–140
Origins	1 from South Africa, China, Australia; 2 from India; 167 from Europe, the US, Canada, or South America	1 from Vietnam, Pakistan, Singapore, China, India; 2 from Philippines; 3 from South Africa; 279 from Europe, US, Canada, or South America

I was also able to gather information about how many languages people know. Figure 2 shows the distribution of language repertoire size among people who participated in the survey. I asked them, "How many languages do you say that you know (spoken and written)?"

Figure 2 shows that people who know more than six languages are rare, but not as rare as those who claim to know eleven or more, who represent the true modern extremes of human language learning. Only two individuals had more than twenty (using their own definitions of "knowing" a language). This finding puts reports of Mezzofanti-size repertoires among modern hyperpolyglots into perspective. Over the entire curve, self-reported talent apparently makes a bigger contribution to language accumulation than does growing up bilingual. However, for the seventeen people with eleven or more languages, six of them grew up with one mother tongue. Thus, we can say that early bilingualism made a larger relative contribution to their overall accumulation than for the whole group.

Here are a few more facts about extreme modern language accumulators. Of the seventeen, 82 percent of them were male. Five were in the United Kingdom, four were in the United States, two each in Canada (one from Quebec) and Germany, and one each in India, Denmark, the Netherlands, and Latvia. They're not particularly mobile; 62.5 percent said they live in the same place they grew up in. Twelve had English as one mother tongue and eleven said that English was now their dominant language. They claimed languages from an average of nine language families; as a group, their language families ranged from five to seventeen. Assuming that they're developing literacy skills, each one worked in an average of five writing systems, ranging from two to nine.

Given the size of their repertoires, it would have been surprising if they were able to learn only major world languages. Among these extreme accumulators, the bulk of these linguistic collections consisted of European languages (representing the Romance, Germanic, Slavic, Finno-Ugric, Celtic, and Hellenic families), most of which are state languages (except for Macedonian, Latgalian, Welsh, Bavarian, Catalan, and Occitan, and historical versions of languages such as Old High German). Nevertheless, non-European languages were also represented: Arabic (in several regional forms), Hausa, Igbo, Afrikaans, Farsi, Hindi/Urdu,

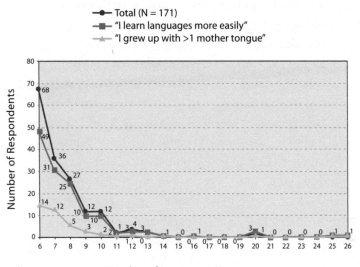

Figure 2. Polyglot language repertoires.

Kazakh, Kinyarwanda, Hawaiian, Japanese, Mandarin, Cantonese, Mongolian, Vietnamese, Malay/Indonesian, Korean, Southern Min, Wu, Thai, Hindi, Marathi, Gujarati, Sanskrit, Innu-aimun, and Cree. Apart from Farsi, Japanese, Mandarin, Cantonese, Korean, Thai, and Hindi, all the languages were reported by only one person apiece. Overall, there were only two Native American languages, Innu-aimun and Cree.

I asked them in what order they learned these languages. A common assumption is that language accumulators learn within language families in order to "rack up numbers," but my analysis shows this isn't strictly true. From language to language, they were more likely to move between different language families (e.g., English → Arabic) than within the same family (e.g., English → German → Dutch). About a quarter of the time, they studied languages from families they'd encountered before. Another interesting pattern was that Asian languages, nonstate languages, and languages with smaller populations of speakers were more apt to be learned later than earlier.

All of them said that learning languages was easier for them than for others. The survey asked them why. Sixty-two percent said it's due to an innate talent; 69 percent said it's because they're more motivated; and 88 percent said it's because they like languages. In other studies with similar findings, motivation is treated as a personality trait, which means you can't predict who will and who won't have it. To the contrary, the neural tribe theory, borrowing from Ellen Winner's descriptions of gifted children, suggests that you're born with the capacity to be motivated to learn foreign languages. How that capacity is developed is a matter of biographical detail and historical circumstance.

In the stairwell of Gregg Cox's house in Bremen, Germany, I'd seen the plaque from *The Guinness Book of World Records*: "Gregg M. Cox of Oregon, USA, the Greatest Living Linguist, is able to read, write and speak 64 languages, 11 different dialects, speaking 14 fluently." It had once hung in the hallway, but his wife, Sabine, moved it to the staircase because her clients (she's a cosmetologist) always wanted to talk about her husband. "You don't want to tell every customer your entire history and who you're married to," Sabine said. "I mean, I'm proud, but . . ." Her sentence trailed off.

The three of us were standing in Cox's office; she was talking while Cox, a short, bald man, rummaged through papers in his desk.

"I got tired of it, so I hung it in a different place," she said. "I go shopping sometimes," she said wearily. "They say, 'Cox, oh, are you his wife?' I say yes."

"Do they expect you to speak a lot of languages?" I asked.

"I get that a lot," she replied. "I say, I only speak two languages. But then I say, it doesn't matter how many languages I speak, because he doesn't understand me anyway."

When Cox and I sat down to talk again, I asked him if there were any myths about hyperpolyglots. He immediately replied, "That they can jump back and forth between all their languages. That's the biggest myth. I've met several other polyglots, and we've been able to bounce back and forth in seven or eight languages, but not further than that," he said. "The most languages that I've ever had back and forth with somebody was seven." (I can attest that I heard Cox speak English, German, and Spanish in our several days together.)

As Cox well knew, there's a persistent myth that hyperpolyglots are able to maintain very high skills in each and every one of their languages. When this can be proven false, then they're considered to be discredited. You can graph this by putting on the *y* axis a global measure of language skills and proficiencies, and on the *x* axis the number of languages, which looks like this:

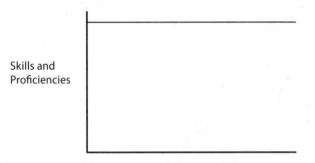

Skills and
Proficiencies

Number of Languages

Figure 3. Imagined distribution of a hyperpolyglot's language abilities.

Yet hyperpolyglots are not unique in this—the same myth applies to bilinguals. The reality, as bilingual researcher François Grosjean notes, is that "some bilinguals are dominant in one language, others do not know how to read and write one of their languages, others have only passive knowledge of a language and, finally, a very small minority have equal and perfect fluency in their languages."

As I had discovered, the actual curve of skills and proficiencies over number of languages looks (roughly) more like this:

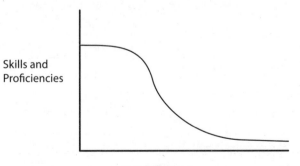

Skills and
Proficiencies

Number of Languages

Figure 4. Actual distribution of hyperpolyglots' language abilities.

Where you can find data for specific people, you can plug them into the curve. Let's use Charles Russell's careful accounting to generate one for Mezzofanti. We know that he didn't speak or read all of his languages to equal degree—one group he had to a very high degree (though the figure of thirty might be exaggerated), and his "surge" languages to some middling degree, along with the "bits of language" on the tail end.

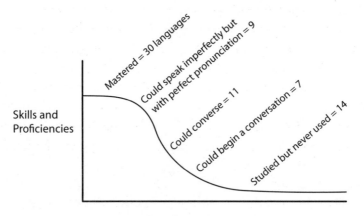

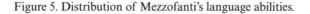

Number of Languages

Figure 5. Distribution of Mezzofanti's language abilities.

You can produce a similar curve by plugging in modern criteria and data from contemporary hyperpolyglots. For instance, Air Force officer Edgar Donovan scored 3 (out of 5) in listening and reading in Spanish, Italian, French, and Brazilian Portuguese, and 2 (out of 5) in European Portuguese. In his other languages, he has negligible proficiency, and he received a number of zeros (meaning that he knows practically nothing of the language) in Arabic, Hebrew, Turkish, and Serbo-Croatian.

A more extensive picture came from Graham Cansdale, the European Commission translator I'd described to Loraine Obler. He possessed a cluster of Geschwind-Galaburda traits (gay, spatially limited, verbally gifted). After meeting Graham in his office, I stayed in touch with him. Later he agreed to rate his abilities in all of his languages using surveys of speaking, listening, and reading that were adapted by the American Council on the Teaching of Foreign Languages. The surveys are based on a scale first developed by the US State Department's

Foreign Service Institute in the 1950s (the test became mandatory for all foreign service officers in 1958) and modified over the following decades by the Interagency Language Roundtable (ILR), an informal group in the federal government that shares information on language teaching and testing.

As is the case with the Defense Language Proficiency Test, the ACTFL scale makes the educated native speaker the pinnacle of achievement. Still, the scale suited my purposes well, especially since everyone knows its shortcomings. Using a full version of a proficiency test would have been expensive and time-consuming. We also know there's good correlation between the skills that someone reports and their actual skill level.*

I interviewed Graham about his language learning history, which provides the basis for the x axis of Figure 6; the y axis is the ratings of the ILR scale. Graham then filled out the self-assessments. The standards grade on a scale from 0 to 5. In speaking, for instance, a 0 means no proficiency, 0+ refers to an ability to use rehearsed utterances, while 5 is a "functionally native proficiency."

Figure 6 is Graham's total language system, which is a patchwork of proficiency. Here's a native English speaker, raised monolingually, who now lives in predominantly Francophone Brussels with a native Slovakian speaker (which explains his strong oral skills on all three) and who uses a range of languages for his work. There are higher scores in reading than in speaking because he's a translator; even so, he said he's reached a "critical mass" in some of the languages, so that his abilities degrade more slowly. Not only does practice matter, but having consolidated certain languages, such as Spanish, by living in a place also helps. (One benefit of his job is substantial opportunities for travel and professional development.)

Figure 7 graphs his total speaking proficiency.

Of particular interest is that he claims no perfect score in any language but English, and in one-third to one-half of the languages he has studied, he has no skills to report in speaking, reading, or listening.

---

* I was also limited to testing Graham's reading, speaking, and listening, because only these skill areas have been targeted for self-assessment.

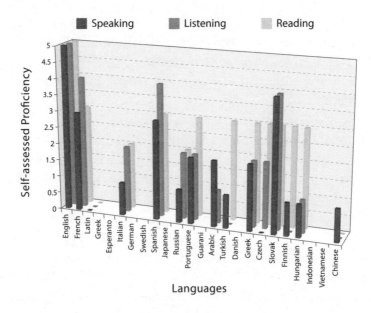

Figure 6. Distribution of Graham Cansdale's self-reported proficiencies in speaking, listening, and reading, arranged by language biography (2010).

This curve appears to map onto Graham's biography, such that his later learned languages appear lower on the curve. Alternatively, it might reflect how much practice he gets in which languages. Or it might map both. The fact that there appear to be three clusters of abilities—very high ones, a set of middling ones, and a long tail of very low ones—reflects the three levels of retained knowledge that linguists Kees de Bot and Saskia Stoessel laid out in an exploration of how people lose and relearn languages. At the highest level is knowledge that remains active. At the next level are items that can be recognized passively. At the third is knowledge that was thought lost but is still there—things that had been "saved." Saved languages are important to hyperpolyglots—over and over, people mentioned their "surge" languages proudly. But such knowledge isn't quantified in the modern language testing world. Aptitude can't account for it, either.

Earlier I suggested that reading and translating activities require less mental effort than speaking. Indeed, in Figure 8 is how Graham assessed his reading proficiency; note that the line doesn't drop off as sharply as the speaking curve. He's able to read more languages than he can speak.

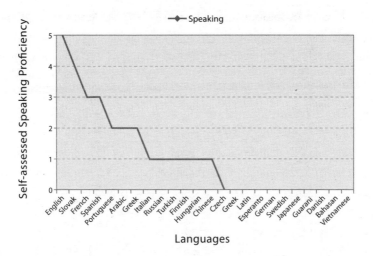

Figure 7. Distribution of Graham Cansdale's self-reported proficiencies in speaking, arranged by score (2010).

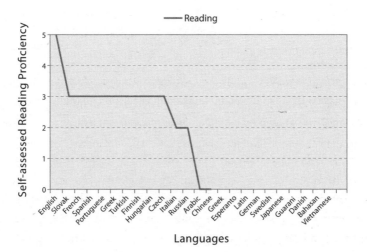

Figure 8. Distribution of Graham Cansdale's self-reported proficiencies in reading, arranged by score (2010).

I also asked experts how many languages a person could control—how many they could switch back and forth between with no confusion. They said that there was no theoretical limit to the number of languages one could learn. Time, not cognition, seemed to be the limiting factor. "There's really no limit to the human capacity for language except for things like having enough time to get enough exposure to the language," said Suzanne Flynn, a psycholinguist at MIT who studies bilingualism and trilingualism. "It gets easier the more languages you know." Harvard University psycholinguist Steven Pinker agreed. Asked if there is any theoretical reason someone couldn't learn dozens of languages, he replied: "No theoretical reason I can think of, except eventually interference— similar kinds of knowledge can interfere with one another."

But there are *real* limits—ask hyperpolyglots themselves. Out of respect for Erik Gunnemark, I'll count only the contemporary superlearners. Gunnemark, in a letter to Alexander, wrote that "if you read or hear that a certain person 'can speak' (or 'speaks') a large number of languages (for instance twenty or more) you should always be a little skeptical." Gunnemark insisted that only thirteen languages be attributed to him, those he spoke "fluently" or "fairly well." He never counted the fifteen languages he spoke at a "mini" level. (Amorey Gethin, who collaborated with Gunnemark on *The Art and Science of Learning Languages,* told me in a phone call that "I don't think [Erik] could speak very many languages very well—but he could read them. He could read quite a few languages.")

A clearer limit came from my survey. Out of 167 respondents, only twenty-eight said they knew ten or more languages; only seven knew fifteen or more; and the highest number claimed was twenty-six. One thing to note is that my standard was very broad—people didn't have to speak the language (they could also write it), and the definition of "knowing" was up to them. I don't know if they were counting all the languages they had ever encountered or all the ones they claimed to have readily accessible. Either way, one consequence is that if you thought Ziad Fazah and Gregg Cox had exaggerated, you'd really think so now. The map of what's possible, even at its extremes, doesn't seem to extend to fifty-nine (for Fazah) or sixty-four (for Cox) languages simultaneously. Among other things, this would seem to invalidate Cox's *Guinness* record. (Yet I'm not inclined to diss *Guinness* record keeping altogether, as you'll see.)

I'd started out looking for what the human limits might be in practice, not in theory. The hypothetical immortal with a million lifetimes to learn everything adds about as much understanding to the phenomenon as the native speaker of one language does—it tells us that exceptional language learning takes place within the very real constraints of our very real world. Since that's the case, we should look to real hyperpoly-glots and the results of their natural experiment.

Because working memory capacity is finite, one could predict that there should be a limit to how many languages someone can keep active. Lomb Kató described active languages as the ones that "lived" inside of her; Claire Kramsch described them as languages one "resonate[d]" with. Indeed, if you want to understand the upper limits of language *control* rather than language *learning* or *memory,* you should look to the hyperpolyglots, too. Lomb said she only had five languages "living" inside her; Cox told me he could switch back and forth only in seven. Gunnemark reported being fluent in six.

Presumably, they could have controlled more languages if they needed them, given that they claimed to have "surge" languages as well. These seem to range between five and nine, though hyperpolyglots are able to manage more for short periods of time. When Helen Abadzi worked as an interpreter at the Athens Olympics, she said she worked in ten languages simultaneously, but she carried a PDA loaded with dictionaries. There was also the polyglot contest she'd participated in—to win that, you'd have to keep many languages powered up for at least a day or two (but not longer).

Such a limit has been proposed before. Psychologist and Russian hyperpolyglot hunter Dimitri Spivak deemed it "the rule of 7." For his book *Kak stat' poliglotom* (or "How One Becomes a Polyglot," which is only available in Russian), Spivak interviewed polyglots across Russia and asked how many languages they felt they really knew. Though his rule is disputed, no one has offered counterevidence. Spivak adds that it doesn't matter if the languages are spoken or written: "The brain tends to treat each set of homogeneous units as a simple set," he said in an email. "There's no substantial difference between storing or recalling from long-term memory seven languages, or seven systems of writing."

The question is, Why is there a limit at all? One scientific model of these working memory limits suggests that items in memory begin to compete with each other, endangering the mind's ability to keep any one item in clear view. Scientists don't really know why there's a limit; it doesn't appear to confer any evolutionary advantage. However, it bolsters the conclusion by linguist Peter Skehan that talented language learners (like C.J. and Chris-topher) are "memory-driven learners." They can put a lot of things into memory and retain them. They can also retrieve them efficiently without mixing them up. It doesn't explain how Mezzofanti was able to maneuver so sprightly among his languages, though. Perhaps there are undiscovered individuals out there with more powerful working memories.

"I don't know many women who collect stamps or coins," Alexander said to me on one of my visits. He wanted to know if I had ever considered polyglottery as a kind of collecting behavior, perhaps an obsessive one. Maybe it would explain why so many hyperpolyglots were men.

Only one famous hyperpolyglot that I'd read about, George Henry Borrow (1803–1881), who had studied forty-two languages, seemed to fit the profile of someone with obsessive-compulsive disorder (OCD), a psychiatric illness that affects about 1 to 3 percent of adults. Borrow had to touch a series of mundane objects in the correct sequence; otherwise, he feared, something would happen to his mother.

Other hyperpolyglots had a touch of this, too. Alexander keeps records—overdetailed ones, some might say—and became visibly agitated if he hadn't put in time on his languages. There was also Elihu Burritt's rigid accounting of studying and blacksmithing, and Christopher, and Krebs. Certainly there were care and focus, but none of them was crippled by a compulsion.

I also didn't meet a hyperpolyglot who resembled a chronic hoarder, who collect such huge masses of worthless items (newspapers, food, scrap metal, car parts, matchbooks) that it interferes with their daily lives and their families. They do take pride in the grammars and dictionaries they amass. Yet stacks of books, as a mere fact, point to bibliophilia, not hyperpolyglottery. The hoarders I read about in the research literature can't turn away from their junk long enough to have a normal life.

Why are there more male hyperpolyglots? One answer is that speaking a lot of languages is a geek macho thing. In addition to my survey of hyperpolyglots, I had one set up for monolinguals, too. By chance, perhaps, this one was answered mostly by women, more than 30 percent of whom said they'd studied three languages or more, though the survey asked for people who spoke only one. It seemed that a woman is less likely to say she "speaks" or "knows" a language if she studied it at some point in the past, while a man, wanting to display his giant repertoire, would include it.

The Geschwind-Galaburda hypothesis interested me the most: the idea that because male hormones in the fetus affect the developing brain, the effects of asymmetrical development of brain hemispheres would be seen mostly in males. Females also have male hormones, but they have fewer and would be less affected.

Male brains. Hormones. This brought me directly to the doorstep of the very thing I'd avoided all along.

Does the hyperpolyglot neural tribe overlap with the autistic population? Like many good questions, it has its traps. After all, there have been some high-profile autistic savants who've performed impressive language feats. Daniel Tammet, a writer and educator with high-functioning autism, once was challenged to learn Icelandic in two weeks and then went on Icelandic television to speak it. Intriguingly, Karl Zilles had mentioned that Emil Krebs seemed like someone with Asperger's. Yet I didn't want to get caught up in people's medical histories, making diagnoses I wasn't qualified to make. Nor did I want to follow the fashion of seeing autism in every eccentric's biography.

I thought I'd be able to recognize someone with autism or Asperger's syndrome fairly easily—someone who seems very socially awkward, with flat affect, who demands routine and fears deviations, and who might be able to perform brilliantly in some area, such as mental calculations. Admittedly, I had gotten this notion from the movie *Rain Man*. The autistic character that Dustin Hoffman plays, Raymond Babbitt, was in fact based on a real-life savant named Kim Peek, but no hyperpolyglot I spoke to resembled either Peek or Hoffman's portrayal of him.

Yet they could be called "neuroatypical." And part of their neuroatypicality might come from something shared with autism, particularly high-functioning autists. British psychologist and autism expert Simon Baron-Cohen has argued that autism represents the extreme form of a cognitive style that is adept at, and given to, "systemizing." When someone systemizes, she (or, more likely, he) is watching inputs and outputs to a system, relating the two, and observing how they vary.

Baron-Cohen defines systemizing as an attribute of the "male brain," which more biological males have (he acknowledges that biological females can also have male brains). Hence Baron-Cohen's "extreme male brain" theory of autism.

Perhaps a tendency to systemize would help explain why scientists score higher than nonscientists on a test that measures autistic traits. It might also explain why mathematicians, physical scientists, computer scientists, and engineers score higher than doctors, veterinarians, and biologists. Baron-Cohen has also found that autism occurs more frequently in the offspring of physics, mathematics, and engineering students than it does of those of literature students.

Baron-Cohen had also done some relevant work on the obsessional interests of children with autism, autism spectrum disorders, and Asperger's syndrome. He hypothesized that systemizers would find mechanical systems more interesting than social systems. Or as he put it, they would be more readily interested in "folk physics"—a commonsense knowledge about how objects and systems behave in the world—than in "folk psychology." In a survey of children with Tourette's, autism, or Asperger's, the autistic children were more often obsessed with machines, vehicles, physical systems, computers, astronomy, building, spinning objects, and lights than with beliefs, crafts, food, or sports. They were also more obsessed with folk physics than the kids with Tourette's.

Could language count as an obsessional interest? Baron-Cohen asked parents whether their kids engaged in "echoing, collecting words, phrases, and learning languages." Only a quarter of the children had this as an obsessional interest, about the same number as those obsessed with sports and games. The desire to make lists or "taxonomies" was three times as large; and surprisingly, only 35 percent of these systemizing children were interested in mathematics and numbers.

This is a small point about people with autism. But it sheds some light on the sort of brains that might be extraordinary at learning languages.

Chapter 17

ne of my visits to Berkeley to see Alexander Arguelles coincided with a conference on brain mapping in San Francisco. As I rode the train across the bay from Berkeley, I hoped that I might find something there to help me connect what I knew about hyperpolyglots with what others knew about brains. At the conference, I was supposed to meet up with Susanne Reiterer, an Austrian neuroscientist pursuing the neurological basis of what she calls "phonetic language talent." Her specialty is a gift for mimicry: people who can "do voices," parodists, actors. A vivacious brunette in dark-rimmed glasses, she described her own phonetic talent, and how her research is an attempt to explain it.

At her university in Germany, she and her research team have been comparing good mimics and bad mimics using psychological tests and brain imaging. Some Germans without any Hindi skills could trick native speakers of Hindi into believing they were themselves Hindi speakers. Each of these exceptional mimics had strong verbal ability, good working memory, and a sophisticated ability to discriminate between musical tones and rhythms, particularly in singing.

She told me that before the study, they had anticipated finding a lot of people like author Joseph Conrad—someone who adopted a new language as an adult, but despite excellent grammatical abilities always spoke with a thick accent.

"We did not find too many clear-cut Joseph Conrads!" she told me. Instead, she observed cognitive trade-offs: someone who is particularly talented in acquiring grammar and words may be a poor mimic, for example. She also found something distinct about the successful mimics' brains. When she did fMRIs, she found that the talented mimics had lower levels of activation in brain regions related to speech—in essence, their brains didn't have to try very hard because they used oxygen supplies efficiently. By contrast, the mimics who couldn't fool native speakers (and who were presumably less talented) used oxygen less efficiently—those regions had to work harder to produce speech.

Interestingly, the good mimics' brains were more efficient whether they were speaking German (their native language) or producing English, Tamil, or Hindi sounds. And the less talented mimics used glucose and oxygen less efficiently when producing either language. Reiterer suspects there may be a structural difference in the neural pathways of the more talented brains that leads to an enhanced connectivity among various parts of the brain during thinking tasks. In turn, this connectivity allows the neural circuits involved in language processing to work more efficiently.

Reiterer's work addresses one component of language aptitude, the ability to hear and produce sounds. One specific brain area that may be involved in this is the primary auditory cortex (also known as Heschl's gyrus). On the brain-as-globe model, it's located right around India. Neuroscientist Narly Golestani has studied the brain structure of phoneticians—those who work with speech sounds in a variety of languages that they don't necessarily speak—and found their primary auditory cortexes to be anatomically more complex than those in non-phonetician brains. Specifically, their cortexes have more finger-like convolutions, or gyri, made of white matter, which give them more surface area.

Unlike other kinds of brain differences (such as the arrangement of cell bodies in Krebs's brain), it isn't likely that this one can arise through practice or training; at least, no one has observed the human brain growing convolutions in this region after birth. This may explain why some people are more likely to take a job in phonetics. And it may further explain why some people find more pleasure in listening to foreign languages than others. In a previous study, Golestani looked at the brain structures of people who learned the sounds of a foreign language more quickly than other people. The faster learners' brains had larger left Heschl's gyri, due to more white matter.

Another neural signature of highly proficient language learners has been located in the left insula, which lies somewhere (to use the brain-as-globe metaphor) under the Arabian Sea. While the insula is long regarded as a mysterious zone dealing with bodily functions, the era of brain scanning has discovered a new role for it: a control center for emotions, consciousness, and working memory. The left insula has been shown in fMRI studies to activate more strongly in bilinguals who have equal abilities in their two languages.* In people whose languages aren't equal, this area shows weaker levels of activation.

The left insula plays a key role in what's known as "subvocal rehearsal." One example of this rehearsal is the automatic process of having a foreign-sounding word in your head before you actually say it. Thus, more active neural circuitry in this area might engrave new sounds into the brain more quickly or durably. "The successful engagement of such neural circuitry," writes the lead researcher, Michael Chee, "may correspond to vocabulary growth."

Hence, Alexander's success with his shadowing technique. Shadowing involves trying to pronounce the sounds of a foreign language (usually from a recording) at the same instant that one hears them. I've tried it and can say that the effect is intense, and very different from the "listen and repeat" format. Shadowing may exploit a mental routine for storing information called the "phonological loop," which is the part of working memory devoted to speech sounds. Someone's ability to automatically remember and accurately repeat nonsense words is a good predictor of foreign-language ability. The converse is also true: people with a disrupted or damaged phonological loop can't learn new foreign

---

*These were Singaporean students being tested on their knowledge of Chinese and English; strictly speaking, exam scores, not abilities, were being compared.

words. If you shadow, you're relying on the loop; shadow a lot, and you can build the loop's strength.

Of the other components of aptitude—the ability to analyze grammar and the ability to learn new words—word learning has been more thoroughly studied, because more is known about where these abilities are located in the brain. Here, too, there are distinct neural signatures of higher performance. A team from Germany observed that people better at acquiring new words had more sustained activity in one part of the brain, the hippocampus (which is heavily involved in long-term memory). The authors speculated that brains vary in how they respond to the tasks of learning languages because there may be differences in the hippocampus, how the hippocampus attaches to the white matter, or what they called "genetic differences in neurotransmitter functions."

In reality, no one would say that language talents reside solely in one area of the brain. Susanne Reiterer says that a talent for mimicry isn't a "splinter skill"—her high performers had higher levels of performance in other language abilities, which suggests they're tied together and involve many parts of the brain. The roles of the phonological loop and working memory suggest that higher-level cognitive skills play a huge role both in learning a sole extra language very well and in learning many languages. And since the biological basis of these skills is hereditary, whole families might belong to the hyperpolyglot neural tribe.

The idea of a genetic component to hyperpolyglottism is supported by evidence that cognitive capacities, such as working memory, executive function, and memory, as well as structural capacities such as plasticity, are hereditary. Back in 2004, when Dick Hudson sent news about N. and his family to the LINGUIST List, one of the respondents was Richard Sproat, a linguist now at the Oregon Health and Science University, who was intrigued by the possibility that language talent itself might be a heritable trait. Since the 1990s, scientists have linked language deficits to a genetic component, as in the case of the KE family, whose inability to produce certain grammatical expressions led to the location of a gene called FOXP2 in the mid-1990s, and a specific mutation of that gene in 2001.

But when it comes to an exceptional language talent, rather than a deficit, it is difficult to get families to sign up for a genetic study, perhaps because they don't need to be cured of anything. Sproat exchanged a few emails with N., but then the replies stopped. When I contacted N. myself, he said he had discussed the issue with his family and did not want to be interviewed.

Before N. stopped writing, however, he did offer Sproat a few more details about his globe-trotting polyglot grandfather. "When we arrived in Thailand, I was sure he did not know any of the language," N. said. But after two weeks his grandfather was arguing with market vendors in Thai. In the late 1960s, N. spent eighteen months in Thailand with the US military, where he learned some of the language. When he later tried conversing with his grandfather in Thai, N. said, "he was able to communicate on a higher level than I knew."

N.'s disappearance is frustrating because in his original message, he mentioned another member of his family: a seven-year-old granddaughter. "She can count in three languages up to one hundred and she is able to pick out words spoken in other languages in public and tell you what they mean," he wrote. N. and his hyperpolyglot family may have retreated from public view for now. But they, and others like them, could provide more fascinating insights into the language abilities we all have.

If the language superlearner's brain has a kind of optimal design, could someone gain advantage by mimicking that design? The US military is particularly interested in neuroenhancements that target language learning. I came across a report that mused on the impact such enhancements would have on military forces and called for more research into improving a variety of cognitive abilities in adults, including learning multiple languages.

At the conference where I met Susanne Reiterer, I was surprised to learn about a technology called transcranial direct current stimulation (or, tDCS), which could be deployed widely tomorrow. Using a small device that's simple enough to make at home (you need only a 9-volt battery, electrodes, and resistors), you can deliver very small amounts of electricity to areas of your brain through your skull. Depending on how you set the current, you can either stimulate or suppress how strongly

neurons fire. If the electrode is attached to the positive part of the battery, the neurons are stimulated; if attached to the negative part, the
neurons' firing is suppressed. Electrical charges could help adults manage their brain plasticity by removing some of the brakes that curtail
plasticity in adulthood.

In some initial studies to test the safety of this device, people who
received currents from the positive part of the battery could recall new
nonsense words 20 percent better than people who got sham currents
or who received currents from the negative part of the battery. After
a week, the positive effect had disappeared. In another study, people's
abilities to generate words that started with a particular letter increased
by 20 percent as well. Direct current has also been shown to increase
people's visual memory by 110 percent.

Before you rush out to buy batteries and electrodes, you ought to
know that the electrodes deliver electricity to the brain haphazardly.
Biomedical engineers have tracked where this electricity flows in the
skull, and it goes all over, flowing through eyesockets and pooling under
the frontal lobe. A cranium full of sustained electrical charge could have
a range of unpredictable effects.

Still, 20 percent increases are substantial, especially if they come
after only a twenty-minute exposure to the device. Would anyone try it?
I asked Helen Abadzi (who had an appetite for technologies that assisted
her language learning) if she'd try tDCS. She replied that she'd worry
about safety risks, especially since the improvements aren't huge. If you
want big improvements, she said, chew gum.

Gum? Sure enough, chewing gum has been shown to improve a person's immediate recall of learned words by some 24 percent. Long-term
recall improves by a larger 36 percent. To get the benefit, you actually
have to chew the gum as you are studying; for some reason you can't
merely move your jaw up and down. I also discovered that drinking sage
tea increases one's recall of words modestly, as does the odor of rosemary.
Something as mundane as coffee provides a benefit, too. Drinking two
cups of coffee increases neuronal activity in the frontal lobe, where working memory is controlled, and in the anterior cingulum (on the brain-as-
globe it sits under eastern Europe), where attention is controlled.

I collected other manipulations that some people mentioned offhandedly. For instance, oxytocin, the so-called love hormone. Children learn best in environments in which they're ideally bonded with caregivers, which means that a lot of oxytocin reception is going on. Maybe, someone said, you could sniff oxytocin before a language class to boost memory function.

Also, dopamine. This is a neurotransmitter that signals pleasure in the brain, but it also has important connections to cognitive functions. It's even been suggested that declining dopamine levels—a symptom of age—are partly responsible for shutting down brain plasticity in language learning. Manipulating these dopamine levels as you learn might allow you to better retain new words.

Manipulating hippocampal activity also makes language learning easier. One way to stimulate the hippocampus is to take amphetamines. In one experiment, use of d-amphetamine and levodopa (a precursor to the production of dopamine, and used in the treatment of Parkinson's disease) accelerated vocabulary learning by 20 percent in healthy subjects. The converse has also been shown: if you suppress hippocampal activity with certain drugs, you can retard associative learning.

Then there are interventions so bold they can only be done on animals. Injections of a protein called brain-derived neurotrophic factor (or, BDNF), which plays a crucial role in helping to shape long-term memories, may improve the ability of rats to navigate mazes. Because physical exercise increases BDNF secretions, at least in rats, this may help explain why exertion improves memory (though it has also been suggested that the memory boost comes from adrenaline).

While it's interesting to speculate about potential neuroenhancers for language learning, the conclusions remain elusive. Caterina Breitenstein, the German neuroscientist who tested d-amphetamine and levodopa, said that the substances in her studies produced rather subtle effects. And not all of the subjects responded to the substances. Presumably, users would want pharmaceutical enhancers to work reliably to be worth any potential side effects.

But could you design a hyperpolyglot in vitro? John Schumann, UCLA applied linguist, equivocated.

"I suppose at some time in the future, it might be possible to enhance the chemical milieu in the womb of a mother as the child is developing," he replied, "and direct a large number of neurons to the left hemi-sphere language areas." There was one problem: you might not produce a hyperpolyglot. The brain is a leaky thing, not a precise machine at all, he noted. You couldn't be sure what you were setting into motion. A bad science fiction plot, for sure.

"If you enhanced aspects of Wernicke's area, you might produce a good signer, or a guy with particularly acute hearing. Broca's is a motor area, a pattern-learning area. The guy could turn into somebody who could count cards at a casino." Then he said something that chilled me. "I'm not sure how this could be enhanced," he said, "without creating a potential monster." And we ignore the tissues of causality at our peril.

Some studies of successful language learners have suggested that they're more "open to new experiences" than the rest of us. Temptingly, psychologist Alexander Guiora proposed that we have a self that's bound up in our native language, a "language ego," which needs to be loose and more permeable to learn a new language. Those with more fluid ego boundaries, like children and people who have drunk some alcohol, are more willing to sound not like themselves, which means they have better accents in the new language.

Such permeability was reflected in answers I received through my online survey. Wrote one person (a native English-speaking male who lives in Taiwan and says he speaks twenty languages), "You have to be a good observer and you have to be able to act and mimic the way others talk, not just accent but body language and intonation and pitch. Most language learners feel embarrassed with this 'acting' and so are blocked from the start from achieving much. Just start by doing this and you'll really go far in your language pursuits. Because it's the adoption of a new identity for yourself."

He added, "I am the epitome of adaptation. Most people who encounter me cannot guess where I'm from because my whole body and actions adopt the culture that I'm in." Someone else wrote, "The good language learner has the ability to accept the role of a child when it comes to speaking/writing a new language. Of being naïve, foolish, stumbling, and inarticulate but also curious, open-minded, and full of energy."

It struck me that the archetypal hyperpolyglot could be a kind of Peter Pan. As long as you're a neophyte in a given language, you never have to present an adult self in it. You'll never be judged for not knowing what an adult would do. Maybe, like Peter Pan himself, you're avoiding reality. And, getting a bit psychoanalytic here, you're revisiting your infant experiences at the maternal lips and ears, that time when the boundaries between yourself and others was more fluid.

But the neural tribe theory suggests that psychological traits—such as ego boundaries and neuroses—don't define the hyperpolyglot, given that cognitive abilities and styles play a bigger role in successful outcomes. It's true that, for some hyperpolyglots, such as Alexander and Ken Hale, delving into language was a response to an emotional trauma. That may be where an identity as a language learner saved them. Yet the question remains: Why did they turn to language? It's useful, I think, to look at some properties of language in order to see how attractive it could be to people who fit Baron-Cohen's definition of systemizers.

To the mind of a systemizer, language's capacity to be ordered is immediately apparent, and lends itself to myriad combinations that can never be fully explored. Some of the order you can impose: you could decide to list all the words you know according to the sounds they start with, the number of syllables in them, when you learned them, how often they're used, what they mean, or which ones in different languages mean the same thing. You can also tally up words, pages, minutes, hours, idioms, errors, parts of speech: How many nouns do you know? How many verbs? And if you get bored with that, you can alphabetize your dictionaries, grammars, and phrase books, or organize them by language family, genre, or publisher.

You can also observe patterns, attempt to "crack the code" and derive rules, make predictions, and look for exceptions. Learning a language involves technical systems of repeating written or spoken words and sentences. These may be borrowed and adopted (by a language-learning tool, such as Assimil, Pimsleur, or Rosetta Stone) or invented (as in the cases of Lomb Káto and Alexander). They can test the way their brain performs, given its inputs, and how well it links to the tongue and hands. Language is also a natural system: you can watch children acquire it, much as you can reflect on your own acquisition and your inevitable loss. It's a social system, linked to cultures, nations, and regions.

Not to be underestimated is the way that the informational richness of language arises out of a finite set of basic units. While the average number of consonants in a language is about twenty-two, and the average number of vowels is five or six,* the possible combinations of these are vast. According to language typologists, there are seven basic ways of arranging subjects, verbs, and objects in sentences (the great majority put the subject first),† and there are only six kinds of words for *no*.‡ (Other ways, if they existed, probably went extinct.)

Let's say that not only are you a systemizer, but also that you're shy. The subtleties of social interaction challenge and maybe frustrate you. One response is simple: avoid people. The other response is to undertake language in a way that makes it the physics of people, tracking the inputs and outputs of sociability and relationships. If you lack a strong ability to empathize with other people, you might use your feel for language's systemic qualities as a crutch. As a result, over a lifetime, your explorations make you intimate with languages rather than with the people who speak them. Yet the dominant paradigm of language learning of your age stresses communication, so you spend time communicating. You haven't abandoned empathizing; you're simulating an empathizer's tools.

A few other cognitive abilities accompany your systemizing. One is memory, perhaps a powerful declarative memory and a durable phonological loop. You also have muscular executive function skills. But neither of these really hooks up to your systemizing tendencies. What

---

* The *World Atlas of Language Structures* says that the number of consonants in a language ranges from 6 to 122; the number of vowels ranges between 2 and 14. Rotokas, a language in Papua New Guinea, has only 6 consonants; southern Khoisan, spoken in Botswana, has 122 (many of which are clicks). http://wals.info/feature/1 Yimas, a language spoken in Papua New Guinea, has only 2 vowels, whereas German has 14. http://wals.info/feature/2.

†The topic of word order is more complicated, however, and an appropriately detailed discussion can be found at http://wals.info/chapter/81.

‡Or as the *World Atlas* puts it, there are six "morphemes signalling clausal negation in declarative sentences." There are multiple other ways to answer a yes-no question in the negative that don't involve morphemes; see http://wals.info/chapter/112.

does, however, is that you're able to manipulate the plasticity of your brain. For adults, plasticity must be regulated with various "brakes," such as regulating new cell growth and manipulating the electrical patterns between neurons.

Scientists are now homing in on ways to biochemically provoke critical periods and their "exuberant plasticity." (Currently, it's the vision system that's best studied; experts presume the same mechanisms also apply to language.) These manipulations are biochemical, and can come from outside or inside the body. Those from the body itself we can find ways to stimulate. As Daphne Bavelier, a cognitive scientist at the University of Rochester, wrote in a 2010 article, "It would be ideal to endogenously recapitulate brain states conducive to plasticity in a noninvasive but targeted manner." In other words, it would be good if you could trigger mental states that are beneficial to learning without doing anything too drastic to the body. Which might produce a monster.

One such noninvasive method—immersive activities—can trigger better learning. In the visual realm, this is done through video games, especially action video games. At a biochemical level, such intense activity over long periods of time involves neurotransmitters, especially the dopamine that signals that a certain behavior is enjoyable. "Gaming is also associated with 'flow,' or the sense that one is able to meet the challenges of one's environment with appropriate skills," Bavelier wrote. This flow triggers biochemical factors that encourage plasticity. This notion of flow is "characterized by a deep sense of enjoyment which goes beyond satisfying a need, and rather occurs when a person achieves something unexpected that has a sense of novelty." The promise of this line of inquiry, says Bavelier, is that they are no longer isolating external or internal factors, but attempting to see how the two sets interact.

In the realm of language, no one knows what optimal organization of cells in the brain should give one the greatest language learning capacity. But we can recognize that hyperpolyglots undoubtedly have an ability to flow with language material. Otherwise, they wouldn't persist in repetitious activities that bore most other people.

———

The two questions I'm most often asked about hyperpolyglots are why and how they pursue languages the way they do. I held off answering both questions for some time, worried that I didn't know enough or that I'd get swamped in biographical particulars and lose a chance at the big picture. I imagined the Italian librarian Franco Pasti punching me in the shoulder, saying, "It was a case study. *A case study.*"

I was right to be apprehensive, because humans seem to be hard-wired to prefer reductive explanations. There is no core to the hyperpolyglot phenomenon. By investigating and explaining the origins of hyperpolyglottism, I discovered that the brain, culture, and individual biography interact with each other to produce someone like Mezzofanti or Graham Cansdale. A person's type of personality doesn't predict whether or not they'll be good at learning languages (though, contrary to the conventional wisdom, introverts are consistently more successful than extroverts).

Cultural background does play a role by incubating cognitive assets and giving talents resources on which to grow. Historical and economic forces also make up an important part of the story, not only by determining which languages one learns and what one does with them, but by calling forth and channeling the neurological traits that serve learning, speaking, and using a lot of languages. Such forces also shape who happens to have access to what opportunities for school, travel, and even literacy. Recall how European wars provided Mezzofanti with sick soldiers in polyglot hospitals, and how European colonialism gave young Cameroonian men the need to learn more languages.

Clearly, the brain is an important part of the story, and hyperpolyglots seem to have unusual neurological origins. Maybe this looks like a nostalgic return to the era when people believed in elite brains, but it's not. The new neuroscience is locating the neural signatures of high performance, figuring out how to manipulate the plasticity of specific brain systems, and trying to understand the genetic factors that impact cognitive abilities as well as disabilities.

I'm describing a neural tribe that existed before but has been made more visible by cultural trends. The polyglot ambition has intensified at the same time that technology has enabled its fulfillment. I've tried to describe how foreign-language learning has taken different forms throughout history—and how, in some cultures, people's brains were occupied with very different sorts of cognitive feats. I've also tried to account for the way certain abilities have been recognized as talents or impairments depending on their context. And I've tried to explain why people in multilingual societies tend to learn far fewer languages than exist in their surroundings.

Hyperpolyglots are made when the linguistic world order gets into certain brains and when certain brains are projected into any given linguistic world order. Hyperpolyglots can't help but be linguistic outsiders, because they're multilinguals who learn more languages than they need to participate in their immediate community but far fewer than they need to participate in an imagined global community. To the degree that they're already educated elites, they're people for whom the exercise of neuroplasticity is *elective,* not required. English is spoken so commonly throughout the world that if one is already a mother-tongue English speaker, pursuing other languages is something of a luxury, in global terms.

When you look at brain plasticity in the context of the global economy, the questions "Why do they do it?" and "How do they do it?" take on a deeper meaning.

Why do they do it? *In order to improve their neuroplasticity.*

How do they do it? *By improving their neuroplasticity.*

They're not ashamed that they'll never sound like native speakers. Rather, they fear being *only* native speakers. They don't care that there's no polyglot community—being outside of a speech community is exactly the point.

What about the rest of us? We resign ourselves to stiff brains. We remain happy as linguistic insiders, staying safely where we feel we belong.

Part 5

ARRIVAL:

The Hyperpolyglot

of Flanders

Chapter 18

As far as I can tell, the neural tribe of hyperpolyglots has been gathered only twice, both times in Belgium. Through a bit of luck, I found the name of the man who had brought them together.

His name was Eugeen Hermans, and I met him in the town square of Leuven, a university town near Brussels, where we sat outside at a café. Bald and handsomely craggy, he was born in 1943 and is retired now, with fond memories of his career as the principal of a language school in Hasselt, where Flemish businessmen came to find more outlets for their goods and housewives came to broaden their minds. In 1986, he told me, he attended a party with a US consul fluent in seven languages. He can't be the only man in the world apart from the Belgians and perhaps the Norwegians and the Dutch who speaks a lot of foreign languages, Hermans thought. Why don't I try to discover if there are other people like him? Let's start with Flanders and see.

After finding a bank to cosponsor the contest, Hermans held a press conference to call for contestants who had oral skills in at least seven languages. He set some thorough, if not ingenious, rules: none could be dialects; all had to be ones that a government would vouch for. No dead languages allowed. None could be artificial languages (Esperanto was out). Even with these restrictions, Hermans had to telephone-screen all the people who wanted to participate in order to pare down the entries to twenty-six contestants who were to be tested in a pool of forty-seven languages. The judges could award up to twenty points in each language, and could also dock points for ignorance. A Dutch speaker might try to fake his way through Afrikaans, a related dialect (though a national language, so it qualified), but if he couldn't speak it to the judge's satisfaction, he lost points. Overall, the point scheme gave several routes to a win. One could accrue many points in relatively few languages. Or one could accrue fewer points per language over a larger number of them.

Hermans knew he'd achieved something special, bringing members of the tribe together in this way. "You had people meeting each other who were in their environment seen as a kind of rarity, who suddenly found themselves with kindred spirits, with people who were more or less alike, interested in the same thing, having the same skills," he said. "They all had the greatest respect for each other."

I asked him if he knew what sort of person the winner might be.

He said he had seen so many students at his school who spoke five, six languages, and he assumed the winner would be one of them. He was surprised, he said, by the person who won.

Among the polyglots, myth is the uncanny double of science. To help me navigate their qualities, I turned, every once in a while, to a book by a French zoologist named Bernard Heuvelmans, *On the Track of Unknown Animals,* where he argued that undiscovered big mammals could still be discovered—if zoologists were willing to listen to folktales.

Consider the okapi, a four-legged animal native to Central Africa. Depending on how familiar you are with African mammals, the okapi looks like either a tan zebra with an unusually long neck or a giraffe with an unusually short one. They're staple exotics in modern zoos. But what the zoo's information plaques won't tell you is that Western naturalists of the nineteenth century once denied that the okapi could be real. They believed that African tribesman had concocted them or had simply seen a mutant zebra. Once zoologists touched okapi skins and then witnessed actual animals with their own eyes, the creatures were accepted as a new species. Heuvelmans discussed other cases, the brown bear of Kamchatka, the mountain gorilla, the Komodo dragon, the bonobo, and the coelacanth, all creatures whose existences were long doubted by scientists but attested to by local people. He had unrelenting faith in scientific progress, but he had a somewhat cynical view of scientists themselves, who (in his opinion) lacked his sense that lost worlds might still exist. To find those creatures, you had to be willing to listen to the locals. Though a scientist himself, Heuvelmans was comfortable living with mythologies. I had to learn the same.

I set out to write *Mezzofanti's Gift* along the lines of a book about, say, some fabled creature like the Loch Ness monster. Such a book would acknowledge the tangle of myth, history, and science behind the monster by investigating old reports of monster sightings, reports which, for any number of reasons, crumble under inspection. Off the author goes to Loch Ness itself, where cameras and sonar are unpacked, crews are assembled, locals interviewed. The author goes out in a boat, criss-crosses the waters, hoping for that crucial face-to-face encounter with the beast. The author does learn what it's like to be on the water, which he rather enjoys, and he likes the culture of Nessie searchers, with their self-serious testing of myth and folklore. From this experience the author develops a list of questions and a set of conclusions about more ordinary forms of biological diversity. He returns from his wanderings enlightened, engaged. But not with the creature in a cage.

Proceeding along those same lines, I came to feel that Heuvelmans was a kindred spirit. However, my project differs from the standard cryptozoological account in this main respect: I made a real discovery, and that discovery was not a single species but an entire tribe.

Recall that I wanted a modern figure, someone with oral skills (not just a reader or translator) whose abilities had been not merely reported by observers or claimed by the speaker but evaluated by a range of educated observers. I wanted evidence, the results to the natural experiment of hyperpolyglottery, and the answer to the question, What is the upper limit of the ability to learn and speak languages?

Johan Vandewalle, possibly a twenty-first-century Emil Krebs, had been in and out of the media since 1987, but he proved elusive. He didn't return my emails begging him for an interview, and when I took the direct route and phoned him, the man who answered pointed to his website, which is in Dutch. The German newspapers at the time of the contest had portrayed him as a solitary young man, a trained engineer obsessed with languages. I wanted to gently prod that image and get his perspective on the Flanders contest. I finally got in touch through his wife, and we arranged a meeting in the small city of Aalst, near Brussels, where he lives.

I arrived in Aalst a day early to see the place, a former manufacturing stronghold, and I wandered through the bubbly shopping district, contemplating a coffee or a beer somewhere far from the rock band that had set up a stage on the square. Suddenly a man caught my eye, a house-husband, dressed in baggy clothes, his shoulders pulled down by all the packages hung in his hands. He seemed lost in thought, as if his body was being operated by remote control. I don't know why it struck me then. I wasn't looking for him, and I couldn't have picked him out from the photos I'd seen. Yet I knew. *That's the hyperpolyglot,* I thought. Then: *That's absurd. You know that bookish scholars don't always look the part.* Briefly I contemplated following him to see where he'd go, but even if it was he, what could I do with that knowledge, except describe how he carried his groceries?

Johan was set to pick me up the next morning, from the Irish pub attached to my hotel. When he shuffled into the pub, I recognized him immediately, not from the photos, but from the town square the day before.

I was glad not to have followed him—his house, a pale yellow row house, was a bit of a drive, which we made in silence. By now I knew we wouldn't sit in his dark basement, sipping water from paper cups. Indeed, in the kitchen of his comfortably furnished house, his wife, Linda, had laid out frangipane tart and coffee, and we sat down to eat with their two children, a boy and a girl. We talked for a long time into a dinner of cheese, fruit, meats, and bread, discussing languages and his hyperpolyglot life.

Johan has brown hair, wears square glasses, and speaks in a soft voice. Nowadays, he's the head of a Turkish-language department at Ghent University College, where he's finishing a PhD in Turkish, Uzbek, and Russian grammar. He appears to be well fed and well loved; he meets one's gaze with equanimity, laughs at jokes, pauses to let Linda finish a comment—and she always has a comment to finish. Herself a language adventurer, she studied Mandarin and Russian in preparation for a trip on the Trans-Siberian railroad, and she wooed Johan in the early 1990s by writing a Christmas card to him in a language he'd invented. Somehow he was lucky enough to find one of what are likely few women on the planet who suit him. Johan grew up in a Flemish family, so he had early experiences with three languages. There are thousands of polyglots in Flanders, he said; learning foreign languages has a lot of prestige, and "it's a normal thing to study a foreign language in one's leisure time, just like doing sports." His first non-Belgian language was Turkish, which he discovered when he was thirteen, on a trip with his father, a mathematics teacher, and which he dove into after another trip two years later, in 1975. Turkish is an agglutinating language, which means that you add grammatical particles to the ends of nouns and verbs. Because of a language reform in the 1930s, most of the exceptions, the language learner's bugbears, had been cleaned out. It was, in other words, the perfect language for a systemizer with a strong memory. "Turkish saved my life," Johan told me. (Later he said this was too strong, and wanted me to say that "Turkish had entered his life to stay.")

When the Polyglot of Flanders contest was announced in 1987, his father pushed him to join. By then he knew Turkish and related languages—Uzbek, Kyrgyz, Kazakh, Turkmen, Azerbaijani—most of which were spoken in then-Soviet territory, so dictionaries and grammars were in Russian. To get at them, he learned Russian. (Because each was an official language of a Soviet republic, Eugeen Hermans would accept them.) To grasp Arabic and Persian loanwords in Turkish that had been cleaned out in the 1930s, he picked up those languages too.

When the contest organizers called him, he gave them a list of the languages he had studied. Only then, he said, did he realize that he had thirty-one. Seven were dead languages; in another seven he described his knowledge as superficial. At the time, he was in the middle of his military service. Before the contest he found an abandoned barracks in which to lay out his books and spent weeks practicing his languages every night.

When I heard this, I was disappointed. In a way he was no different from the hyperpolyglots who kept half a dozen or so languages active with many more on ice. I'd hoped that he stepped from his life straight into the contest, all of his languages at the ready. Even the Polyglot of Flanders didn't work that way.

Would it have been possible to keep all those languages activated? I asked.

Johan scoffed at the idea. "What is the use of this?" he asked. "My Kyrgyz is not as good as it's been, but I don't expect a Kyrgyz to ring my bell today or tomorrow." To keep all the languages up, he'd need a schedule: get up at six o'clock, do some Tajik, switch to Turkmen at seven, and so on. "I find such a thing absurd," he said. He had never aimed to know as many languages as he could. "What I like is going to the country and functioning in that language, in that society." (I recalled Rainer Ganahl's shopper/tourist paradigm of language learning.) Last summer, he said, they traveled to Egypt; he had bought a book on hieroglyphics and happily deciphered temple walls and obelisks. "Some people may be indifferent to that," he said, "but for me, I find it important, to have that kind of amazement. To stay amazed by language."

He used to think anyone could learn languages, and that one didn't need to be special to do it well. He stated this opinion over and over in his early interviews. Now, he's of a different mind. After twenty years of teaching languages, he doesn't think that hard work is solely central to success. "I think some people really have a predisposition for learning languages or are better equipped than other people," he said.

On the day of the competition, which took place in a drab meeting hall in a government building, contestants went from table to table and talked for ten minutes in each language with native-speaker judges. They took only five-minute breaks between. Vandewalle was tested in twenty-two languages. Five of these were languages he knew superficially. Several weeks afterward, his father met him at the train station with a garland on the car. "That's when I knew," Johan said. He was twenty-six years old. He'd won with a grand point total of 251, with nineteen languages in which he had "proven to possess communicative competences." The runner-up, a Russian professor, had scored only 181 points. Some languages, like Gaelic, Vandewalle hadn't scored in (he could only say, "I'm a soldier"); others, like Latin and Old Slavic, hadn't counted.

The shy student, now king of the language pile, the *Polyglot van Vlaanderen,* was about to have a grand whirl. He did more than seventy interviews for radio, print media, and television. An appearance on Turkish television won him hundreds of marriage proposals. Champagne corks popped on flights to Turkey. So great was the Turkish girls' faith in his fame, or in the Belgian postal service, that some of them addressed their envelopes to The Polyglot of Flanders, Venice of the North.

Johan Vandewalle after winning the Polyglot of Flanders/Babel Prize, 1987. (*Courtesy of Linda Gezels*)

In his own mind, Vandewalle had a clear sense of what had happened. Hermans had come up with rules; the contest had applied the rules; and he'd won. With different rules, someone else might have won. In the resulting frenzy of attention, this was overlooked. "Johan Vandewalle speaks 22 languages fluently," blared the headlines. The attention amused him, but also bored him. "I had been asked the same questions . . . hundreds of times, and didn't want to start it again," he told me. "That really was the reason why I didn't participate in the second contest."

The *second* contest?

It was 1990, the blast of attention from the Polyglot of Flanders contest had worn off, and Eugeen Hermans, who had a promoter's flair, was looking for another hit. We couldn't do the same thing, he thought; Vandewalle, if he enters, will win again.

He decided to broaden it to the (then twelve) countries of the European Union. The Belgian changed some rules. You now had to have at least nine languages to enter, and provide diplomas, certificates, or letters from professors proving that you'd studied the languages. Scoring was now different, too. Instead of having a flat twenty points to award in each language, judges were to use a five-level scale (a "survival" level of at least fifteen hundred words; a pre-intermediate level; an intermediate level in which mistakes were occasional but vocabulary measured five or six thousand words; an advanced level, "achieved by a university graduate in foreign language studies"; and a mother-tongue level) and a precise number of points assigned to each level.

Judges could also give points for the overall repertoire. "If you learn all the Germanic languages and all the Romance languages, that's relatively easy," Hermans told me, "but if you have Chinese and Arabic and Spanish, that's an intellectually bigger performance than Spanish, French, and Italian," which might get more overall points. That would eliminate the possibility of a win based on using all the languages from a single family very well. The winner would be someone like Vandewalle.

Hermans also instructed judges to interrupt the contestants with questions of their own—to have a real conversation, something dynamic, in the moment. In the earlier contest, the best hyperpolyglots had very skillfully started the interaction, "because they know exactly what they can say and can't say."

Nearly two hundred people applied for the Polyglot of Europe contest, out of whom twenty finalists were identified: three Greeks (one of whom was Helen Abadzi), three English, two Scots, three Belgians, two Italians, two Danes, and one apiece from France, Germany, Portugal, the Netherlands, and Luxembourg. Johan Vandewalle wasn't one of them. He'd grown tired of telling the same story to every newspaper, every weekly magazine, every small local radio station, and answering the same questions, being treated like a curiosity, seldom with any scientific interest. *How many languages do you speak? Why do you study languages? What is your method? Always the focus on the method. What is the method?* Hermans was reluctant to push Johan into participating. Hermans himself had begun to wonder if he was doing something of value. Was it just showbiz? Was he exposing this person to too much attention? Was it really worth it?

———

Derick Herning, a Scotsman who grew up north of Edinburgh and now lives in the small town of Lerwick on the Shetland Islands, won the Polyglot of Europe contest after being tested in twenty-two languages. Because the rules of the second language game were more rigorous, we might say that Herning was more prodigious than even Vandewalle. Born in 1932 and now in his late seventies, Herning gives tours and plays organ for his church (he's a devout Christian, though he identifies himself as a "Jesuite," his own neologism) and relies on his wife, a Russian artist, to "turn on the Internet" for him (which, feistily witty, Herning phrases that way on purpose, I'm certain).

In a series of phone calls, he described his life of language learning, a familiar pattern I'd heard before. There was an early fascination with German during World War II, which he heard on BBC propaganda broadcasts, because it was the language of the enemy. High school French (which he rejected as "sissy" but was forced to study) and more German. Latin ("which was dry at the time, but helped in the long run") provided vocabulary for the Romance languages and grammatical preparation for the elaborate case systems of Russian, Finnish, Estonian, and Hungarian.

At Edinburgh University he majored in German, taught himself Dutch, became fascinated by Frisian; entered the army and learned Russian (another enemy's language), then worked in intelligence. He traveled a lot in Russia and Germany, fell in love with a German woman and lived in Germany for four years, learned Romanian in preparation for a trip to Moldova, and taught himself Gaelic.

He spun out a familiar narrative of accumulation, extended plasticity, and linguistic homelessness (but not despair). He moved to Lerwick in the late 1960s, learned Swedish, Icelandic, Faroese, the Swedish-Danish-Norwegian clump, and more Slavic languages. To me, Lerwick sounded like the far ends of the earth, but Derick assured me, it's a cosmopolitan harbor filled with sailors, fisherman, and yachters from all over Europe. In the mid-1990s, he made a name for himself as an interpreter for Bulgarian sailors who were on strike aboard a factory ship; once he escorted a psychotic Russian sailor back to Moscow.

I asked him why he saw opportunity where others might see a language barrier.

Derick thought for a moment. "I suppose it's an addiction. Other people get stuck on drugs. It's quite a healthy form of addiction."

"It's an interesting comparison, because when people don't have access to the thing they're addicted to, they have a negative physical reaction."

He then told me the following story. "At one time, I applied for a job as a headmaster at the Outer Hebrides, and I was on the short list for that job. The more I thought about it, the less it appealed to me. Okay, headmaster, oh, lovely. And then I thought, what am I going to do at the nights? The only language I could develop here is my Gaelic. I could have been desperately wrong about that. But I don't think the Western Isles have the same cosmopolitan atmosphere as the port of Lerwick. For my purposes, it was supreme. I thought, well, what am I going to do apart from going to the local pub and talk Gaelic to the locals? I could probably find a Gaelic-speaking wife, but the thought of speaking only Gaelic at home, Gaelic during the day, Gaelic at the night—that didn't appeal to me either."

In 1990, his life took a new turn. He related the contest and his sudden rise to fame in tones of alternating exasperation and pride. He was teaching German and some French at a Lerwick school whose headmaster told him about the Brussels contest. I think you should go in for it, he told Derick.

"I said 'No, I haven't a chance,'" Derick replied.

No, Derick, you try, the headmaster said.

"So I did. I applied."

Soon Hermans called and said they would call in a week to ask him questions in up to ten languages. "It was quite difficult to participate in this conversation," he said, "just one language after another without a pause. It was like being under machine-gun fire." But he did well enough and was invited to Brussels.

Like Johan Vandewalle and Helen Abadzi, he didn't keep many languages cranked up for use. "In the last month before the contest, I had to do a lot of concentrated swotting. I used to get up two hours earlier than usual every morning and just work through one language after the other, and when I came home at night I did the same again. I did that day in, day out until I was absolutely sick of languages." He laughed.

When the contest day of multilingual conversations was over, the contestants all went out and revealed facts about themselves. A lot of us were born in the middle of the summer, Derick said. Quite a few of us are left-handed.

"Are you left-handed?" I asked.

"Yes," he said.

Later that night, he learned that he'd won, scoring points in twenty-two languages, and had more minority languages than any other contestant. There was bad news, too. His polyglot feats weren't over: as the winner, he had to produce a speech, in nine languages, for the very next day. And it was already ten o'clock. Exhausted, Herning started working, even though he was also "absolutely fed up with languages." By 2:00 a.m. his speech was written, but the excited Scotsman couldn't fall asleep. At the ceremony, he received a bronze sculpture, which he seems to delight in complaining about, along with the other parts of the experience. "I took the sculpture back to the hotel, they didn't even give me a box, it was sharp, I had to carry that blooming sculpture through three airplanes."

"Do you still have it?" I asked.

"Oh, yes," he said. "My wife uses it for hanging her hat."

Derick was inducted into *The Guinness Book of World Records* in 1991, and his record stayed until 1994, until Ziad Fazah's spectacle. In Lerwick he's known as the "man who knows every language," an exaggeration he no longer tries to correct. To the "intelligent people," he says he has a "nodding acquaintance" with more than thirty languages but only twelve that he "speaks readily"—the rest he'd need to give himself a crash course in in order to use. But even these twelve aren't so handy, and in order to establish this, I found myself chasing the hyperpolyglot around the bush.

"How many languages would you say that you can speak readily right now?"

"Well, twelve. Twelve, let's say."

"Without any crash course?"

"Oh, we'll say ten. I don't try to keep up with these languages—it's impossible."

I ask, "So you're actively keeping up ten of them?"

"No, no," he said, laughing. It depends on the language. In some he'd have to read some things to reactivate his memory, but in German, Dutch, and Russian, he wouldn't need to warm up. For French he says he'd want a few hours. Gaelic he uses frequently. The others? He'd have to prepare to use them, I surmise.

"It's fairly easy for me to learn a foreign language," he said. "I have to recognize that for most people it's exceedingly difficult."

"Would you say that anyone could do with languages what you've done?" I asked him.

"Probably not," he replied.

"Why not?"

"Hmm," he said, and paused for a long time. "You could say, most people seem able to swim. I can't swim very well. I'm a hopeless swimmer. You think it would be natural, just like where some people take to a language like a duck to water, while I don't take to water like a duck. I take to water like Derick Herning and wave my arms about and sputter. It's just something that I have."

Chapter 19

W hat does it take for someone to learn many languages at a very high degree of proficiency?

This question was posed to me by Andrew Cohen, an applied linguist at the University of Minnesota who happens to be also a hyperpolyglot. A muscular, balding man in his late sixties, he's a quick, voluminous talker who has learned four languages to a very high level (of the thirteen he's studied), mostly to take advantage of opportunities to teach and lecture around the world. When I told him about the hyperpolyglots I'd met, he insisted that I pay attention to what they can actually do. His gold standard is working professionally in his languages, teaching and giving lectures, as he's done.

"I'm good at memorizing vocabulary," he said, "and figuring out the grammar. I'm an extrovert—I'll go out there and practice. I can retain stuff and I'm willing to be laughed at. Part of the talent shows up as a talent for having words, for finding the words and not being at a loss for words. Fluency. For learning the grammar so it's functional, so that I can use it, being interested in the pragmatics of the language and practicing that pragmatics once I've used it, so I know how to apologize and complain, to try to fit in and be more of a chameleon. I have a talent for finding things to talk about.

"But," he added, "a lot of it is hard work. It's just being willing to put in all those long hours and study the language."

Despite the fact that he'd answered his own question, I replied anyway. Based on my observations, you need three things, I said: some neural hardware that's exceptionally suited to the activity of learning languages and to the ability to use many of them; a sense of mission about learning languages; and an identity as a language learner. This "hardware" is a set of either structural or anatomical features that act as precursors to exceptional outcomes—if they are recruited by the right sorts of practice in the right sort of context (one, say, that recognizes foreign language abilities as a desirable trait). These precursors might include a high-performing phonological loop; an anatomically larger primary auditory cortex, which enables the learner to hear distinctions in speech sounds in the non-native language more easily; differences in the hippocampus that enable the learning and easy recall of new language material; some as-yet-unidentified ability to control multiply represented languages; or some variations in hormones or neurotransmitters that may increase plasticity and encourage the building of language circuits.

Maybe it's not as definitive an answer as some people might like. But there are still lessons to be drawn from hyperpolyglots for other foreign-language-learning adults.

If you want to get good at languages, you should find—or construct—your niche.

As the Hippo Clubs know, being a linguistic outsider isn't easy; what you need to do is create a social inside. There, you can all be outsiders together.

Belonging in this way might have helped my gawky preadolescent self be more than a French speaker *manqué*; it would have also helped me retain my other languages when I returned home. Even better if you can be driven by your own goals. I admire people who were such fans of Japanese anime that they took up the language. Living and working in a context where multiple languages are used, and where learning and using them are socially and materially rewarded, are big assets, especially if that place respects a "something and something" view of languages—where one's capacity in languages, at whatever level, is regarded as meaningful multilingualism.

This observation comes from hyperpolyglot lives. In the library and at the Propaganda Fide, Mezzofanti constructed his niche; Helen Abadzi found hers at the World Bank; Graham Cansdale at the European Commission. When I first met Alexander Arguelles, he was nicheless and a bit bereft; ever an iconoclast, he wants his own polyglot college. He seems happier in Singapore among multilinguals who appreciate his languages and his seriousness.

But it also comes from what I saw in south India, where some strata of the society are so fluidly multilingual, there seems to be no other way to live your life.

If you want to be better at languages, you should use native speakers as a metric of progress, though not as a goal. Try to get a sense of what it is that bilinguals you admire can do in their languages. Embrace your linguistic outsiderness—it's the way of the world.

A language isn't reserved for the perfectly calibrated native speaker. Words have currency even if they're not perfectly wrought. We don't need to pretend that those cooks in the Manhattan Japanese noodle restaurant whom I overheard or the billions of other people who speak (or even sign) some amalgamated code are locked in a mute, fruitless shuffling of feet, saying "Tan, tan." In fact, they're dancing quite happily.

Does this mean that speaking like a native is no longer important? It depends on the language. Take English, which, thanks to Mickey Mouse and General Patton, has become a global lingua franca. Belonging to everyone, a lingua franca will be spoken and written in a vast array of ways that will have to be tolerated—and learned—by everyone, even native speakers themselves. Of course, some versions of English will continue to have more status than others. I recently heard about Australians and Irish who must acquire American accents if they want to get English-teaching jobs in South Korea. The point is, we live in a world where there are many different types of Englishes and English speakers.

On the other hand, speakers of less widespread languages won't be familiar with such accommodations. Japanese, for instance, is spoken by a good number of people—around 127 million—but only about one million speak it as a second language. Polish has the twenty-third largest group of native speakers in the world but no measurable number of second users at all. You'll never sound like a native to these native speakers, so unused are they to hearing their language spoken by foreigners. So the pressure should be off.

If you want to improve at languages, you should manage your dopamine.

Dopamine is the neurotransmitter that operates in the brain's reward circuit. When we do certain things, a little dopamine is released in our brains, telling it that we just did something pleasurable, which ensures that we do that pleasurable thing again. People who learn many languages do it because they're attached to the pleasure of it. More than 95 percent of all the respondents to my online survey reported, "I like languages" as the reason they could learn languages more easily than other people.

I've argued that this liking is brain-related, as in "I like what happens to my brain when I'm studying languages." Of course, someone who says she "likes languages" could be covertly admitting that she likes the social status conferred on people who have many languages. I didn't get this sense from my survey, though. "Learning a language is an utmost pleasure to me," one person wrote on the survey. "The pleasure of a large interior world," someone else wrote. "Appreciating the beauty of human speech sounds." "Exercising the brain just for the fun of it." These don't seem to be people motivated by climbing the social heap—they enjoy the neurological rewards of learning.

If you want to promote brain plasticity, you should find flow.

That the respondents appear to be hooked on a brain chemical suggests that they can promote flow states in order to learn languages. I recall that when I first met Alexander, he seemed a bit distressed to be taken from his scriptorium; he craved studying. Derek Herning reported a physical need to be speaking in other languages. Helen Abadzi exercises and listens to language tapes, which heightens the sensation of flow as she learns. Others have said similar things. Generating these flow states is a way to use the body's own power to lift the brakes on brain plasticity— perhaps this is why some commercial language-learning programs are so popular, because their simplicity and repetitiveness can put anyone into a zone.

If you want to improve at languages, you should build executive function and working memory skills.

Numerous studies have shown that individuals have cognitive skills like executive function to varying degrees, and that these skills run in families. Geneticist Naomi Friedman gave executive function tasks to nearly three hundred same-sex twin pairs (divided between identical twins, who share all their genes, and fraternal twins, who share half of the same genetic material). She found that nearly all of the differences between individuals' skills could be explained by what they'd inherited genetically. In an email, Friedman was careful to say that people can still improve their executive function through training. But the raw material of training is genetically determined, as is one's capacity to be trained. Call it one's plasticizability. Working memory can also be trained— somewhat. The problem is, the improvement is not dramatic. You can get better at performing a single task over and over, but you're not likely to transfer that skill to other areas.

If you want to improve at languages, you should develop a feel for language.

Hyperpolyglots say they have a "feel for language." Graham Cansdale said, "I can see some of the people in my Arabic class—they fundamentally don't get the feel for the language." We were sitting in his office, and he held his hand out, rubbing his fingers. This "feel" for the language he called the *Sprachegefühl* (literally, "language feeling"). "In each language," he said, "you have to take it at its own terms. When you ask 'why?' you demonstrate that you don't get it. You can only ask why in the language's own terms."

Lomb Kató probably put it best: "Spend time tinkering with the language every day." *Tinkering.* I love it.

Some of this *Sprachegefühl* is an expectation of how languages behave—they'll have nouns and adjectives, for instance, but in which order? Maybe there are prepositions, or they're postpositions (as in Japanese, where "on the bark of the young tree" is literally "young tree of bark on"). Ever attentive to common constructions found in each language, the hyperpolyglot will, when working within a language family, group commonalities and separate exceptions. (Emil Krebs once said that when one knows twenty-five languages, the twenty-sixth comes without much effort.) When working between families, the hyperpolyglot asks: Will the adjective be before the noun or after the noun? Will the gender of the adjective be changed to the gender of the noun? The way to get *Sprachegefühl* is by learning how languages behave, and one way to do this is by studying a lot of them.

One note about hands and speaking. Even in monolinguals, scientists have observed that arm movements (and other movements) and spoken language are controlled in the same part of the brain. Graham's finger-rubbing gesture, which mirrored Ziad Fazah's odd head-scraping gesture in the Chilean television video, may be more than a gesture. It may also be an indication that this part of the brain is constantly stimulated.

As lovers of patterns, hyperpolyglots are attached to languages as structures, as well as to memories of encountering those structures. "I can't imagine not knowing French—it would just be impossible to me. I've known French my whole life, it would be such a blank," Alexander said to me. Cutting languages back because he doesn't have time is painful for him once he's gotten to know and respect them. Hyperpolyglots also know what they can remember and what they can't—a sort of metamemory about what they've known once and what they never have.

"I know whether it's a word that I have known and have forgotten," Graham Cansdale said, when I visited him in his Brussels office. He mused for a moment. "'Rabbit.' I know that I have learned the Arabic word for 'rabbit,' but I cannot think for the life of me what it is. But 'crocodile,' I know that I have never come across that word in Arabic."

If you want to be skillful at languages, you should find your tribe.

The hyperpolyglot tribe is finding itself and becoming unlost. It's cohering as a real community online, on blogs and on forums like http://how-to-learn-any-language.com. There they can express themselves directly, demanding to be admired because they've touched a common thread that runs through languages that, otherwise, wouldn't be known. One of their gathering places is on YouTube, where more and more people are posting videos of themselves speaking in multiple languages (though whether they're reciting, reading, or actually speaking fresh lines, it's hard to tell). The community there is nascent, but growing. The videos have the tenor of a warrior's posturing to opponents or perhaps to aspirants. The message is, Here's the gauntlet you'll have to run if you want to join this tribe.

Finally, if you want to improve at languages, whatever the method is, stick to the method. Or as Rainer Ganahl puts it, "At a certain point, you have to tolerate the absence of quick success."

On one of the days on my trip to Bologna, while I was walking down Via Malcontenti, a very unurban shade of blue caught my eye. It was a raft, pulled up next to a canal. In fact, a number of rafts were lined up, crowded with passengers. To float down a canal in the middle of Bologna! The murky brown channel of water, called the Moline, ran through a narrow urban canyon. Since the canal turned a corner about two hundred meters away and disappeared, I assumed the raft trips would be going under the city itself. I hurried to the join the rafting party and was soon putting on a fire engine–red spelunking helmet, tipped with a hand-crank headlamp, that the passengers wore. Men in hip waders held each raft in place as I approached the canal by scrambling over railings, rafts, oars, other rafters. About two dozen of us had settled in when some women in my boat snickered; heads turned. Two latecomers clambered into our boat: a young man in jeans and a ratty shirt, and a young woman with long, dark hair, wearing a miniskirt and high heels. Would she puncture the raft climbing across it? Would she topple across the assembled laps? For every wife who hoped she would was a husband who hoped so, too.

After our boatman pushed us off, we settled in for a leisurely sail. But the canal narrowed and the speed of our tiny craft increased, and without rudders or oars the boat began to spin. A murmur went up from the rafters. The young man was shouting something at me, pointing at my head. *Attento! Attento!* he cried. I looked over my shoulder to see the column of a bridge rushing straight at me. I held out a hand to catch the brick and stone and push us away. I smiled at him—thanks. No time for introductions, though. The raft now swung in the other direction. He readied his stick to push us off while his girlfriend smoothed her hair and checked her polished toenails. Behind her, a column on the opposite side of the boat was headed straight for her. I pulled out my new Italian word: *Attento! Attento!* She ducked and the stone brushed by, as the canal sucked us down. *Grazie,* she said.

Beyond the bridge, the water slowed, and the rafts were tethered in a cluster so that we could hear a short lecture about the waterways of Bologna. Afterward, we resumed our float, and I wondered, what other hidden depths of the city would we be privileged enough to see? By then I knew the name of Gerolamo, a musician, and Xenia, an economics student.

No sooner did I settle in for a long drift than the rafts were pulled along a landing. Get out, we were ordered. Next to us, the canal poured through a chute opening and fell, who knew how far. Headlamps whirred, their beams fluttered into the dark, the cranking of hand generators swallowed by the roar of the water disappearing through a grate into the city's guts. We climbed out of the rafts and shuffled along a corridor, up eight narrow stone steps, nearly as steep as a ladder, the passageway strangely quiet as the sounds of the falling water faded. Were we moving to a higher or lower level? Would we be met by rafts on the other side to continue our journey? The beam of my headlamp stabbed in front of me. We turned, climbed more stairs. I expected the stairs to turn downward. Why were we still going up? A metal door flashed open. I plunged through it and found myself on some Bolognese street. I pulled off my helmet and saw that the skies were darker and streetlights more yellow than the ones I'd left. We paused to get our bearings. "I'm going to teach you something about your own city," I told Gerolamo and Xenia. Via Malcontenti was nearby, and when we reached the corner with the plaque, I pointed up at it and told them a little about Mezzofanti.

"Wow," Gerolamo said. "That's incredible."

Yes, it's *incredible*, isn't it? I thought. Incredible that someone could do what he wanted in so many languages. Incredible that someone could spend his lifetime accumulating more languages than twenty ordinary people would use in theirs. Incredible that his hometown had done so little to commemorate his passage through this life.

Every morning, *"Buongiorno!"* in the Archiginnasio's manuscript room had brought new boxes with bona fide treasures: the unpublished manuscript in which Mezzofanti analyzed the Codex Cospi, or the description of Luiseño, written by Pablo Tac, a young student from Southern California. I found lists of languages. Not one but six of them, scattered among different boxes, undated, untitled, and unusable. Surely they were Mezzofanti's—they were written in the cardinal's cramped handwriting that by then was dancing in my dreams. But the lists were inconsistent. One had 24 languages, another 123. They could have been books in his library or poems for the *Accademia Poliglotta*. Two lists didn't even mention Latin or Italian.

Then, on my last day in the archive, I found something entirely unexpected. There was one final box, what the *inventario* labeled as "miscellaneous." After days of looking at files and flat pages, I was surprised to see, when I opened the lid, squarish lumps. My heart jumped. I took out a lump. It was a block of paper, about three inches long and one inch wide on each side, wrapped in dry paper and tied with red waxed string. I untied the string's tiny knot and peeled back the cover. It contained a stack of thin paper slips, darkened with age. On each slip of paper was written a word with a corresponding word in a different language on the reverse.

Flash cards? Is that was these were? Was this the Holy Grail that Starchevsky said he'd found?

"It does not appear that the Cardinal possessed any extraordinary secret," Charles Russell wrote, "or at least that he ever clearly explained to any of his visitors the secret process, if any, which he employed." Some, like the Russian Starchevsky, ignored this and sought one anyway.

The universe had been smiling on my mission. I had discovered the ponderous reality of the *massimo poliglotta*'s language learning.

In Mezzofanti's own time, his methods must have seemed sensibly industrious. Today they dazzle us only by their vigor and persistence. Mezzofanti himself once said that, even as an adult, he learned languages like a schoolboy: writing out words and verb conjugations and memorizing them. He made good use of his time, making it more abundant. He talked to himself in his languages while he was alone. He read dictionaries, catechisms, vocabularies, and literature of great variety. He sought people to talk to, and he took notes on their conversations. He also translated among his various languages. Labors and games, routines and diversions, he invented or discovered them all. And whatever his method was, he stuck to it. The story of his life said he'd been rescued from carpentry. If his language life had really been such drudgery, one wonders whether it amounted to a rescue at all.

Discovering hard work is a disappointment if, like Starchevsky, you were looking for Bolognese potions or gnostic formulas. But hard work, a superior ability to switch among languages, and an excellent memory for language don't disappoint if you have the advantage of some neuroscience with which to understand it. So what did Starchevsky take home with him? I'm confident that it was nothing, *nada, awan, nashi, niente, niets*—it was linguistic snake oil, the Russian's attempt to dig up hyperpolyglot relics to sell under his own counterfeit brand.

Most of the flash cards were in Mezzofanti's hand. The first was labeled as Georgian; the next one, thinner, was Hungarian. The librarians, as surprised by the discovery as I was, became alarmed at seeing me unpack them all at once to take a photograph and excitedly pantomimed that I could examine only one packet at a time.

The paper was brittle, the string dry, the wax seals of another set of cards crumbling. In all, I counted thirteen packets, all different sizes, for Georgian, Hungarian, Arabic, Turkish, Persian, Algonquin, Russian, Tagalog, and three unlabeled sets in Arabic writing. Some packets were thin—there were only twenty-two cards in Armenian. But the Russian cards made a stack ten inches thick; Tagalog (though not in Mezzofanti's handwriting) was three inches thick.

Stack of flash cards from the
Mezzofanti archive.

Box of flash cards from the
Mezzofanti archive.

One reason that Mezzofanti and people like him are so fascinating is that they seem to have leapfrogged the banality of method. They don't learn languages; they "pick them up." They don't sit down and read lists of words; they absorb them. We hope that the methods are magic, and that if we adopt those methods too, we might achieve great things. The truth is, Mezzofanti and others haven't escaped the banality of methods at all; they make the banality more productive. Their minds *enjoy* the banality. The nature of the methods themselves doesn't seem to matter. Johan Vandewalle told me something that bears repeating: "Whatever the method is," he said, "stick to the method. That's the method."

Think of the polyglot spectacle that Mezzofanti became: the popes and the cardinals, the poets and the emperors, the Russian princesses, the Texan colonels and the German barons. Then imagine him shuffling home through the quiet arcaded streets, flipping through his Tagalog verbs, and blowing out the candle. It's difficult to hold these two images together. But this little collage is an instructive reminder: before there was a myth, there was a man whose pleasure in language never faltered, and because of that pleasure—with no hope of future rewards—he would do what he did, leaving no followers and no intellectual heirs, no students. As certainly as he'd lived, he was gone, leaving us with our fascination and few answers. A miracle? No, a parable. *Parabole. Parábola. Npumчa. Līdzība. Mfano. Ddameg.*

Acknowledgments

The generosity of the Ralph Johnston Foundation enabled me to write and research a good portion of this book as a Dobie Paisano Writing Fellow. I am enormously grateful to the University of Texas at Austin and the Texas Institute of Letters for their support.

Dozens of people have contributed in great and small ways to every page of this book, and I can mention only a small number of them, though I would much prefer to invite everyone to a big party. At the top of the list are all those devoted language learners who let me into their lives and helped me understand their passion, for which I'm extremely grateful. I was also aided immeasurably throughout by the patient efforts and companionship of Richard Hudson, Loraine Obler, Susanne Reiterer, Ellen Winner, and Andrew Cohen, and those of other experts who provided their insights into massive multilingualism, including Neil Smith, Ianthi Tsimpli, David Birdsong, Claire Kramsch, Robert DeKeyser, Arturo Hernandez, Rita Franceschini, and Stephen Krashen. To each and every expert in neuroscience, anthropology, applied linguistics, sociolinguistics, American immigration, psycholinguistics, and language typology whom I interviewed or exchanged emails with, thank you.

Loren Coleman, cryptozoologist, was a helpful early inspiration, and Ben Zimmer sent hard-to-find information about polyglots abroad. In Düsseldorf, Katrin Amunts, Karl Zilles, and Peter Sillmann were gracious hosts at the Vogt Brain Institute. Hannes Kniffka provided early encouragement, as well as a big lunch and tour of Köln. I'm exceptionally grateful for Franco Pasti's tour of the University of Bologna's library, and to Paola Foschi at the Archiginnasio. For conversations about Hippo/Lex Language Project, I would like to thank Yash Owada, Elizabeth Victor, Miguel Duran, Nayiba Thomas, Kenshi Suzuki, and Chad Nilep for their insights and, to the Salas family in Chihuahua City, their hospitality. For the India trip, I would like to thank Sri, Kala, and all of their family members; also Zainab Bawa, Robert King, Gail Coelho, Reena Patel, Krishnamuthy Nagamangala, Joshy Eapen, and Aparna Mohan. I am grateful for the statistical expertise of Kris Arheart, James Ha, and Amanda Erard. Individuals at the Foreign Service Institute, the Defense Language Instititute, and the Center for Applied Linguistics assisted in the development of my survey and answered related questions. Michael Adams at the University of Texas at Austin was a huge help during my stay at the Paisano Ranch.

I would also like to thank the families of Lomb Kató, Ken Hale, and Erik Gunnemark for answering questions and providing photos. Thanks to Helen Abadzi, Alexander Arguelles, and Johan Vandewalle for the permission to use photos. I also thank the editors of *Glot* for permission to excerpt their interview with Ken Hale.

A number of early readers provided excellent feedback on portions of the manuscript; I'd like to especially thank Stephanie Bush, Jill Nilson, Colleen Moore, Lynn Davey, Cara Schlesinger, Roger Gathman, Gary and Deana Gurney, Ron Peek, Stefano Bertolo, Scott Blackwood, Neil Sattin, Deborah Snoonian Glenn, Katherine Gibbs, and my parents, Michael and Jeanette Erard.

From its early inception, Dan Green and Simon Green of POM, Inc. were wonderful stewards of a nebulous project about polyglots, first as a magazine article and as it morphed into a book, and I am eternally grateful to David Patterson of Foundry Literary + Media who has been both the best friend and best agent a writer could hope for through all the lives of this book. Roger Gathman supplied his innate gifts to excellent translations and brilliant editing, as did Mimi Bardagjy with thoroughness and insight into facts and typography. I also thank Pilar Archila of the University of Houston for neurological fact-checking advice. The succinct brilliance of Hilary Redmon at Free Press transformed the manuscript several times over; her favorite Japanese noodle shop in Manhattan is, by chance, the one that opens chapter 2. I also have to thank Sydney Tanigawa and Anne Cherry, a polyglot copyeditor, for improving the details of the story I had to tell.

I am exceptionally indebted to my wife, Misty McLaughlin. The greatest untold story about the making of this book is the deepening discovery of her companionship, support, and wisdom.

Appendix

In my online survey, I asked people for their top three methods of learning new languages. For simplicity, I focus here on the reports from people who said they know eleven or more languages. Some of their answers were straightforward, such as "I relax and enjoy the language; I accept mistakes and uncertainty; I listen and read a lot" or "I learn the grammar; I read; I speak." More detailed accounts with some interesting strategies I quote on the following pages, with the caveat that these are methods developed by highly passionate individuals to match their own cognitive styles. As one researcher told me, a method is like a medication: for some people it works; for some it has no effect; for some it's toxic.

One person wrote in the survey that, "Rather than sheer, blind repetition, I do consistent, continuous and regular mindful practice. I do shadowing (listening) with various audio sources and speaking. I use as many resources (paper, audio, online) as I can get my hands on and adapting them for my specific purposes. I also try to get short periods of immersion." Someone else wrote:

> In the beginning: I make hyperliteral translations of genuine written texts, using grammars, dictionaries, and "ordinary" translations. I also make three-column wordlists (target, base,

target, divided into blocks of 5–7 words) and repeat them on a schedule. I also learn grammar from my own tip sheets; these include morphological points. I also write small bits about difficult points.

One of the most detailed accounts was this:

I draw mind maps of the phonological system and vocabulary roots to connect them with languages I already know. In this way I build memory anchors so that I have the ability to increase vocabulary at a very fast rate (as many as several thousand words in the first week). I also build lists of relationships between words and build working memory through organized repetitions, which is a method I've developed and teach. I work through conversational dialogues that cover nine major areas of everyday life: home, school, work, leisure (eating/shopping), travel, transportation, business, medical, emergency.

This comment also contained useful detail:

First I acquire a working knowledge of the structure of a language with minimum vocabulary, so that I am able to apply that structural knowledge to my own understanding and production of the language. The Michel Thomas courses are good for this, as they provide me with the structure of the language that I can immediately use. Next, I develop my passive listening skills as well as furnishing the structure I have learnt with vocabulary and idioms. This is followed by applying my new vocabulary to the previous learned structure and developing my active speaking skills. Dialogues are a good way to do this. However, they must be spoken dialogues that appear in a written form, as I have to hear the pronunciation of the words and sentences. Assimil's method is perfect for this. Finally, I would perfect my knowledge by spending an extended period of time in a country where the language is spoken. I am therefore immersed in the language and fully develop my skills as well as building my knowledge of vocabulary and idiom.

The Assimil and Michel Thomas courses, as well as products from many other companies, can be easily found online. Other further resources with perspectives from successful language learners that I can recommend are all in English: Andrew Cohen, *Strategies in Learning and Using a Second Language* (Longman, 2011); Andrew Cohen and Ernesto Macaro (eds.), *Language Learner Strategies: Thirty Years of Research and Practice* (Oxford University Press, 2008); Earl Stevick, *Success with Foreign Languages: Seven Who Achieved It and What Worked for Them* (Prentice-Hall, 1989); and Carol Griffiths (ed.), *Lessons from Good Language Learners* (Cambridge University Press, 2008). Other books, written by polyglots themselves, will be of special interest, including: Amorey Gethin and Erik V. Gunnemark, *The Art And Science of Learning Languages* (Intellect Books, 1996); Claude Cartaginese (ed.), *The Polyglot Project* (available online, 2010); and Brendan Lewis, *Language Hacking Guide* (available online).

Notes

PART 1 QUESTION: Into the Cardinal's Labyrinth

Introduction

3 account of his narrow escape: Charles Russell, *The Life of Cardinal Mezzofanti, with an Introductory Memoir of Eminent Linguists, Ancient and Modern* (London: Longman, Brown, and Co., 1858), 168–71.

3 "but will you tell me yourself?": Ibid., 343.

4 fifty on display: For a full list, see Thomas Watts, "On Dr. Russell's *Life of Cardinal Mezzofanti*," *Transactions of the Philological Society* (1859), 255.

4 "monster of languages": Ibid., 228.

5 "correctness of accent that amazed me to the last degree": Ibid, 243.

5 "not stuttering and stammering": Ibid., 243.

5 "was a most inferior man": Charles Lever, "Linguists," *Blackwood's Edinburgh*, XCVI: DLXXXV (1864), 12.

5 "'never said anything'": Russell, *Life*, 484.

5 Roman priest quoted in a memoir: George Borrow, *The Romany Rye* (London: John Murray, 1857).

5 "does not seem to abound in ideas": Russell, *Life,* 345.

6 "rather of a monkey or a parrot": Ibid., 390.

6 "He is the Devil!": Ibid., 201.

6 "but an ill-bound dictionary": Ibid., 395.

6 Mezzofanti could not be bested: Ibid., 314.

Chapter 1

9   the most popular language to learn: See David Graddol, *English Next* ([2006]: www.britishcouncil.org/learning-research-english-next.pdf), 14.

9   thirty thousand companies offering English classes: Greg Dyer, "English Craze Highlights Chinese Ambitions," *Financial Times,* Jan. 19, 2010.

9    $83 billion worldwide language-learning market: Gregory Stone, "Rosetta Stone: Speaking Wall Street's Language," *Time,* April 25, 2009.

9   70 percent of college students in foreign-language classes: Modern Language Association, "Enrollments in Languages Other than English in United States Institutions of Higher Education" (Washington, DC: MLA, Fall 2009), www .mla.org/2009_enrollmentsurvey.

10   London . . . the most multilingual city in the world: See Andrew Buncombe and Tessa MacArthur, "London: Multilingual Capital of the World," www .independent.co.uk/news/london-multilingual-capital-of-the-world-1083812. html, March 29, 1999.

11   "grasped the language's sounds and rhythms": Russell, *Life,* 46, 158.

11   "flexibility of the organs of speech": Ibid., 157.

11   One writer compared it to "a bird flitting from spray to spray": Guido Görres, quoted in Ibid., 420.

13   "don't take this claim seriously": Carol Myers-Scotton, *Multiple Voices: An Introduction to Bilingualism* (New York: Wiley-Blackwell, 2006), 38.

15   "When I'm an adult": *Daily Mail,* Oct. 29, 2007.

Chapter 2

16   puzzled the language genius by speaking to him in Ukrainian: "Russia's Polyglot College," *San Francisco Bulletin,* Sept. 12, 1885.

Chapter 3

27   gates to the Archiginnasio public library: Nadir Maraldi, Giovanni Mazzotti, Lucio Cocco, and Francesco A. Manzoli, "Anatomical Waxwork Modeling: The History of the Bologna Anatomy Museum," *The Anatomical Record* (New Anat.), 26:1 (2000), 5–10.

33   the cutoff for acquiring a native-like pronunciation: See, for example, Kenneth Hyltenstam and Niclas Abrahamsson, "Who Can Become Native-like in a Second Language? All, Some, or None?" *Studia Linguistica,* 54:2 (2000), 150–66.

34–35 "a riot of linguistic variation": Martin Maiden, "The Definition of Multilingualism in Historical Perspective," in A. Lepschy and A. Tosi (eds.), *Multilingualism in Italy Past and Present* (Oxford: Legenda, 2002), 29–46.

35   Jesuit missionaries who had been expelled: Charles Russell, *The Life of Cardinal Mezzofanti, with an Introductory Memoir of Eminent Linguists, Ancient and Modern* (London: Longman, Brown, and Co., 1858), 133.

36   "Through the grace of God": Ibid., 54.

37   "I made it a rule to learn every new grammar": Ibid., 156–57.

37   noted one writer, "indicates delicacy": Ibid., 263.

37   "monkey-like, restless motion": Ibid., 389.

37 "never . . . permitted himself the indulgence of a fire" Ibid., 161.
37 *scaldino* (or *scaldén*): Pietro Mainoldi, *Vocabolario del dialetto bolognese* (Bologna: Arnaldo Forni Editore, 1996).
37 would not let people kiss his ring: Russell, *Life*, 429.
37 confer God's forgiveness before they went to the gallows: Ibid., 129.
38 enough Sardinian to hear the maid's sins: Ibid., 158–59.

Chapter 4

41 disparate accounts of the Bolognese lion of languages: Thomas Watts, "On the Extraordinary Powers of Cardinal Mezzofanti as a Linguist," *Transactions of the Philological Society*, 5 (Jan. 23, 1852), 115. See also Thomas Watts, "On M. Manavit's *Life of Cardinal Mezzofanti*," *Transactions of the Philological Society*, 7 (1854), 133–50; Thomas Watts, "On Dr. Russell's *Life of Cardinal Mezzofanti*," *Transactions of the Philological Society* (1859), 227–256.
41 Watts himself was said to read fifty languages: George Borrow, *Isopel Berners* (London: Hodder and Stoughton, 1901).
42 British traveler Tom Coryat: Charles Russell, *The Life of Cardinal Mezzofanti, with an Introductory Memoir of Eminent Linguists, Ancient and Modern* (London: Longman, Brown, and Co., 1858), 120.
42 who said that he knew twenty-eight languages: By Jones's own admission. Russell quotes a document written by Jones: Ibid., 89.
42 "Cardinal Mezzofanti" will be found: Ibid., 121.
43 "pronunciation, at least, is described as quite perfect": Ibid., 470.
43 "and with a purity of accent, of vocabulary, and of idiom": Ibid.
43 "speak it correctly and idiomatically": Ibid., 460.
43 "on a level with the majority of the natives": Watts, "On the Extraordinary Powers," 112.
43 "great spirit and precision": Watts, "On Dr. Russell's *Life*," 237.
44 eleven linguistic families: Russell, *Life*, 467.
44 reduced the overall repertoire to sixty or sixty-one: Watts, "On Dr. Russell's *Life*," 242.
45 Arab audiences also prefer truthful speech: "Arabic Media and Public Appearance Forum" (Washington, DC: Center for the Advanced Study of Language, 2005), 16.
45 are born to hearing, nonsigning parents: Brendan Costello, Javier Fernández, and Alazne Landa, "The Non-(existent) Native Signer: Sign Language Research in a Small Deaf Population," paper presented at Ninth Theoretical Issues in Sign Language Research Conference, 2006.
45 no native signing community: MLA, 2009. Also see Tamar Lewin, "Colleges See 16% Rise in Study of Sign Language," *New York Times*, Dec. 8, 2010.
46 *"too correct to appear completely natural"*: Russell, *Life*, 403.
46 knowing French to the satisfaction of Harvard College: "A knowledge of the language itself, rather than of the grammar, is expected; but proficiency in elementary grammar, a good pronunciation, or facility in speaking the language will be accepted as an offset for some deficiency in translation," read the Harvard handbook. Cited in David Barnwell, *A History of Foreign Language Testing in the United States* (Tempe, AZ: Bilingual Press, 1996), 1.

47 fluent, though accented, Arabic: See Fawn M. Brodie, *The Devil Drives* (New York: W. W. Norton, 1984). Brodie's book has notes to sources of the claim of twenty-nine languages and eleven dialects that I mention in the footnote. The information about Burton's Hindustani exam comes from Edward Rice, *Sir Richard Francis Burton: A Biography* (New York: Da Capo Press, 2001). See also James Milton, "The Lessons of Excellence: Sir Richard Francis Burton and Language Learning," *The Linguist*, 40:5 (2001), 135–39.

48 who made the fastest progress: Joseph De Koninck, "Intensive Language Learning and Increases in Rapid Eye Movement Sleep: Evidence of a Performance Factor," *International Journal of Psychophysiology*, 8 (1989), 43–47.

48 improved the most: Joseph De Koninck, "Intensive Learning, REM Sleep, and REM Sleep Mentation," *Sleep Research Bulletin*, 1:2 (1995), 39–40.

49 [the language] they used right before they slept: David Foulkes, Barbara Meier, Inge Strauch, et al., "Linguistic Phenomena and Language Selection in the REM Dreams of German-English Bilinguals," *International Journal of Psychology*, 28:3 (1993), 871–91.

49 greener, less purple color: Leigh Caskey-Sirmons and Nancy Hickerson, "Semantic Shift and Bilingualism: Variation in the Color Terms of Five Languages," *Anthropological Linguistics*, 19 (1977), 358–67.

49 even conceptualize time differently from monolinguals: Panos Athanasopolous and C. Kasai, "Language and Thought in Bilinguals: The Case of Grammatical Number and Nonverbal Classification Preferences," *Applied Psycholinguistics*, 29 (2008), 105–23.

49 aren't equally disordered in each of their languages: F. I. de Zulueta, N. Gene-Cos, and S. Grachev, "Differential Psychotic Symptomatology in Polyglot Patients: Case Reports and Their Implications," *British Journal of Medical Psychology*, 74 (2001), 277–92. See also R. E. Hemphill, 1971, "Auditory Hallucinations in Polyglots," *South African Medical Journal*, Dec. 18, 1971, 1391–94.

50 spoke in English, he went 'mad'": F. I. de Zulueta, "The Implications of Bilingualism in the Study and Treatment of Psychiatric Disorders: A Review," *Psychological Medicine*, 14 (1984), 541–57.

51 "a community imagined by language": Benedict Anderson, *Imagined Communities* (London: Verso 1983).

52 "not failed native speakers": Vivian Cook, "Going Beyond the Native Speaker in Language Teaching," *TESOL Quarterly*, 33:2 (1999), 204.

52 two or three monolingual speakers' worth of language in his or her head: Vivian Cook, "Multicompetence and the Learning of Many Languages," *Language, Culture, and Curriculum*, 8:2 (1995), 94.

53 current European Commission standard: Brian North, *The Development of a Common Framework Scale of Language Proficiency* (New York: Peter Lang, 2000), 281.

53 language competitions . . . German government: J. R. Campbell, H. Wagner, and H. Walberg, "Academic Competitions and Programs Designed to Challenge the Exceptionally Talented," in Kurt A. Heller, Franz J. Mönks, Robert J. Sternberg, and Rena F. Subotnik (eds.), *International Handbook of Giftedness and Talent*, 2nd ed. (Oxford, UK: Elsevier, 2000).

54 Yet only 2 of the 104 pilots: Patricia Sullivan and Handan Girginer, "The Use

of Discourse Analysis to Enhance ESP Teacher Knowledge: An Example Using Aviation English," *English for Specific Purposes,* 21:4 (2002), 397–404.

55 only about one-quarter . . . concerns the actual flying: Jeremy Mell, "Dialogue in Abnormal Situations of Air Traffic Control," *Cahiers du Centre Interdisciplinaire des Sciences du Langage,* 10 (1994), 263–72.

55 "What does 'pull up, pull up' mean?": Atsushi Tajima, "Fatal Miscommunication: English in Aviation Safety," *World Englishes,* 23:3 (2004), 456.

55 confusion was a major cause of the accident: David A. Simon, "Boeing 757 CFIT Accident at Cali, Colombia, Becomes Focus of Lessons Learned," *Flight Safety Digest,* May/June 1998, 1–31.

55 couldn't convey his misgivings to the crew: Peter Ladkin, "AA965 Cali Accident Report near Buga, Colombia, Dec 20, 1995," http://sunnyday.mit.edu/accidents/calirep.html.

57 about the period of Mezzofanti's life between 1812 and 1831: Franco Pasti, *Un poliglotta in biblioteca: Giuseppe Mezzofanti (1774–1849) a Bologna nell etá della restaurazione* (Bologna: Patron Editore, 2006).

Part 2 APPROACH: Tracking Down Hyperpolyglots

Chapter 5

67 a popular forum with language scientists: LINGUIST 7.881, Wed., June 12, 1996.

68 Hudson passed the mail on to linguists: LINGUIST 14.2923, Sun., Oct. 26, 2003.

71 £1.3 billion a year: David Graddol, *English Next* (2006), www.britishcouncil.org/learning-research-english-next.pdf.

71 the most multilingual city on the planet: Philip Baker and John Eversley, *Multilingual Capital* (London: Battlebridge, 2000).

Chapter 6

73 read his *Washington Post* obituary: Joe Holley, "George Campbell Dies; Spoke 44 Languages," *Washington Post,* Dec. 20, 2004.

74 Elizabeth Kulman: "Mastering Languages," *Dakota Republican,* 14:45, Supplement 4 (Nov. 12, 1874).

74 should be content to serve the humble role of a blacksmith": "Rome's Learned Vulcan," *Idaho Daily Statesman,* Oct. 27, 1898, 5.

74 manual labor and reading foreign languages: Ibid., 21.

75 granted Burritt thirty languages: Peter Tolis, *Elihu Burritt: Crusader for Brotherhood* (Hamden, CT: Archon Press, 1968), 16–17.

75 carried his Greek and Latin grammars to work in his hat: Elihu Burritt, "Autobiography of the Author," in *Ten-Minute Talks on All Sorts of Topics* (Boston: Lee and Shepard, 1873), 11.

76 "His compulsive and erratic study of languages: Tolis, *Elihu Burritt,* 21.

77 "there was something to live for": Elihu Burritt, *Lectures and Speeches* (London: Sampson Low, Son, and Marston, 1869), 174.

77   never paid for a hotel room or riverboat passage: Ellen Strong Bartlett, "Elihu Burritt—The Learned Blacksmith," *New England Magazine*, 16: 4 (1897), 21–22.

77   Sanskrit Lessons for Young Yankee Ladies: Letter from Burritt to "Miss Butler," 1878.

77   a plaster cast of Burritt's skull was taken: Everything in this section comes from Lorenzo Fowler, *The American Phrenological Journal and Miscellany*, OS Fowler (ed.) Fowlers and Wells, 9 (1847), 269. There was also an earlier note that appeared in the *American Phrenological Journal and Miscellany*, 3, (1841).

79   Sidis was also doing at the age of four: "Give Easy Recipe for Child Prodigies," *New York Times*, Oct. 31, 1920.

79   probably didn't speak those seventeen languages, either: "Winifred Stoner Plea Calls Count a Faker," *New York Times*, March 19, 1930.

79   world tour to "find geniuses": "Stoners to Start Hunt for Geniuses," *New York Times*, Aug. 3, 1927.

80   had her marriage annulled: "Winifred Stoner Plea Calls Count a Faker," *New York Times*, March 19, 1930.

80   couldn't say "no" in any of them: The joke was first written in 1931 by a *Chicago Tribune* columnist, Richard Henry Little, though it has also been attributed to Dorothy Parker. Little's version goes, "Winifred Stackville Stoner II, now twenty-nine and who is reported in the public press as having just left her third, was renowned at the age of six, when she wrote a book, as a child genius. And a few years later, with her hair still in pigtails, it was proudly proclaimed that Winifred could speak twelve languages. But apparently Winifred never learned to say 'no' in any of them and hiked up to the altar as fast as anybody suggested the idea."

80   by lunchtime, Hale . . . would be conversing fluently: See the MIT tribute web page for Ken Hale, which contains many of these and other stories, here: http://web.mit.edu/linguistics/events/tributes/hale/testimonies.html.

80   admiring lore was matched by his colleagues' regard: Victor Golla, "Hale, Wurm, and Mezzofanti," *SSILA Newsletter*, 20:4 (Jan. 2002), 2–4.

82   denials were rejected: Lisa Cheng and Rint Sybesma, "The Excitement Comes from the Language Itself!," *Glot*, 2: 9/10 (Dec. 1996).

84   he quips in one video: www.ganahl.info/videos/Wojia.mp4.

84   something of a manifesto: Rainer Ganahl, "Travelling Linguistics," www.ganahl.info/t_travelling_linguistics.html.

85   191 million in 2005: Department of Economic and Social Affairs, Population Division, *Trends in Total Migrant Stock: The 2005 Revision* (New York: United Nations, 2006).

85   World Bank statistics from 2005: Dilip Ratha and William Shaw, *South-South Migration and Remittances*, World Bank Working Paper no. 102 (2005), 2.

85   The bulk moved within Europe/Central Asia: Ibid., 7.

85   anticipates 1.6 billion a year by 2020: World Tourism Organization, *Tourism 2020 Vision*.

85   "The will to plasticity" . . . among them, language circuits: To borrow a phrase from Pierre Kosslowski (Daniel W. Smith, trans.), *Nietzsche and the Vicious Circle* (Chicago: University of Chicago Press, 1997), 46.

86   "Plasticity is an intrinsic property of the human brain," Alvaro Pascual-Leone, Amir Amedi, Felipe Fregni, and Lotfi Merabet, "The Plastic Human Brain Cor-

tex," *Annual Review of Neuroscience*, 28 (2005), 377. See also Peter Huttenlocher, *Neural Plasticity: The Effects of Environment on the Development of the Cerebral Cortex* (Cambridge, MA: Harvard University Press, 2002).

86 self-help guru Tim Ferriss published "language hacking" guides on his website: www.fourhourworkweek.com/blog/2007/11/07/how-to-learn-but-not-master-any-language-in-1-hour-plus-a-favor/.

86 A New York–based writer, Ellen Jovin, has a blog: www.ellenjovin.com.

Chapter 7

94 "He spends most of his waking hours digging in the garden": Neil Smith and Ianthi Tsimpli, *The Mind of a Savant: Language Learning and Modularity* (London: Wiley-Blackwell, 1995), 2.

94 Christopher can translate from and communicate in: Ibid., 12.

96 Given a newspaper in one of his languages: Ibid., 82.

96 didn't get better at distinguishing syntactically: Ibid., 92.

96 Normal second-language learners have a harder time: Gary Morgan et al., "Language Against the Odds: The Learning of British Sign Language by a Polyglot Savant," *Journal of Linguistics*, 38 (2002), 4.

96 "basically English with a range of alternative veneers": Smith and Tsimpli, *Mind of a Savant*, 122.

97 experiment they document: Neil Smith, Ianthi Tsimpli, Gary Morgan, and Bencie Woll, *The Signs of a Savant: Language Against the Odds* (Cambridge UK: Cambridge University Press, 2011).

98 "a working knowledge of French, Spanish": Bernard Rimland, "Savant Capabilities of Autistic Children and Their Cognitive Implications," in G. Serban (ed.), *Cognitive Defects in the Development of Mental Illness* (New York: Brunner/Mazel, 1878), 43–65. Quoted in David Birdsong's *Contemporary Psychology* review of Smith and Tsimpli, *Mind of a Savant*, cited above.

98 or that his fascination with languages was so remarkable: Elizabeth Bates. "On Language Savants and the Structure of the Mind." *International Journal of Bilingualism*, 1:2 (1997), 163–79.

98 rote memory, considered one hallmark: S. Bölte and F. Poustka: "Comparing the Intelligence Profiles of Savant and Nonsavant Individuals with Autistic Disorder," *Intelligence*, 32 (2004), 121–31.

98 "Christopher is not so much a successful learner of languages": David Birdsong, "An Interesting Subject Indeed," *Contemporary Psychology*, 41:8 (1996), 837–38.

98 "no relevant evidence" for language talents: Ibid., 182.

98 "supremely gifted at learning new languages": Smith, Tsimpli, Morgan, and Woll, *Signs of a Savant.*, 40.

99 a very nearly complete handbook: Amorey Gethin and Erik V. Gunnemark, *The Art and Science of Learning Languages* (Oxford, UK: Intellect Books: 1996).

100 "three pillars" of language learning: Ibid., 26.

101 She'd also written a memoir: Scott Alkire, "Kató Lomb's Strategies for Language Learning and SLA," *The International Journal of Foreign Language Teaching*, 1:4 (Fall 2005), 17–26.

101 learning her seventeenth language, Hebrew: Stephen Krashen and Natasha Kiss, "Notes on a Polyglot: Kató Lomb," *System*, 24:2 (1996), 207–10.

102   they "acquire" it: Stephen Krashen, "Case Histories and the Comprehension
        Hypothesis," Plenary Address, English Teaching Association Conference, 2007,
        www.eslminiconf.net/september/krashen.html.

102   "(I was fifty-four at the time)": Ibid.

103   "remove the mystical fog": Kató Lomb, *Polyglot: How I Learn Languages* (Ádám
        Szegi and Kornelia DeKorne, trans.; Scott Alkire, ed.) (Berkeley, CA: TESL-EJ,
        2008).

103   "Be firmly convinced that you are a linguistic genius": Lomb, Ibid., 161.

103   "The language learning method that is good": Ibid., 76.

103   "all I suggest is that monologues be silent": Ibid., 77.

103   the difference between finding entertainment: Peter Skehan, *A Cognitive
        Approach to Language Learning* (Oxford, UK: Oxford University Press, 1998), 17.

103   "I will sooner see a UFO than a dative case": Lomb, *Polyglot,* 122.

104   "live inside me simultaneously with Hungarian": Ibid., viii.

104   ability to "switch between any of these languages": Ibid.

104   English at the age of twenty-four: Ibid.

104   Russian at thirty-two: Ibid.

104   brush up for half a day: Ibid., xvii.

104   "the same level of ability": Ibid.

Chapter 8

106   1996 news report: All the biographical information here comes from Tova
        Chapoval, "One-Man Tower of Babel; Fluent in 58 Languages, Brazilian Tries
        to Sell Method," *Washington Post,* Dec. 27, 1996, B8.

108   In 2006, when Israel bombed and invaded: Alexander Arguelles's account was
        published in the *San Jose Mercury News* on Aug. 13, 2006, "Deliverance: Thou-
        sands Fled Israeli Bombs Pummeling Lebanon. This Is the Story of One Ameri-
        can Family's Escape."

109   everyone could see Fazah's spectacular failure. As of April 2011, the video was
        posted at www.youtube.com/watch?v=_XA1Ifi-ntE.

110   "one of billions of people who are unable to speak fifty-nine languages":
        http://ardentagnostic.blogspot.com/2009/03/ziad-fazah-man-who-does-not
        -speak-59.html.

Chapter 9

123   that work for them and use them more often": See Charlotte Kemp. "Strate-
        gic Processing in Grammar Learning: Do Multilinguals Use More Strategies?"
        International Journal of Multilingualism, 4:4 (2007), 241–61.

134   He recommended reviewing any learned material . . . at intervals: Paul
        Pimsleur, "A Memory Schedule," *Modern Language Journal* 51 (1967), 73–75.

134   what one remembers doesn't decline steadily over a lifetime: Harry Bahrick,
        "Semantic Memory Content in Permastore: Fifty Years of Memory for Span-
        ish Learned in School," *Journal of Experimental Psychology: General* 113:1 (1984),
        1–31.

135   "including learning, reasoning, and preparation for action": Alan Baddeley and

Graham Hitch, "Working Memory," in G. A. Bower (ed.), *The Psychology of Learning and Motivation,* vol. 8 (New York: Academic Press, 1974), 47–90.

135   the best predictor of intelligence: See, for example, R. Kyllonen and R. Chrisal, "Reasoning Ability Is (Little More than) Working Memory Capacity," *Intelligence,* 14:4 (1990), 389–433.

135   four to five words every second: From Willem Levelt, *Speaking: From Intention to Articulation* (Cambridge, MA: MIT Press, 1989).

137   "Have you ever tried on a pair of green spectacles?": Charles Russell, *The Life of Cardinal Mezzofanti, with an Introductory Memoir of Eminent Linguists, Ancient and Modern* (London: Longman, Brown, and Co., 1858), 421.

138   also known as the Feast of the Languages: www.newadvent.org/cathen/12456a.htm.

138   he was dazzled: Russell, *Life,* 411–20.

138   A speaker has to do two things: J. Abutalebi and David Green, "Bilingual Language Production: The Neurocognition of Language Representation and Control," *Journal of Neurolinguistics,* 20 (2007), 251; J. Crinion et al., "Language Control in the Bilingual Brain," *Science,* 312 (2006), 1537–40.

139   requires some powerful neural hardware. J. Lipski, "Code-switching or Borrowing? No sé *so* no puedo decir, *you know,"* in Lofti Sayahi and Maurice Westmoreland (eds.), *Selected Proceedings of the Second Workshop on Spanish Sociolinguistics* (Somerville, MA: Cascadilla Proceedings Project, 2005), 1–15.

139   Think of executive function as how you control your mental airspace: This metaphor comes from Nathaniel Kendall-Taylor, Michael Erard, Adam Simon and Lynn Davey. *Air Traffic Control for Your Brain: Using a Simplifying Model to Clarify the Science of Executive Function,* (Washington, DC: FrameWorks Institute, 2010).

139   "Standing that means *ständig ständig führen stein":* Ellen Perecman, "Spontaneous Translation and Language Mixing in a Polyglot Aphasic," *Brain and Language,* 23 (1984), 51.

140   builds up a "reserve" that people carry into older age: See, for example, Ellen Bialystok, "Cognitive Effects of Bilingualism: How Linguistic Experience Leads to Cognitive Change," *The International Journal of Bilingual Education and Bilingualism* 10:3 (2007), 210–23; Ellen Bialystok et al., "Bilingualism as a Protection Against the Onset of Symptoms of Dementia," *Neuropsychologia,* 45 (2007), 459–64.

142   one works hard at tasks that one finds rewarding: Ellen Winner, *Gifted Children: Myths and Realities* (New York: Basic Books, 1996), 146.

142   "they are intrinsically motivated to acquire skill": Ellen Winner, "The Rage to Master: The Decisive Role of Talent in the Visual Arts," in K. Anders Ericsson (ed.), *The Road to Excellence: The Acquisition of Expert Performance in the Arts and Sciences, Sports, and Games* (Mahwah, NJ: Lawrence Erlbaum Associates, 1996), 271–301.

PART 3 REVELATION: The Brain Whispers

Chapter 10

148   as late as 1800, more than 100 languages were spoken: Lyle Campbell, *American Indian Languages: The Historical Linguistics of Native America* (Oxford, UK: Oxford University Press, 1997), 16.

148 contained half of the entire world's linguistic diversity: Lyle Campbell, personal communication, 2010.

148 living their lives in their native tongues: See Gillian Stevens. "A Century of US Censuses and the Language Characteristics of Immigrants," *Demography*, 36:3 (1999), 391.

148 23 percent . . . reported that they couldn't speak English at all: Ibid. 394.

148 illegal to speak any language but English: Bill Piatt, *¿Only English? Law and Language Policy in the United States* (Albuquerque: University of New Mexico Press, 1990).

148 By 1960, the number had fallen to 29: J. Holmquist, *They Chose Minnesota* (St. Paul, Minnesota Historical Society Press, 2003), 178.

148 showed up at the teacher's desk speaking French: Mazat, W. (2000). *"Emil Krebs (1867–1930), das Sprachwunder, Dolmetscher in Peking und Tsingtau. Eine Lebensskizze."* (Wilhelm Matzat, "Emil Krebs (1867–1930) The Language Wonder— Interpreter in Peking and Tsingtau,") *Bulletin of the German China Association*, 1, 31–47.

149 By then, he had studied: Ibid., 1

149 "I want to learn the hardest one": Ibid., 2

149 One day an exacting Chinese imperial official: Krebs's relationship with the Empress Dowager is described by Matzat, 7, quoting Ferdinand Lessing, "Emil Krebs," *Ostasiatische Rundschau* (1930).

150 "a striking example of the linguistic outward-lookingness that has pervaded the Indian Ocean world": Benjamin Zimmer, "Linguistic Imaginations of the Indian Ocean World: Historical Viewpoints from Western Java," Paper presented at the International Conference on Cultural Exchange and Transformation in the Indian Ocean World, 2002.

151 "Then he was a master of them too": Werner Otto von Hentig, "Memories of Emil Krebs," undated typescript.

152 He had translated the phrase: "Man Who Knew 65 Languages," *Western Argus*, 15 April, 1930, 26.

152 Hentig described having to fetch Krebs for a meeting: Hentig, "Memories."

152 With a book in hand, he walked around and around: This portrait is compiled from Hentig's account.

153 His Tuscan dialect was so good: Ibid., 7.

153 "this wonderful talent bites its thumb": Ibid., 15.

153 more daily newspapers published in other languages: "Polyglot America," *The Brisbane Courier*, Feb. 14, 1929, 12.

153 cluster of real hyperpolyglots at Ellis Island: Barry Moreno, personal communication.

154 eventually was sold to the US Library of Congress: Shuzhao Hu, *The Development of the Chinese Collection in the Library of Congress* (Boulder, CO: Westview Press, 1979), 83–84. "While the bulk of his collection was devoted to rare lexicographical aids to the study of central European languages, the Chinese items alone numbered 236 works in 1,620 volumes. They are richest in Chinese novels, popular lyrics, histories, government documents, and early examples of *pai-hua* (vernacular) literature."

154 "surrendering to his great ambition for language study": Eckhard Hoffmann

has written and talked about Krebs extensively; one example is available here: http://ueberFlieger.qoalu.com/artikel/den-kopf-voller-sprachen.

154 The request came from Oskar Vogt: E. G. Jones, "Review of *Cécile and Oskar Vogt: The Visionaries of Modern Neuroscience,* by Igor Klatzo," *Nature,* 421 (2003), 19–20.

154 "It also appeared a brilliant idea to obtain": Igor Klatzko, *Cécile and Oskar Vogt: The Visionaries of Modern Neuroscience (Acta Neurochirurgica Supplement 80)* (New York: Springer Wien, 2002), 30.

Chapter 11

156 languages are controlled in other places besides "Broca's area": Harry W. Whitaker, "Paul Broca," in Robert Andrew Wilson & Frank C. Keil (eds.), *The MIT Encyclopedia of the Cognitive Sciences* (Cambridge, MA.: MIT Press, 2001), 97–98. See also F. Dronkers, O. Plaisant, M. T. Iba-Zizen, and E. A. Cabanis, "Paul Broca's Historic Cases: High Resolution MR Imaging of the Brains of Leborgne and Lelong," *Brain,* 130:5 (2007), 1432–41.

158 "dual stream" model: Gregory Hickok and David Poeppel, "Dorsal and Ventral Streams: A Framework for Understanding Aspects of the Functional Anatomy of Language": *Cognition,* 92:1–2 (2004), 67–99.

158 engaged mainly on the left side of the brain: See, for example, G. Vingerhoets et al., "Multilingualism: An fMRI Study," *NeuroImage* 20 (2003), 2181–96. Also Rita Franceschini et al., "Learner Acquisition Strategies (LAS) in the Course of Life: A Language Biographic Approach," paper presented at the Second International Conference on Third Language Acquisition and Trilingualism, Fryske Akademy, Sept. 13–15, 2001.

Chapter 12

161 galvanizing work that promised many answers: Katrin Amunts, A. Schleicher, and Karl Zilles, "Outstanding Language Competence and Cytoarchitecture in Broca's Speech Region," *Brain and Language,* 89 (2004), 346–53.

162 exploring the "neurological substrate" of talent: Loraine Obler and Deborah Fein (eds.), *The Exceptional Brain: Neuropsychology of Talent and Special Abilities* (New York: Guilford Press, 1988).

163 aren't held back from hearing and producing: See, for example, B. McLaughlin and N. Nayak, "Processing a New Language: Does Knowing Other Languages Make a Difference?" in H. W. Dechert and M. Raupach (eds.), *Interlingual Processes* (Tübingen: Narr, 1989), 5–16.

164 his answer was a resolute yes: Peter Skehan, *A Cognitive Approach to Language Learning* (Oxford, UK: Oxford University Press, 1998), 211.

164 They "would have a high range of lexicalized exemplars": Ibid., 250.

164 "do not seem to have unusual abilities with respect to input or central processing": Ibid., 233.

165 part of the memory system that remembers facts and words, and which remains robust as one ages: This paragraph draws from Michael Ullmann's

Declarative/Procedural Model, described in "A Cognitive Neuroscience Perspective on Second Language Acquisition: The Declarative/Procedural Model," in Cristina Sanz (ed.), *Mind and Context in Adult Second Language Acquisition: Methods, Theory, and Practice* (Washington, DC: Georgetown University Press, 2006), 141–78. His account contains many intriguing possibilities for understanding individual variations that might explain very high levels of language abilities, including gender differences and seasonal/hormonal effects, as well as chemical interventions for enhancing procedural and declarative memories.

165 they just have declarative memories with a lot of capacity: One possibility might be that language accumulators choose certain languages to compensate for relative limitations of procedural memory. That is, they would opt for inflected languages over isolating languages, the notion being that inflections encode grammatical relationships in the words themselves that would otherwise rely on procedural memory. Of the 172 language repertoires I collected in my online survey, only 20 contained Mandarin. Moreover, only 5 had more than one Chinese language or other Southeast Asian language. Typical repertoires were ones like "Portuguese, English, Latin, French, Spanish, Italian, German, Russian, Polish" or "Hungarian, Serbian, German, English, Italian, Esperanto." People were clearly choosing languages whose words are combined of many smaller parts. (This doesn't seem to explain Emil Krebs, however, whose mental resources weren't exhausted by Chinese.) Surely this bias toward a certain type of language has partly to do with the fact that the survey circulated on English-language forums and blogs.

165 asymmetry could create clusters of talents and deficits: Norman Geschwind and A. M. Galaburda, "Cerebral Lateralisation: Biological Mechanisms, Associations, and Pathology: I," *Archives of Neurology*, 42 (1985), 428–59; "Cerebral Lateralisation: Biological Mechanisms, Associations, and Pathology: II," *Archives of Neurology*, 42 (1985), 521–52; "Cerebral Lateralisation: Biological Mechanisms, Associations, and Pathology: III," *Archives of Neurology*, 42 (1985), 634–54.

167 left-handers often reported having speech problems: K. M. Cornish, "The Geschwind and Galaburda Theory of Cerebral Lateralisation: An Empirical Evaluation of Its Assumptions," *Current Psychology*, 15:1 (1996), 68–76.

167 people with autism have higher rates of non-right-handedness: See Senole Dane and Nese Balci, "Handedness, Eyedness and Nasal Cycle in Children with Autism," *International Journal of Developmental Neuroscience*, Vol. 25, No. 4 (2007), 223–26. Also, P. R. Escalante-Mead, N. J. Minshew, and J. A. Sweeney, "Abnormal brain lateralization in high-functioning autism," *Journal of Autism and Developmental Disorders*, Vol. 3, No. 5, (2003), 539–543.

168 more males than females who perform both very high and very low: G. M. Grimshaw, G. Sitarenios, and J. K. Finegan, "Mental Rotation at 7 Years: Relations with Prenatal Testosterone Levels and Spatial Play Experiences," *Brain and Cognition* 29 (1995), 85–100.

Chapter 13

173 the tool that Amunts used on Krebs's brain slices: This project, called the Human Brain Mapping Initiative, constructs maps of the probability that any given point of a brain belongs to a certain named region. Such a mapping avoids

one of the pitfalls of traditional brain anatomy, in which individual brains vary so much in size (ranging in weight from 1,000 grams to 1,700 grams) and in structure that the brain areas (such as Broca's) don't line up.

173 Amunts found that in Krebs's brain: See Katrin Amunts, A. Schleicher, and Karl Zilles, "Outstanding Language Competence and Cytoarchitecture in Broca's Speech Region," *Brain and Language,* 89 (2004), 346–53.

174 "meta-linguistic abilities far beyond automatic speech": Ibid., 351.

174 may also have something to do with Krebs's Chinese: J. Crinion et al., "Neuroanatomical Markers of Speaking Chinese," *Human Brain Mapping* 30:12 (2009), 4108–15.

174 Italian research team revealed in 2009: C. Bloch et al., "The Age of Second Language Acquisition Determines the Variability in Activation Elicited by Narration in Three Languages in Broca's and Wernike's Areas": *Neuropsychologia,* 47:3 (2008), 625–33.

Chapter 14

177 Different languages activated overlapping areas of the brain: R. S. Briellmann, M. M. Saling, A. B. Connell, et al., "A High-Field Functional MRI Study of Quadri-Lingual Subjects," *Brain and Language,* 89:2 (2004), 531–42.

179 training increases the number of synapses: A. Norton et al., "Are There Preexisting Neural, Cognitive or Motoric Markers for Musical Ability?," *Brain and Cognition,* 59 (2005), 130.

180 "Automatic acquisition from mere exposure": Eric Lenneberg, *Biological Foundations of Language* (New York: Wiley, 1967), 176.

181 If a child learning Swedish can't become a native speaker: Niclas Abrahamsson and Kenneth Hyltenstam, "Age of Onset and Nativelikeness in a Second Language: Listener Perception Versus Linguistic Scrutiny": *Language Learning,* 59:2 (2009), 287.

181 Some have figured that only 5 percent: Larry Selinker, "Interlanguage," *International Review of Applied Linguistics in Language Teaching,* 10 (1972), 209–31.

181 at fewer than 1 percent: R. Coppetiers, "Competence Differences Between Native and Near-Native Speakers," *Language,* 63:3 (1987), 545–73.

181 a type of sentence that's hard for people to learn: Sonja van Boxtel, T. Bongaerts, and P. A. Coppen, "Native-like Attainment of Dummy Subjects in Dutch and the Role of the L1," *International Review of Applied Linguistics,* 43 (2005), 355–80.

182 In another project, an exhaustive battery: Stefka Marinova-Todd, *Comprehensive Analysis of Ultimate Attainment in Adult Second Language Acquisition,* PhD dissertation (unpublished), Harvard University, 2003.

PART 4 ELABORATION: The Brains of Babel

Chapter 15

189 Sorensen wrote in an article about the place: Arthur Sorensen Jr., "Multilingualism in the Northwest Amazon," *American Anthropologist,* 69 (1967), 670–84.

190 typical person will "speak only two or three": Leslie Moore, "Language Mixing at Home and School in a Multilingual Community (Mandara Mountains, Cameroon)," *Georgetown University Round Table on Languages and Linguistics* (2006), 1.

191 "speaks *pelasla, wuzlam,* and French fluently": Scott MacEachern, *Du Kunde: Processes of Montagnard Ethnogenesis in the Northern Mandara Mountains of Cameroon* (London: Mandaras, 2003), 274.

191 four languages was the norm: Ibid., 275.

196 The languages borrowed each other's sound patterns: Murray Emeneau, "India as a Linguistic Area": *Language,* 32:1 (1956), 7.

196 For instance, Sanskrit: Ibid., 9.

197 Added to this mix was the third invasion: See, for example, N. Krishnaswamy and L. Krishnaswamy, *The Story of English in India* (New Delhi: Foundation Books Ltd., 2006).

197 range from 5 to 50 percent of the population: David Graddol, *English Next* (2006), www.britishcouncil.org/learning-research-english-next.pdf, 94.

197 the power structure along with independence: Krishnaswamy and Krishnaswamy, *Story of English,* 109.

197 "over which one language is spoken from end to end": George Grierson, *Linguistic Survey of India,* vol. I, part 1, 93.

198 newspapers are published in at least 34 languages: From the 2001 linguistic census of India.

198 The next most populous Indian languages are Bengali, with 70 million speakers, and Telugu, with 69 million: All of the figures here from Paul M. Lewis (ed.), *Ethnologue: Languages of the World,* 16th ed. (Dallas, TX: SIL International, 2009).

198 one house with many mansions": Wendy Doniger, *The Hindus* (New York: Penguin Press, 2009), 197.

198 Bangalore, bringing Tamil with them: The history is related in S. M. Lal, *Convergence and Language Shifts in a Linguistic Minority: A Sociolinguistic Study of Tamilsi in Bangalore City* (Mysore: CIIL, 1986).

200 Hindu fundamentalists attacked Indian women dressed in Western clothes: See Somini Sengupta, "Attack on Women at an Indian Bar Intensifies a Clash of Cultures," *New York Times,* Feb. 9, 2009. Also, "Police to Invoke Goondas Act Against Hindutva Extremists," *The Hindu,* Jan. 27, 2009.

200 "They were being forced into a clipped and compromised existence": Raju Srinivasaraju, *Keeping Faith with the Mother Tongue: The Anxieties of a Local Culture* (Bangalore: Navakarnataka Publications, 2008), 15.

201 "Within two generations, the Indian literary past": Sheldon Pollock, "The Real Classical Languages Debate." *The Hindu,* Nov. 27, 2008.

201 the notion is obvious in the painting *Goddess English:* www.bbc.co.uk/news/world-south-asia-12355740.

202 "Goddess English is all about emancipation": http://blog.shashwati.com/2006/11/04/goddess-english-ii/.

202 assume that anyone working with computers is a Brahmin: From a study by Gail Omvedt, quoted in www.rediff.com/news/2007/mar/05inter.htm.

202 "if I say the same things in English, I am heard and applauded":www.rediff.com/news/2007/mar/05inter.htm.

203 until you see that he knows languages in four families: A. K. Srivastava et al., *The Language Load* (Mysore: CIIL, 1978).

207   successful interactions 89 percent of the time: Josep Colomer, "To Translate or
      to Learn Languages? An Evaluation of Social Efficiency," *International Journal of
      the Sociology of Language*, 121 (1996), 181–97.
209   "bilinguals know their languages to the level that they need them": François
      Grosjean, www.francoisgrosjean.ch/myths_en.html.
211   we need is something brain-based: See, for example, Joan Kelly Hall, An Cheng,
      and Matthew T. Carlson, "Reconceptualizing Multicompetence as a Theory of
      Language Knowledge," *Applied Linguistics*, 27:2 (2006).

Chapter 16

215   "trust their guts": Madeline Ehrman and B. L. Leaver, "Cognitive Styles in the
      Service of Language Learning," *System*, 31 (2003), 395.
215   not enough for them to call something "green": Madeline Ehrman, "Personal-
      ity and Good Language Learners," in Carol Griffiths (ed.), *Lessons from Good
      Language Learners* (Cambridge, UK: Cambridge University Press, 2008), 67.
215   They *notice* (which was a key skill): Madeline Ehrman, "Variations on a Theme:
      What Distinguishes Distinguished Learners?," October 2006.
216   "functionally equivalent" to the well-educated native reader or listener: http://
      www.uscg.mil/hq/capemay/education/dlpt.asp.
221   "some bilinguals are dominant in one language": www.francoisgrosjean.ch
      /myths_en.html.
222   based on a scale first developed by the US State Department's Foreign Service
      Institute: www.govtilr.org/Skills/IRL%20Scale%20History.htm.
223   good correlation between the skills that someone reports and their actual
      skill level: D. M. Kenyon, V. Malabonga, and H. Carpenter, "Effects of Exam-
      inee Control on Examinee Attitudes and Performance on a Computerized
      Oral Proficiency Test," paper presented at the 23rd Annual Language Testing
      Research Colloquium. Cited in D. M. Kenyon, V. Malabonga, and H. Carpenter,
      "Response to the Norris Commentary," in *Language Learning and Technology*, 5:2
      (2001) 106–10, http://llt.msu.edu/vol5num2/response/default.html.
223   5 is a "functionally native proficiency": www.govtilr.org/Skills/ILRscale2.htm.
224   exploration of how people lose and relearn those languages: Kees de Bot and
      Saskia Stoessel, "In Search of Yesterday's Words: Reactivating a Long-Forgotten
      Language," *Applied Linguistics*, 21:3 (2000), 333–53.
227   suggests that items in memory begin to compete: K. Oberauer and R. Kliegl, "A
      Formal Model of Capacity Limits in Working Memory," *Journal of Memory and
      Language*, 55 (2006), 601–26.
228   a psychiatric illness that affects 1 to 3 percent: L. Friedlander and M. Desrocher,
      "Neuroimaging Studies of Obsessive-Compulsive Disorder in Adults and Chil-
      dren," *Clinical Psychological Review* 26 (2006), 32–49.
229   When someone systemizes, she (or, more likely, he): Simon Baron-Cohen,
      "The Extreme Male Brain Theory of Autism," *TRENDS in Cognitive Sciences*, 6:6
      (2002), 248.
230   higher than doctors, veterinarians, and biologists: Simon Baron-Cohen et al.,
      "The Autism-Spectrum Quotient (AQ): Evidence from Asperger Syndrome/
      High-Functioning Autism, Males and Females, Scientists and Mathematicians,"
      Journal of Autism and Developmental Disorders 31 (2001), 14.

230 has also found that autism occurs more frequently: Simon Baron-Cohen, "Does Autism Occur More Often in Families of Physicists, Engineers, and Mathematicians?," *Autism* 2 (1998), 296–301.

230 relevant work on the obsessional interests of children with autism: Simon Baron-Cohen, "Obsessions in Children with Autism or Asperger Syndrome," *British Journal of Psychiatry*, 175 (1999), 487.

Chapter 17

232 talented mimics had lower levels of activation in brain regions related to speech: Many of these results and others are discussed in Grzegorz Dogil and Susanne Reiterer (eds.), *Language Talent and Brain Activity* (Berlin: Walter de Gruyter, 2009).

232 anatomically more complex than those in non-phonetician brains: Narly Golestani, Cathy J. Rice, and Sophie K. Scott, "Born with an Ear for Dialects? Structural Plasticity in the Expert Phonetician Brain," *Journal of Neuroscience,* 31:11 (2011), 4213–20. See also N. Golestani, T. Paus, and R. J. Zatorre, "Anatomical Correlates of Learning Novel Speech Sounds," *Neuron,* 35 (2002), 997–1010; Narly Golestani and R. J. Zatorre, "Learning New Sounds of Speech: Reallocation of Neural Substrates," *Neuroimage* 21 (2004), 494–506.

233 left insula . . . more strongly in bilinguals who have equal abilities in their two languages: Michael Chee et al., "Left Insula Activation: A Marker for Language Attainment in Bilinguals," *PNAS,* 101:42 (2004), 15265–70.

233 "may correspond to vocabulary growth": Ibid., 15269.

233 ability to automatically remember and accurately repeat nonsense words: Alan Baddeley, *Working Memory, Thought, and Action* (Oxford, UK: Oxford University Press, 2007), 8.

233 can't learn new foreign words: Alan Baddeley and Graham Hitch, "Working Memory," in G. A. Bower (ed.), *The Psychology of Learning and Motivation,* vol. 8 (New York: Academic Press, 1974), 17.

234 "genetic differences in neurotransmitter functions": Caterina Breitenstein et al., "Hippocampus Activity Differentiates Good from Poor Learners of a Novel Lexicon," *NeuroImage,* 25 (2005), 965.

235 called for more research into improving a variety of cognitive abilities on adults: Some of this research was reported in Cathy Doughty and Anita Bowles. "A Talent for Language." *The Next Wave,* 18:1 (2009), 33–41.

235–236 suppress how strongly neurons fire: M. B. Iyer, U. Mattu, J. Grafman, et al., "Safety and Cognitive Effects of Frontal DC Brain Polarization in Healthy Individuals," *Neurology,* 64 (2005), 872–75.

236 the positive effect had disappeared: Agnes Flöel, Nina Röser, Olesya Michka, et al., "Noninvasive Brain Stimulation Improves Language Learning," *Journal of Cognitive Neuroscience,* 20: 8 (2008), 1415–22.

236 abilities to generate words that started with a particular letter increased by 20 percent: Iyer et al., "Safety and Cognitive Effects."

236 to increase people's visual memory by 110 percent: R. P. Chi et al., "Visual Memory Improved by Non-invasive Brain Stimulation," *Brain Research,* 1353 (2010), 168–75.

236   as does the odor of rosemary: M. Moss and J. Cook, "Aromas of Rosemary and
      Lavender Essential Oils Differentially Affect Cognition in Healthy Adults,"
      International Journal of Neuroscience, 113 (2003), 15.
236   two cups of coffee increases neuronal activity: F. Koppelstatter and B. Rubin,
      "Influence of Caffeine Excess on Activation Patterns in Verbal Working Mem-
      ory," paper presented at the annual meeting of the Radiological Society of
      North America, Chicago, 2005.
237   d-amphetamine and levodopa . . . learning by 20 percent in healthy subjects:
      Caterina Breitenstein et al., "D-amphetamine Boosts Language Learning Inde-
      pendent of Its Cardiovascular and Motor Arousing Effects," *Neuropsychophar-
      macology,* 29 (2004), 1704–14.
241   "conducive to plasticity in a noninvasive but targeted manner": Daphne Bave-
      lier, Dennis M. Levi, Roger W. Li, et al., "Removing Brakes on Adult Brain Plas-
      ticity: From Molecular to Behavioral Interventions," *The Journal of Neuroscience,*
      30:45 (2010), 14968.
241   flow is "characterized by a deep sense of enjoyment": Ibid.
241   "It would be ideal to endogenously recapitulate brain states": Daphne Bavelier,
      Dennis M. Levi, Roger W. Li, et al., "Removing Brakes on Adult Brain Plasticity:
      From Molecular to Behavioral Interventions," *The Journal of Neuroscience,* 30:45
      (2010), 14964–71.

PART 5 ARRIVAL: The Hyperpolyglot of Flanders

Chapter 18

251   Seven were dead languages; in another seven he described his knowledge as
      superficial: Vandewalle has helpfully posted documents from the contest on his
      website, http://users.telenet.be/orientaal/oprichter.html.

Chapter 19

263   individuals' skills could be explained by what they'd inherited genetically:
      Naomi P. Friedman et al., "Individual Differences in Executive Functions Are
      Almost Entirely Genetic in Origin," *Journal of Experimental Psychology,* 137:2
      (2008), 201–25.
263   not likely to transfer that skill to other areas: Torkel Klingberg, *The Overflowing
      Brain: Information Overload and the Limits of Working Memory* (Neil Betteridge,
      trans.) (Oxford, UK: Oxford University Press, 2009), 120.
263   "Spend time tinkering with the language every day": Kató Lomb, *Polyglot: How
      I Learn Languages* (Ádám Szegi and Kornelia DeKorne, trans.; Scott Alkire, ed.)
      (Berkeley, CA: TESL-EJ, 2008), 159.
264   the same part of the brain: Agnes Flöel, T. Ellger, Caterina Breitenstein, and S.
      Knecht, "Language Perception Activates the Hand Motor Cortex: Implications
      for Motor Theories of Speech Perception," *European Journal of Neuroscience,*
      18:3 (2003), 704–8, M. Gentilucci and R. Dalla Volta, "Spoken Language and
      Arm Gestures Are Controlled by the Same Motor Control System," *Quarterly
      Journal of Experimental Psychology,* 61:6 (2008), 944–57.

267   Pablo Tac, a young student: Tac also described what happened to his people
      during the Conquest in a book, *Indian Life and Customs at Mission San Luis Rey*.
      He died in Rome at the age of nineteen.
267   "secret process, if any, which he employed": Charles Russell, *The Life of Cardinal
      Mezzofanti, with an Introductory Memoir of Eminent Linguists, Ancient and Modern*
      (London: Longman, Brown, and Co., 1858), 475.

INDEX

Page numbers in *italics* refer to illustrations.
Page numbers beginning with 277 refer to end notes.

Abadzi, Helen, 132–37, *132*, 139, 141–43,
    169, 175, 212, 227, 236, 254, 256,
    261–63
Abadzi, Theodore, 136
Académie Française, 208
Accademia Poliglotta, 137–38, 267
accents, 5, 8, 11, 33, 84, 238
    American, 261
    British, 21, 204
    Colombian *altiplano,* 19–20
    native, 123
    pure, 19
    thick, 18, 232
ADHD, 214
adrenaline, 237
Africa, 3
    sub-Saharan, 85
    tribal and village languages of, 21
Afrikaans language, 118, 218, 248
Afroasiatic language family, 44*n*
Aikhenvald, Alexandra, 190
Air Force, U.S., 176
air traffic controllers, 54–55, 281
Albanian language, 4, 31, 43
Algonquin language, 31, 40–41, 43, 60, 210,
    268
Alliance Française, 203
alphabets, 30, 34, 39, 44
    Greek, 31
al-Qaeda, 71

"Amarinna" language, 43
Amazon basin, 189–90
American Airlines Boeing 757 jet crash
    (1995), 55, 281
American Antiquarian Society, 75
American Council on the Teaching of
    Foreign Languages (ACTFL), 222–23
American University, Beirut, 106
Americas, indigenous languages of, 31, *35,*
    40–41, 42, 43, 76, 82, 148, 219
Amharic language, 4, 31
Amunts, Katrin, 171–74, 177–79, 212, 287,
    289
Angolana language, 30
Angolese language, 43
Annamalai, E., 208–9
aphasia, 156
Arabic language, 3, 4, 8, 30, 31, 39, 42, 43,
    45, 47, 58, 60, 61, 152–53
    study and teaching of, 9, 33, 35, 106, 131,
    161, 162
Arabic numbers, 117
Aramaic language, 150
Ardaschir, King of Persia, 107*n*
Ardaschir, *see* Arguelles, Alexander
Arguelles, Alexander, 107–8, 110–27, *116,*
    129–31, 136, 137, 140–43, 152, 166, 169,
    175–76, 212, 226, 231, 233, 239, 261–62,
    264, 284
Arguelles, Ivan, 118–21, 166, 210

Arguelles, Joseph, 118–19
Arguelles, Max, 113, 119–20
Aristotle University, 94
Armenian language, 30, 57
   ancient, 43, 151
   modern, 43
Armstrong, Thomas, 214–15
Army, U.S., 163
Art and Science of Learning Languages, The
   (Gunnemark and Gethin), 99–101, 226,
   283
Asperger's syndrome, 175, 229, 230, 291
Assimil, 239, 275–76
Assyrian language, 154
Athens, University of, 153
atherosclerosis, 154
attention spans, 33
Australia, 80
   aboriginal language of, 81, 82
autism spectrum disorders, 95, 165, 167,
   175, 214, 229–30, 288, 291–92
aviation industry, 54–55

Babylonian language, 154
Bahrick, Harry, 134
Bangalore School of English, 204
Bangladesh, 85n
Baron-Cohen, Simon, 229–30, 239, 291–92
Basque language, 4, 31, 43
Bavelier, Daphne, 241, 293
Bawa, Zainab, 203
BBC, 202, 255
Béarnais language, 47n
Beijing, 8, 20, 149, 153
Bel Canto (Patchett), 21–22
Belgium, 247
   multilingualism of, 25–26
Bengali language, 119n, 194, 203
Berber language, 95
Bible, 34, 79
   translations of, 58–59, 60
*Bilingual Brain, The: Neuropsychological and
   Neurolinguistic Aspects of Bilingualism*
   (Obler and Albert), 162
bilingualism, 13, 33, 49, 51, 63, 140, 180,
   190, 226
Bimbarra language, 42
Bohemian language, 31, 43, 75n
Bologna, 3, 16, 17, 19, 21, 27–38, 56–62, 134,
   265–69
   Allied bombing of, 28
   Archiginnasio public library of, 27–32, 52,
      61–62, 267–69, 278
   as linguistic cross roads, 34–38, 58, 242

Bologna, University of, 3, 35
   library of, 57–60
Bolognese language, 4, 31, 37, 124
Boothe, Ryan, 125–26
Borges, Jorge Luis, 125
Borrow, George Henry, 228
Boucheron, Carlo, 6
brain-as-globe metaphor, 157–60, 171, 173,
   232, 233, 236
brain-derived neurotrophic factor (BDNF),
   237
brain imaging technologies, 14, 157, 159,
   232, 233
brains, 124–25
   anterior cingulum of, 236
   of babies, 69
   biochemistry of, 237, 241, 262
   Broca's area of, 156–57, 160, 171–74, 238,
      287, 289
   cognitive aging and disorder in, 140, 162
   development of, 229
   disease and damage of, 73–74, 94–95, 113,
      139, 156, 157, 161, 171, 174, 233–34
   executive function of, 139, 263, 285
   frontal lobe of, 236
   as globe, *see* brain-as-globe
   hippocampus of, 234, 237, 292
   of hyperpolyglots, 14, 15, 28, 140,
      142–43, 154, 155, 170–75, 212, 231–43
   insula of, 233
   language as separate function of, 97–98
   language centers in, 24, 69, 74, 139,
      156–60, 171–74, 178, 238
   limitations of, 10
   neural circuits of, 33, 86, 139, 140, 143,
      155, 158–60, 162, 171–74, 205–6,
      233–34, 236–38, 241–43, 262
   oxygen use in, 159, 178, 179
   plasticity of, 8, 9, 14, 33, 72, 85–86, 122,
      158, 180–81, 237, 241, 243, 262–63,
      282–83
   posterior parietal cortex of, 139
   prefrontal cortex of, 139, 155, 157
   preservation and analysis of, 154–56, 160,
      161, 171–75, 177–80
   primary auditory cortex (Heschl's gyrus)
      of, 232–33, 260
   right and left hemispheres of, 157–58,
      165–66, 173–74, 229, 238
   streams of, 157–59, 287
   study of, 41, 154–60, 170–75
   Wernicke's area of, 157, 160, 238, 289
Brazil, 9, 10, 106, 109
Breitenstein, Caterina, 237, 292, 293

Briareus, 4
British Sign language (BSL), 97
Broca, Paul, 156–57, 287
Brodmann, Korbinian, 173
Bruch, Charles Philip Christian, 79–80
Brussels, 25, 136, 166, 223, 247
Bulgarian language, 43, 104, 132
Bunsen, Baron, 5
Bunyan, Paul, 75
Burmese language, 31, 42
Burritt, Elihu, 74–78, 76, 77, 104, 141–42, 228, 281–82
Burton, Sir Richard Francis, 47, 104, 280
Byron, George Gordon, Lord, 4–5, 58

California, University of:
   at Berkeley, 21, 120, 129
   at Irvine, 158
   at Los Angeles, 160, 237
"Californian" language, 31, 43
calques, 96–97, 99
Campbell, George, 73, 281
Cansdale, Graham, 166–67, 222–25, 224, 225, 242, 261, 263, 264
Caronni, Felix, 3
cartoons, 53
Catalan language, 39, 119
catechism, 31
Catherine, Saint, 32
Cécile and Oskar Vogt Institute of Brain Research, 170
cell phones, 8
Celtic languages, 75, 76, 218
Central Institute for Indian Languages, 205
Chaldaic language, 75
Chaldean language, 4, 43, 76
Chee, Michael, 233, 292
Chicago, University of, 108, 208
Chihuahua, 87–89
child prodigies, 79, 282
China, 8, 44, 55, 147, 149–53
   value of English language in, 9
Chinese language, 4, 30, 31, 35, 41, 43, 44–45, 57, 120, 123, 147–48
   Cantonese, 106, 109
   characters of, 39, 113, 117, 150
   Mandarin, 9, 10, 20, 52, 81, 97, 106–7, 109, 123, 124, 149, 151, 251
   study of, 9, 110, 149, 174
Chinese University of Hong Kong, 164
Chippewa language, 42
Christianity, 150
Christopher, 94–99, 124, 141, 162–65, 169, 210

language abilities of, 69, 94–96, 98–99, 134, 175, 227–28
   mental impairment of, 69, 94–96, 97, 162
Cispadane Republic, 35
Cixi, Empress Dowager of China, 149
C.J., 162–66, 168–69, 227–28
Cochin-Chinese language, 42
Codex Cospi, 60, 267
Cohen, Andrew, 128, 259–60
cold war, 90
Coleman, Loren, 169
colloquialisms, 53
Colloquial Romanian, 119
Colombia, 19–20, 55, 91
Colomer, Josep, 206–7
colonialism, 84, 242
colors, 49, 280
Columbia University, 107–8, 200
Columbus, Christopher, 79
Confucius, 151
Conrad, Joseph, 231–32
Cook, Vivian, 52–54, 197, 280
Cooper, James Fenimore, 40
Coptic language, 3, 4, 31, 433
Cornish language, 42, 118
Coryat, Tom, 42
Costello, Elvis, 120
Cox, Gregg, 176–77, 220–21, 226–27
Cox, Sabine, 220
creole languages, 106
cryptozoology, 169, 248–49
Curtin, Jeremiah, 78, 78
Czech language, 35, 43, 104, 207
Czerniawski, Eugen M., 100, 105

d-amphetamine, 237, 293
Danish language, 31, 43, 75, 104
Dart, Frédéric, 203
Dead Souls (Gogol), 102
deafness, 45, 279
de Bot, Kees, 224, 291
Defense Language Institute (DLI), 176, 216–17
Defense Language Proficiency Test (DLPT), 216, 223
DeKeyser, Robert, 24–26, 134, 136
De Koninck, Joseph, 48, 280
Delaware language, 42
dialects, 5, 6, 10, 47n, 115
   Florentine, 35
   local, 35, 90
   Parisian, 51
   regional, 51
   Tuscan, 153
   versions of, 45

dictionaries, 5, 11, 31, 37, 39, 75, 84, 95, 122, 148, 227
diffusion tensor imaging (DTI), 157
digital language repeater, 133
Doniger, Wendy, 198
Donovan, Edgar, 216–17, 222
dopamine, 237, 241, 262
Dravidian languages, 191, 196, 200, 208
Dreaming in Chinese (Fallows), 86
Dreaming in Hindi (Rich), 86
Duran, Miguel, 88–89
Dutch language, 4, 25, 30, 31, 39, 43, 95, 106, 114–15, 124, 181–82, 207, 248, 250
dyslexia, 165, 166, 214

Eapen, Joshy, 204
East India Company, 47n
Eats, Shoots & Leaves (Truss), 207
Edinburgh University, 255
Egypt, 85n
Ehrman, Madeline, 163n, 215, 291
Einstein, Albert, brain of, 160
Elements of Style, The (White and Strunk), 207
Elizabeth I, Queen of England, 197
Ellis Island, 153–54
Emlen, Deborah, 59
English and Foreign Language University, Hyderabad, 202
English language, 4, 5, 8, 17, 18, 30, 43, 49, 96
    aviation industry's use of, 54–55
    as global lingua franca, 9, 10, 85, 261
    Middle, 108, 118
    native vs. non-native speakers of, 9
    Old, 108
    pidgin version of, 7
    prestige and utility of, 9
    as second language, 9
    spread of, 9
    standardized foreign versions of, 9
    study and teaching of, 9, 20, 25, 182, 261
Enki (god), 12
Enlil (god), 12
enunciation, 46
Esperanto, 247
Estonia, 31
Estonian language, 54, 75n
Ethiopian language, 31, 43, 75
Euclid, 35
Eurobarometer poll of 2005, 91n
European Commission, 25, 53, 166
European Union, 9, 71
    bilingualism advocated in, 91

Everett, William, 74–75
Exceptional Brain, The: Neuropsychology of Talent and Special Abilities (Obler and Fein, eds.), 162, 212, 287
eyes, 10, 77

Fallows, Deborah, 86
Farsi language, 109–10
Fazah, Ziad, 100, 105–7, 108–10, 125–27, 176, 210, 226, 257
Ferriss, Tim, 86, 283
Finnish language, 81, 109, 152
Finno-Ugric languages, 218
flash cards, 131, 267–68, *269*
Flemish language, 35, 43, 75
Flume, Harvey, 214
Flynn, Suzanne, 226
Foreign Service Institute, 223, 291
    School of Language Studies of, 215
Foschi, Paula, 29
Fowler, Lorenzo Niles, 77–78, 282
FOXP2 gene, 234
French language, 4, 8, 10, 18, 25, 30, 35, 41, 43, 46, 124
    dialects in, 51
    Old, 108
    study of, 9, 19, 20, 33, 48, 148–49
French Revolution, 51
Friedman, Naomi, 263, 293
Frisian language, 42, 118, 255
functional magnetic resonance imaging (fMRI), 157, 232, 233, 287, 289

Gaelic language, 42, 75, 111, 252, 255, 256, 258
    Manx, 118
    Scottish, 118
Galaburda, Albert, 165–66, 288
Galvani, Luigi, 27
Ganahl, Rainer, 83–85, 86n, 140–41, 252, 265, 282
Genesis, Book of, 31, 60
Geneva, 17, 18
Gentleman Prefer Blondes (Loos), 102
Georgian language, 43, 54
Germanic languages, 44, 96, 115, 218
German language, 4, 5, 10, 25, 30, 35, 44, 60, 96, 124, 148
    Austrian dialect of, 5
    Middle High, 118
    Old High, 108, 118, 218
    Saxon dialect of, 5
    study of, 9, 33
    Swabian dialect of, 5

Geschwind, Norman, 165–66, 288
Geschwind-Galaburda hypothesis, 165–68, 170, 173, 212, 216, 222, 229, 288
gestures, 28, 110, 211, 264, 294
Gezels, Linda (wife of John Vandewalle), 250–51
Gethin, Amorey, 226
Ghent University College, 250
Giordani, Pietro, 59
globalization, 8, 11
glyphs, 60
God, 4, 11, 12, 37, 60, 122
Goddess English, 201–2
Gogol, Nikolay, 102
Golestani, Narly, 232–33, 292
Golla, Victor, 80
Google, language tools of, 18
Gould, Stephen Jay, 177
grammar, 18, 37, 38, 42, 45, 56, 69, 97, 158, 207, 259
  loss of control over, 9
  patterns of, 34, 163
  rules of, 24, 33, 103, 134
  shared, 48
  word order in, 97, 99, 122–23, 141, 210, 240n
grammar books, 11, 75, 95
Great Britain, 85
  lack of foreign-language training in, 71, 72
Greek language, 23, 32, 43, 58, 95, 116, 150
  alphabet of, 31
  ancient, 33, 34, 75, 84, 118, 119
  modern, 39, 120, 149
Greenblatt, Stephen, ix
Gregory XVI, Pope, 6, 109, 137
Grierson, George, 197, 290
Grosjean, François, 209, 221, 291
Guarani language, 167
Guinness Book of World Records, The 106, 176, 220, 226, 257
Guiora, Alexander, 238
Gujarati language, 4, 43, 47n, 219
Gunnemark, Dan, 105
Gunnemark, Erik, 91–93, 92, 99–101, 102n, 105, 107, 137, 140, 215, 226, 227
"Gypsy" language, 43

Hale, Ezra, 81
Hale, Ken, 80–83, 141, 169, 212, 239, 282
hallucinations, 49–50, 280
Harvard University, 46, 75, 86, 149–50, 162, 279
HB (patient), 139

Hebrew language, 31, 76, 150, 161, 207
  Biblical, 4
  Rabbinic, 4, 43
  study of, 33, 101, 132, 1490
Hellenic language family, 44, 218
Hentig, Werner Otto von, 151–53, 286
Hermans, Eugeen, 247–48, 251, 253–54, 256
Herning, Derick, 255–58, 262
Heuvelmans, Bernard, 248–49
Hickok, Gregory, 158, 287
Hindi language, 9, 14, 20, 26, 111, 119n, 120, 127, 129–31, 188–89, 191–94, 197–99, 203, 211, 231
Hindu, The, 200–201
Hindustani language, 4, 42, 43, 47, 75
Hippo Family Club, 86–89, 260
  official seven languages of, 87n
historical archives, 13, 17, 27–32
Hmong language, 123
Hoffmann, Dustin, 229
Hondurans, 8
How I Learn Languages (Lomb), 101, 102–3, 293
Hudson, Dick, 67–73, 91, 94, 159, 168n, 209, 234
Hungarian language, 4, 5, 35, 39, 43, 104
Hungary, 101, 104
Hurro-Urartian language family, 44n
hyperlexia, 162
hyperpolyglots, 12–20, 28, 46–47
  characteristics of, 12–13, 14–15, 34, 83, 209–10, 214–30
  as cryptids (out of time, out of place, out of scale), 15, 169
  definition of, 12
  as freaks and geeks, 101n, 106, 212, 228
  gender and, 101n, 228–29, 230
  lack of modern scientific literature on, 73
  language-learning lessons of, 82–83, 102–3, 111, 114, 133–36, 260–65
  legends and myths about, 13, 79n, 81–82, 126, 189, 220–21, 248, 249
  mental impairment and, 69, 94–99
  memoirs of, 13, 59, 86, 170
  modern, 92, 100–105, 218, 247–58
  neural tribe theory of, 15, 213, 214–16, 229, 234, 239, 242–43, 247, 265
  newspaper account of, 78
  skepticism about, 6, 13, 14, 25, 42, 61–62, 67, 101, 105, 108–10
  study of, 13–19, 67–143
  surveys of, 13, 56, 217–26, 217, 219, 274–76
  testing of, 6, 16–17, 109–10

hyperpolyglots (*cont.*)
    unusual neurological resources of, 14, 15,
        62, 94, 98, 231–35, 240–41, 260
    uses of languages by, 13, 14, 15, 16, 50,
        62, 812–16

Icelandic language, 42, 75
    Old, 119
idiomatic expressions, 53
Illyrian language, 43
India, 8, 14, 42, 107*n*, 149, 187–89
    caste system in, 197, 201–2
    multiple languages of, 5, 9, 188–89,
        191–205, 207–9, 290
Indian Army, 47*n*
Indo-Aryan languages, 196
Indo-European languages, 34, 196
Indo-Iranian language family, 44*n*
intelligence quotient (IQ), 94, 162–63, 216,
    217
    performance vs. verbal, 163
    testing of, 214
Interagency Language Roundtable (ILR),
    223
intermarriage, 21
International Civil Aviation Organization
    (ICAO), 54–55
Internet, 8
    fraudulent email scams (419s) on, 10
    language learning on, 107, 168, 265
    translations on, 10, 18
    see also Skype; Twitter; YouTube
iPods, 133
Iran, 85*n*, 183
Iraq, 124
Irish language, 42, 80
Israel, 108, 161, 195, 284
Italian language, 10, 14, 17–18, 28–30, 31,
    35, 43, 50, 59, 130
    Latin basis of, 17
Italy, 3, 16, 46
    1860 establishment of republic in, 35
    linguistic variations of, 34–35
    northern, 34, 35
    papal states of, 35, 59

Jackson, Jean, 190
Jacobson, Marcus, 85*n*
Jaillet, Lorraine, 80
Jampijinpa, George Robertson, 80
Japan, 45, 109
Japanese language, 7, 8, 42, 79*n*, 80, 106,
    152, 261–62
Jesuits, 35

Jesus Christ, 150
Johnny Appleseed, 75
Jones, Sir William, 42
Joseph of Copertino, Saint, 32
Jovin, Ellen, 86
Juutilainen, Arvo, 100, 105

Kak stat' poliglotom ("How One Becomes a
    Polyglot") (Spivak), 227
Kala, 188–89, 193, 199
Kalmuck language, 151
Kannada language, 188, 191, 193, 196,
    198–200, 203
Kashmiri language, 203
Kazakh language, 118
Kazakhstan, 10
Keeping Faith with the Mother Tongue
    (Srinivasaraju), 200, 290
Kenrick, Donald, 100, 105
Keyser, Samuel Jay, 83
Khmer language, 133
Klatzo, Igor, 154
Knight's Cyclopedia of Biography, 75
Korea, 45, 108
Korean language, 9, 10, 49
Kramsch, Claire, 21, 22–24, 56–57, 227
Krashen, Stephen, 101–4, 284
Krebs, Amande Heyne, 147, 151, 175
Krebs, Emil, 100, 105, 147–49, 151–55, 157,
    170–75, *170*, 177–80, 212, 228, 229, 249,
    264, 286–87
    personal library of, 147, 154
    preserved brain of, 154, 155, 156, 160,
        161, 169, 171–75, 177–80, 232, 288–89
Kulman, Elizabeth, 74
Kurdish language, 43

language CDs and tapes, 87, 88, 114, 119,
    130, 133
language competitions, 53, 109, 136–37,
    247–48, 250–57, *253*
language exercises, 31, 111, 137
language games, 25–26
language labs, 34
language learning, 67–72
    of adults, 9, 10, 12, 100
    aptitude for, 70, 100, 103, 122, 126
    biological elements of, 10, 11, 68–69, 77
    of children, 10, 12, 21, 33, 69, 86*n*, 100,
        102*n*, 122, 142, 238–40
    compulsory, 9, 148
    dedication to, 163
    developmental problems with, 68
    difficulties of, 14, 21, 71–72, 205

ease of, 11–13
economic demands and, 8, 9, 10, 25, 71, 89, 204
educational systems of, 9, 24, 70–72, 86–89, 239, 247, 275–76, 291
emergentist theory about, 69–70
genetics and, 68, 160, 164, 166, 179–80, 234–35
in government, spycraft and diplomacy, 70, 71–72, 149, 176
impetus and motivation for, 12, 15, 19, 24, 83–84, 90–91, 103
innatist theory about, 69
on Internet, 107, 168, 265
language "acquisition" vs., 87, 102, 180–81
lessons of hyperpolyglots on, 260–65
limitation of, 71–72, 226–28
methodology of, 11, 16, 17, 20, 24, 36–37, 38, 51, 72, 82–83, 86–89, 99–100, 102–4, 107–9, 111–13, 123, 133–35, 239, 259–69, 269, 274–76
native-like proficiency as goal of, 14, 23, 25
from people vs. books, 35–36, 40
practice and training in, 11, 25, 54, 61, 100, 117–18, 137, 141, 251, 259, 274–75
pseudo-immersion in, 89
speed of, 9, 11, 14, 16–17, 36, 38, 50, 71, 86
state subsidy of, 25
thrill of, 20–21, 142
languages:
artificial, 99, 247
"bits" of, 50–52, 53, 81, 89, 134
codes and pragmatics of, 22–23, 51, 57, 164, 259
"code switching" in, 51, 139
cognitive investment in, 48–50
conversation in, 40, 43, 47, 55, 92
cultural capital of, 8, 12, 23, 91
dreaming in, 48–49
emotional attachment to, 22, 141–42, 262
endangered, 9–10
extinct, 9–10, 247, 251, 293
fatal failure and confusion in, 55
"feel" for, 263–64
fluency in, 20, 24–25, 43, 46, 48, 53, 72, 74, 92, 95, 247, 259
interpreting of, 21–22, 36, 45, 71, 149, 153–54
keeping up skills of, 24–25, 105, 251, 257–58

"knowing" of, 22–24, 48, 50–51, 54, 56
"living" in, 24
love of, 141–42
mastery of, 44, 46, 53, 74, 108, 142
memory decay and, 18, 73, 102n, 137
mimicking of, 46, 63, 71, 231–32
minority, 80
miscommunication in, 12, 55, 157
national, 51, 84
native speakers of, 9, 10, 14, 18, 23, 44–46, 51, 56, 63, 243, 261
new languages connected to ancestral, 10
non-native speakers of, 7–10, 18, 53–54, 84
official, 51, 54–55, 218
proficiency in, 51, 53, 54, 61, 104, 140–41, 182, 259
reactivation of, 9–10, 216
reading of, 12, 19, 21, 34, 39, 40–41, 47–48, 56, 116, 226
receptive skills of, 47–48
related, 10, 17
religious myths of, 5, 12
repetition and clarification in, 55
retention of, 164–65
simultaneous multilingual uses of, 7–8, 10, 11
singing in, 10, 88–89, 136, 231
sounds and rhythms of, 11, 231–32
spoken, 9, 12, 19–24, 43, 49, 56, 81, 87
structure of, 11, 56
switching easily among, 11, 63, 95, 137–40, 225, 227, 228
testing of ability in, 6, 16–17, 51, 53, 109, 126, 136–37, 140–41, 152, 182, 233n
thinking in, 49
tribal, 21
unification of, 51
written, 9, 10, 12, 21, 34, 39, 56
without written forms, 21
language savants, 94–99, 283
language scientists, 13, 16
Lanveur, Miss, 57
Lappish language, 42
Latin language, 4, 6, 8, 23, 30, 32, 43, 79, 104, 118, 138, 252
Italian language related to, 17
study of, 33, 34, 107
translating into, 34, 39, 58
translation of, 30
Vulgate, 58
Latinos, 22
Latvia, 31, 91n
Leatherstocking Tales (Cooper), 40

Lebanon, 108, 126
Leborgne "Tan Tan," 156
Leischner, A., 73–74
Lenin, Vladimir, brain of, 154–55, 172
Lenneberg, Eric, 180–81, 289
Lessing, Ferdinand, 153
Lettish language, 42
Lever, Charles, 5
levitation, 32
levodopa, 237, 293
Lewan, Magnus, 110
lexicon, 22
Lex Language Project, *see* Hippo Family
    Club
Library of Congress, U.S., 154, 286
Library of Pisa, 6
Life of Cardinal Mezzofanti, The (Russell),
    41–44, 277, 285, 294
linguistic creativity, 46
linguistic families, 34, 42, 44
linguistic relativity hypothesis, 49
linguistics, 16, 68, 70
LINGUIST List, 234, 281
linguists, 13, 22, 25, 50, 67–68, 80–83
literacy, 12, 22, 33, 39–40, 70, 150
literature, 11, 13
Lithuania, 91n
Livonian language, 31
Lomb Kató, 100, 101–4, *101*, 138–39, 212,
    215, 227, 239, 263, 283–84, 293
London, 41
  as most multilingual city, 10, 71, 278
Longfellow, Henry Wadsworth, 75
Lord's Prayer, 11
Luiseño language, 31, 267

McDonnell Douglas MD-82 jet crash (1993),
    55
MacEachern, Scott, 190–91, 206
magnetic resonance imaging (MRI), 159
Mair, Victor, 149
Malayalam language, 196
Malay language, 42, 88, 131
Maltese language, 4, 31, 43
Manavit, Augustin, 36
Manchurian language, 149, 151
Mandinka language, 112
Marathi language, 47n, 193, 194, 202
Marvelous Possessions (Greenblatt), ix
Maryland, University of, 24
Massachusetts Institute of Technology
    (MIT), 81, 83, 190, 226
Massachusetts language, 76

Maswary, Dave, 109
Mayan calendar, 119n
Mecca, 47
Mediterranean Sea, 3
memory, 11, 24, 25, 34, 36, 38, 62, 63, 95,
    163–65, 175, 240, 259
  boosting of, 237
  decay and loss of, 18, 73, 102n, 137
  declarative, 288
  long-term, 133, 134, 135, 143, 234, 236,
    237
  photographic, 92
  procedural, 165, 287–88
  verbal, 163
  visual, 236
  working, 98, 134–37, 139–40, 227–28, 233,
    236, 263, 275, 293
metaphors, 31, 96
"Mexican" language, 43
Mexico, 14, 87–89, 118
  pre-Columbian, 60
Mezzofanti, Francis, 32, 35
Mezzofanti, Giuseppe Cardinal, 4, 18, 24,
    48, 50–54, 67, 78, 84, 92–93
  asceticism and humility of, 37, 60–61
  biographies of, 16, 36, 37, 40, 41–44, 45,
    58, 137–38, 277, 285, 294
  birth of, 32, 33, 58
  celebrity of, 58, 81
  childhood and adolescence of, 32–36, 148
  correspondence of, 30–31, 39, 61, 93
  death and burial of, 33, 59
  education of, 32–35, 36–37
  extraordinary linguistic skills of, 3–6, 11,
    12, 16–17, 19, 30–32, 35–44, 56–63, 74,
    100, 113, 115, 137–38, 210, *222*
  handwriting of, 30–31, 39, 60, 93, 268
  historic archive of, 27–32, 36, 38–40,
    57–62, 93, 267–69, *269*
  illnesses of, 35, 37, 124
  knowledge and humor of, 11
  as librarian, 3, 57–62, 261
  personal library of, 58–60, 267
  poetry of, 30, 31, 57, 60–61
  priesthood of, 3, 33, 35–38, 46, 58–60
  skepticism about, 42, 61–62, 92–93, 101,
    105, 140
  social rank of, 46
  teaching of, 35
  testing of, 6, 16–17, 109
migration, 8, 84–85, 90–91, 140, 190
Mikolainis, Peter, 153–54
Milton, John, 194, 280

Mind of a Savant, The: Language Learning and Modularity (Smith and Tsimpli), 94–97, 98, 283
Minnesota, University of, 259
Mismeasure of Man, The (Gould), 177
Mithridates, King of Persia, 4, 12, 42
mnemonics, 99
Moby-Dick (Melville), 17
Modern Language Aptitude Test (MLAT), 163
modularity, 97–98
Mongolian language, 149, 151
monolingualism, 8, 20, 35, 47, 52, 63, 90, 140
  culture and, 18, 206
Moore, Leslie, 190, 206, 290
morphology, 22
Mozart, Wolfgang Amadeus, 23, 83
multicompetence, 52–56
multilingualism, 18, 21–26, 34, 52–54, 68, 89–93, 174
  countries strong in, 85, 188–205
  political evolution of, 90–91
musical ability, 23, 57, 99, 163, 171*n*, 179, 231
Muslims, 47, 191, 192, 197, 200
Myers-Briggs personality type test, 215
Myers-Scotton, Carol, 13

Napoleón I, Emperor of France, 35
Narraganset language, 76
nationalism, 51, 84, 90
Native Americans, 40, 76, 148, 219
"natural education," 79
Navajo language, 82
nervous system, 85*n*, 86
neural tribe, 15, 213, 214–16, 229, 234, 239, 242–43, 247, 265
neurodiversity, 214
Neurodiversity (Armstrong), 214–15
New Age movement, 119*n*
New Testament, 58–59, 75, 76
New York, N.Y., 7, 10, 67, 80, 119, 153–54
New York Times, 79*n*
New York University, 158
Nietzsche, Friedrich, 85
Nigeria, 8
Nilep, Chad, 89
Norwegian language, 75, 81, 97
nouns, 11, 34, 82, 239
Nurmekund, Pent, 100, 105
nursery rhymes, 79

Obler, Loraine, 161–62, 164–66, 168–71, 175, 176, 178, 212, 222, 287

O'Brien, Ira T., 74
obsessive-compulsive disorder (OCD), 228, 291
Oceanica languages, 42
Odyssey, The (Homer), 75
Olympic Games of 1968 (Mexico), 95
"On the Extraordinary Powers of Cardinal Mezzofanti as a Linguist" (Watts), 41
On the Track of Unknown Animals (Heuvelmans), 248–49
oral skills, assessing of, 25–26
Oregon Health and Science University, 234
Owen, Steven, 149–50
oxytocin, 237

Paget, Polyxena, 5–6, 37
Papiamentu language, 106
Papua New Guinea, 9
Parkinson's disease, 237
parts of speech, 4, 11
Pascual-Leone, Alvaro, 86
Pasti, Franco, 57–62, 242
Patchett, Ann, 21–22
Pattanayak, D. P., 191
Peace Corps, 162
Peek, Kim, 229
Peguan language, 43, 138
Pennsylvania, University of, 149
Perecman, Ellen, 139
Persian language, 4, 31, 42, 43, 58, 61, 119, 120, 197
"Peruvian" language, 43
Philippines, 85*n*
Philological Society, 41
philology, 5, 42, 131, 141, 153
phrenology, 77–78
piano playing, 23
pidgin languages, 7, 36
pilots, 54–55
Pimsleur, Paul, 134, 284
Pimsleur method, 134, 239
Pinker, Steven, 226
Pius IX, Pope, 59–60
Poeppel, David, 158, 287
Polish language, 4, 5, 35, 43, 75*n*, 207, 262
Pollock, Sheldon, 200, 201, 290
"Polyglot, the," 150
Polyglot in the Library, A (Pasti), 57, 61
Polyglot of Europe contest, 253–57
Polyglot of Flanders contest, 247–48, 250–53, *253*
polyglots, 5, 15, 17, 25, 29–30, 41–42
  psychotic, 49–50, 280

polyglots (*cont.*)
  see also hyperpolyglots
Polyglottery Today (Gunnemark), 92
Porter, E. X., 79*n*
Portuguese language, 4, 18, 30, 39, 43, 106, 119
positron emission tomography (PET), 157
Prasad, Chandrabhan, 201–2
pronunciation, 9, 11, 22, 36, 37, 40, 89, 158
  perfect, 43
  social, gender and geographic variations in, 45
Provençal language, 47*n*, 118, 119
psychosis, 49–50
Punjabi language, 47*n*, 194

Qing dynasty, 150
quadrilingualism, 190
Quakers, 59
Quechua language, 31, 42

Rain Man, 229
Real Academia Española, 208
recombination, 11
Reiterer, Susanne, 231–32, 234, 235, 292
Renaissance, 28
Renkema, Jan, 207
Respighi, Father, 32
Reuters, 106–7
Ricci, Matteo, 35
Rich, Katherine Russell, 86
Rigby, Christopher Palmer, 47*n*
Rio de Janeiro, 10
Rochester, University of, 241
Romaic language, 43
Roman Catholic Church, 32, 33
  baptism in, 59*n*
  books banned by, 59
  confession in, 35–36, 37–38
  conversion to, 59
  evangelism and missionary work in, 137–38
  excesses of, 46
  feast days in, 137–38
  Propaganda Fide of, 137–38, 261
Romance languages, 34, 44, 96, 115, 119, 120, 218, 254
Romanian language, 4, 104, 119, 255
Romani language, 35
Romanticism, 41, 46
Rome, 3, 4, 16, 33, 41, 57, 59, 137

Rosetta Stone, 239
Rugh, William, 45
Russell, Charles William, 41–44, 45–46, 48, 100, 137–38, 222, 267, 285, 294
Russia, 17
Russian language, 5, 8, 17, 23, 30, 35, 43, 74, 102, 109, 110, 124, 137
  study of, 127–29, 251
Russian revolution, 17
Ruthenian language, 42, 153
RWTH Aachen University, 171

Saami language, 109
St. Patrick's College, Maynooth, 41
St. Petersburg, 17, 74
Sakakibara, Yo, 86, 88
"Salamanic" language, 74
Samaritan language, 75, 76
Sanskrit language, 42, 47*n*, 77, 108, 119, 149, 194–97
Sapir-Whorf hypothesis, 49
Sardinian language, 38
Saudi-Arabia, 85*n*
Sauerwein, Georg, 73–74, 172
schizophrenia, 214
Schrijfwijzer "Style Guide" (Renkema), 207
Schumann, John, 159–60, 237–38
science, 11, 14
  empirical, 41
  language, 13, 16
  medical, 28
  neurological, 15, 16, 41, 156–62, 170–75
  polyglottery as, 92
Scoresby-Jackson, Robert, 172
Seashore, Carl, 163
Seashore Tests of Musical Ability, 163
self-confidence, 34, 46, 131
Semitic language family, 44
sentences, 18
  bilingual, 51
  construction of, 11, 22, 56, 82, 83, 96, 99, 142
  "dummy subject," 181*n*
September 11th, 2001 terrorist attacks, 71
Serbian language, 43
Shakespeare, William, 194
Sharma, Arpan, 15
Shaw, George Bernard, 194–95
Shogun, 80
Sicily, 3
Siddhartha, 194–95, 201
Sidis, William James, 79, 282

sign language, 45, 279
Signs of the Savant, The: Language Against the Odds (Smith and Tsimpli), 97–99, 283
Sillmann, Peter, 170–71
Simon, Paul, 72
Sindhi language, 47n
Singapore, 131, 208
Singer, Judy, 214
Sinhalese language, 42
Sino-Tibetan languages, 44n, 112
Skehan, Peter, 164, 227, 284, 287
Skype, 109
slavery, 3
Slavic languages, 44, 75, 153, 218, 252
   East Slavic subgroup of, 17
sleep, 143
   dreaming in, 48–49
   rapid eye movement (REM), 48, 280
Smith, Neil, 94–99
Somali language, 47n
Sorenson, Arthur, 189–90, 289
sound:
   mimicking of, 63, 71, 160
   perception of, 33
   production of, 33, 163
South America, 31
Southern California, University of, 101
Soviet Union, 129, 154–55, 251
Spain, 35
Spanish language, 4, 7, 10, 14, 30, 35, 43, 45, 49–50, 55, 82, 88, 118, 122, 192
   Italian relation to, 18
   study of, 9, 19–20, 102, 134
speech:
   defective, 95
   loss of coherence in, 161
   mimicking sounds of, 63, 71, 160
   monitoring of, 24
   organs of, 10, 11, 77
   phonetic sounds of, 46
   truthful, 45, 279
Spivak, Dimitri, 227
Sprachbund, 195–97, 208
Sprachegefühl, 263–64
Sproat, Richard, 234–35
Sri, 188–89, 192–94, 199, 204
Srinivasaraju, Sugata, 200, 201, 290
stammering, 5
Stanford University, 79
Starchevsky, A. V., 16–17, 267–68
   "polyglot college" of, 17
State Department, U.S., 222–23, 291
Stieda, Ludwig, 172

Stoessel, Saskia, 224, 291
Stoner, Winifred Sackville, 79–80
Stoner, Winifred Sackville, Jr. "Cherie," 78–80, 282
street signs, 10
strokes, 74, 171, 174
Strunk, William, 207
stuttering, 5, 166
Sumerian language, 154
superlearners, *see* hyperpolyglots
Suzuki, Kenshi, 88
Suzuki, Tomoko, 87–88
Svenska Akademien, 208
Swahili language, 9, 47n, 133
Swedish language, 10, 35, 43, 60, 75, 91, 109, 148, 181
Switzerland, 17–18
syntax, 21, 22, 96–97, 99
syphilis, 154, 156
Syriac language, 43, 75
Syrian language, 4

Tac, Pablo, 267, 294
Tagalog language, 35, 268, 269
Taiwanese language, 20
Tamil language, 75, 120, 131, 188, 194, 196, 198–200, 202, 208, 210, 290
Tammet, Daniel, 229
Teach Yourself Finnish, 81
television, 106, 109
   languages on, 10
   satellite, 8, 90
Teluga language, 47n, 188–89, 191–94, 196, 198–200, 202
tenses, 123
testosterone, 165, 166
Thai language, 123
Thomas, Michel, 275–76
Tibetan language, 42, 149
Time, 78–79
Toda language, 47n
Tok Pisin language, 9
Tolis, Peter, 75–76
tongues, 10
Tongue-Tied American, The: Confronting the Foreign Language Crisis (Simon), 72
"Tonquinese" language, 42
total language system, 52
Tourette's syndrome, 230
tourism, 84, 85, 140
Tower of Babel, 5, 12, 44, 197
transcranial direct current stimulation (tDECS), 235–36

translation, 11, 12, 30, 40, 46, 47–48, 53,
        58–59, 92, 104
    technologies of, 10, 274–75
travel, 8, 14, 24
    sea, 68, 147, 154
    train, 17–19, 147–48
"Travelling Linguistics" (Ganahl), 84–85
trilingualism, 226
Truss, Lynn, 207
Tsimpli, Ianthi-Maria, 94–99, 283
Tukano language, 190
Turin, University, 6
Turkic language family, 44n
Turkish language, 4, 39, 42, 43, 54, 132, 151,
        181, 250–51
Twitter, 15
    languages featured on, 10
typewriters, 79

Ukrainian language, 16–17, 104
ultimo dei Mohicani, L' (Cooper), 40
United Arab Emirates (UAE), 8, 15, 85n
United Nations, 54
United States, 14
    counterterrorism strategy in, 71
    economic and military power of, 85
    English-speaking predominance in,
        71–72, 147, 148, 206
    intelligence community in, 53–54, 71
    language learning in, 9
    Latinos in, 22
University College, London, 67, 94
Uralic language family, 44n
Urdu language, 191, 192, 197

Vandewalle, Johan, 249–56, 253, 269, 293
Vatican, 5
    library of, 3
verbs, 11, 31, 34, 82, 123, 124, 239
Victor, Elizabeth, 87
Vietnam, 8
Vietnamese language, 167
visuospatial abilities, 165
Viva el lunes, 109
vocabulary, 34, 42, 45, 99, 233, 275
    gaps in, 103
    memorizing of, 24, 259
    recall of, 11, 96

shared, 48
Vogt, Cécile, 154, 172
Vogt, Oskar, 154–55, 171–73, 175, 178
voices, hearing of, 50
Volovick, Reuben, 153–54

Walkman, 114
Wallachian language, 43
Warlpiri language, 81, 82
Washington, D.C., 70, 132
Washington Post, 73
Watts, Thomas, 41, 43, 44, 100, 279
Welsh language, 10, 43, 75, 118
Wernicke, Carl, 157
White, E. B., 207
Will to plasticity, 14, 85–86, 107, 122, 209, 212
Wikipedia, 73
William II, Kaiser, 147
Williams, Harold, 73
Winner, Ellen, 142, 220, 285
wordplay, 11
words, 22, 33, 37, 38, 163
    choosing of, 142
    color, 49, 280
    connecting of, 46
    meaning of, 53, 124
    order of, 97, 99, 122–23, 141, 210, 240n
    recognition of, 162
    rhyming of, 57
    spelling of, 78, 96
    structure of, 96
World Atlas of Language Structures, 249n
World Bank, 85, 132–33, 261, 282
World Tourism Organization, 85
World War I, 147, 148
World War II, 28, 255

Yemen, 45
Yiddish language, 148, 153
YouTube, 73, 109, 121, 127, 265
Ysaÿe, Eugène, 171n

Zach, Baron von, 5
Zilles, Karl, 171, 172, 175, 177–79, 212, 229,
        287, 289
Zimmer, Benjamin, 150, 272
Zoraida, 19
Zulueta, Felicity de, 49–50

About the Author

Michael Erard is not a polyglot. He considers himself a monolingual with benefits. A native speaker of American English, he has lived in South America and Asia, where he learned Spanish and Mandarin Chinese, but please don't ask him to say anything in those languages. He has graduate degrees in linguistics and rhetoric from the University of Texas at Austin. His writing about language, linguists, and linguistics has appeared in *Science, Wired, Atlantic, The New York Times, New Scientist, Slate,* and many other publications, and he is a contributing writer for *Design Observer.* His first book, *Um . . . : Slips, Stumbles, and Verbal Blunders, and What They Mean,* a natural history of things we wish we didn't say (but do), as well as a look at what happens in our culture when we do (and wish we didn't), was published in 2007. Michael was awarded the Dobie Paisano Writing Fellowship in 2008 to work on *Mezzofanti's Gift.* See more at www.michaelerard.com.